GRAHAM GREENE
THREE LIVES

Anthony Mockler

In Memoriam

This book is dedicated
to Marjorie Mary Mockler
who saw its inception but
did not live to see its end.

BY THE SAME AUTHOR:

A History of Mercenaries
Lions under the Throne
Francis of Assisi: The Wandering Years
Hostage (with Glenn Dixon)
The New Mercenaries
Our Enemies the French
Haile Selassie's War

King Arthur and His Knights
Sir Yvain the Gold-Green Knight

To Jack

GRAHAM GREENE

THREE LIVES

Anthony Mockler

With Best Wishes

Anthony Mockler

HUNTER MACKAY
SCOTLAND

First published in 1994 by
Hunter Mackay
The Guynd
by Arbroath
Angus

ISBN 0 947907 01 7

Printed in Great Britain.

A CIP catalogue record for this book
is available from the British Library.

Contents

There is, deliberately, no index to this edition. An index covering the whole of Graham Greene's life will be included in the next, and final, volume.

Contrairement à une opinion peureuse et reçue, un écrivain de fond n'a rien à craindre de sa biographie. Non, un écrivain n'a rien à redouter d'une enquête minutieuse sur sa vie et du récit de cette vie, *au contraire*. Une existence d'écrivain est, par définition, pleine de bombes à retardement. Ses ruses, ses dissimulations, ses mensonges, ses bonnes actions cachées, ses vices, ses lâchetés, ses abandons, son héroisme, bref sa tactique et sa stratégie, font partie intégrante de ses livres.

Seule l'œuvre a de l'importance? Mais non. Seule la vie? Mais non. Les deux sont inextricablement liées, et c'est cela qui effraie...

Philippe Sollers

Preface

An Open Letter to Graham Greene's Literary Executors

Gentlemen,

Five years ago now – five long years! as the future Mrs Graham Greene might have put it – this book (as you will probably recollect) was about to be published. But as Graham Greene himself once said – I cannot for the life of me remember where or in what context, though the phrase has stuck in my mind – "Books are a labour to write and a hell to publish." Events occurred. The particular event that, effectively, scuppered this book's publication was the appearance of a series of long extracts from it in the *Sunday Telegraph*.

As soon as I saw a proof of the proposed extracts, my heart sank into my boots. "Graham Greene will go through the roof if this comes out like this," I warned my then publishers, "and I wouldn't blame him." They pooh-poohed the idea. I reasoned with them, suggesting I be allowed to tackle the *Sunday Telegraph* personally and try and persuade them to alter the text, to make it more of a genuine extract, and less of a patchwork of 'private life' paragraphs. I was warned off very firmly. On no account, was I told, must I interfere. In any case, it appeared, I had no legal standing in the matter: the contract was between the publishers and the newspaper; and though it was my text that was being used (or, as I thought, misused) I had no right even to protest. Metaphorically I shrugged my shoulders, let them get on with it – and went into hiding in a small seaside boarding house. Early on the Sunday morning I ventured out and bought the *Sunday Telegraph*. It was even worse than I had feared. The headline, in big black bold letters, announced: "How Graham Greene Proposed a Sexless Marriage".

To be fair to Peregrine Worsthorne, the then editor of the *Sunday Telegraph*, when I wrote to him strongly protesting against this sensationalist headline, he replied courteously and apologetically and agreed to tone the next two extracts down. But by then it was too late. The damage had been done. Thunderous telegrams were coming from Antibes. Threats of legal action were raining down. The publishers reacted with that mixture of self-righteous arrogance and unsupportive cowardice which seems typical of large publishing firms when things go wrong. Of course they were still keen to do the book, but – and here their smiles became full of teeth and their turn of phrase unctuous – I must realise that our interests might diverge. They have.

★ ★ ★

The book that follows is very different from the book of five years ago. For one thing it is immensely shorter. Five years ago it was due to come out neck-a-neck with Professor Sherry's official biography – and it would have been almost as long. It has since been rewritten twice – the first time reduced from nearly a thousand pages to five hundred, the second time reduced again to its present length. It is probably none the worse a book for that, though I am very conscious that there are certain episodes of Graham Greene's early life that have had to be skipped entirely – like for example the curious role he played in the General Strike of 1926 when he became, briefly, a Special Constable – or, as in the case of the Russian Roulette 'legend', rather summarily dismissed in a mere footnote. (This had a whole chapter devoted to it in the original text; which was probably over-kill.) But all these can be found in Professor Sherry's meticulously detailed first volume that covers Graham Greene's life up to 1939.

The second major difference is that I have had to cut out all direct quotations from Graham Greene's private papers – his letters, diaries and so on. This was his retribution for the *Sunday Telegraph* débâcle. I had been to see him at Antibes just a couple of months earlier – it was the only time we met. He received me with courtesy and (I think) a touch of curiosity; offered me several neat vodkas; took one or two himself; and gave me permission to use a long list of quotations that I submitted to him. At the same time he made it plain that he was not too keen on a book like mine being published in his lifetime. (Indeed he had always made it clear that he viewed the whole idea with little favour; but would not actually object provided that I did not bother him with requests for interviews or send long-distance questionnaires.)

As it has turned out, therefore, his wishes are being met in the sense that the book is not coming out during his lifetime. Personally I regret it. I would very much like to have had his reactions to the various theories and critical interpretations put forward in its text; fulminous though some of these reactions might have been.

He was generous about the quotations. There was only one he objected to, a remark of his about Shirley Temple that he thought might cause her offence. All the rest had his approval.

I hoped that in time, when Professor Sherry's authorized biography had come out and the dust had settled, he would remove his veto. He did not – indeed rather the contrary. The bizarre result is that at various universities and learned institutes (mainly American) there are folder upon folder of Greene papers acquired, usually at auction and at great price, by these institutes precisely in order to help scholars, researchers and biographers write about Graham Greene; which can be read *in situ* but which, nonetheless, cannot be quoted unless the original author (or his literary executors after his death) so permit. For the acquiring institutes, legally speaking, own the actual bits of paper but not the copyright of what is written on the bits of paper – though that was their reason for acquiring them in the first place.

But the law of copyright is such that things get curioser and curioser. All the lawyers seem to agree that copyright is "a grey area". Non-lawyers might simply describe it as a complicated morass designed (if for any rational purpose) to enrich those who thus describe it; (and, incidentally, likely to get more complicated and restrictive still when the dreaded Third European Directive on The Term of Copyright comes into force, unless stopped, next year). For, although I cannot quote from these private papers, I can (if I have understood the law correctly) freely use the facts that can be gleaned from them. Clearly in the case of diaries and appointment books this is a great help to a biographer; one can tell where Graham Greene was on such and such a day, whom he saw, what he was writing, even how many words he managed. With the letters things become more complicated; for what precisely is a fact? Or, to put it another way, is a dream as much of a fact as a dinner-party? An opinion as an intention? An expression of emotion as a critical reaction? Sophists can have a field-day here...

At any rate let me assure you, Gentlemen, that I have cut out every direct quotation that Graham Greene originally gave me permission to use; and let me plead for your indulgence in any borderline cases which you may, with your eagle-eyed professional advisors, spot and which I have failed to do.

For after all the law of copyright was basically designed to stop pirated editions of complete works being published, to an author's obvious detriment, and, in the case of private letters, diaries etc, to prevent whole series being 'scooped' when as yet unpublished and thereby, as it were, make their subsequent publication by the rightful proprietors unprofitable. It was not intended to be used as an instrument of repression or oppression. It was not intended to protect every sentence or every phrase as if it were gold dust. *De minimis non curat lex*.

As for quotations from Graham Greene's novels and stories and indeed travel books and other published writings, I believe I am right in saying that there are agreed conventions here – agreed between the Society of Authors and The Publishers Association "with a view to removing doubt and saving all concerned needless bother". I can quote – provided it is for purposes of criticism or review, and duly acknowledged – a series of extracts of up to 800 words from any prose work (but no extract is to exceed 300 words) and from any poem, 40 lines provided that that does not represent more than a quarter of the total of a poem. This without breach of copyright.

Let me assure you, Gentlemen, that I have counted and recounted the words used – and that I think that I can safely say that nowhere have I come near to overtopping the limit.

As for the "fair dealing" aspect, I would argue that this whole book is designed as a critical study of Graham Greene's life and writings, both '*inextricablement liées*' – inextricably intertwined. You may not perhaps care for parts of the book: in places it may seem over-critical or over-speculative or both. All I can say is that biographies always seem *ex natura* to cause some offence; and urge you not to try and use the law of copyright as a weapon of censure.

⋆⋆⋆

Indeed I would go further; and ask you to take a broad view, not a niggardly one.

All books that stimulate interest in, and argument about, Graham Greene are positive. And, from your point of view, Gentlemen, all books that send the readers back to the original texts must be a very good thing indeed. I hope very much that this book of mine will have readers in their droves out buying Graham Greene's novels again – and not only the novels – if only to see for themselves whether the hypotheses put forward carry conviction, or not.

Indeed I will go further still than that. I very much hope this book will induce you to reprint some of Graham Greene's early works: in particular his first unpublished novel, *Anthony Sant* (which I would willingly – and freely – edit, for the interest of the thing); and his second published novel *The Name of Action*. His early poems too (not just those in *Babbling April*) and his early short stories (particularly those in *Oxford Outlook* and *Cherwell*) would, I am sure, both be of great interest if published in annotated editions. In a way it is easier, now that the great man is dead, to throw open all his works again, even those of which he later came to disapprove. It is a truth universally acknowledged that no writer even in possession of a great critical acumen is the best judge of his own books…

⋆⋆⋆

Gentlemen, you have in one sense the advantage of me. I do not know who you are; I do not know how many of you there are; I am not indeed at all sure whether I should not be addressing you as 'Ladies and Gentlemen'; or indeed simply as 'Ladies'. I am sure, however, of one thing, that this book will very soon fall into your hands. It is a small edition; and if there is anything in it you particularly would like to see changed, I am most willing to listen most carefully. All I dare hope is that you will find it, as it now stands, interesting, stimulating even.

Graham Greene was an extremely complex man, alert in his own defence certainly – and in the defence of those dear to him. I hesitate to predict his reaction. But I rather think he would be more amused than enraged at having his complexities examined; and – wherever he is now and assuming that he is reading as avidly as ever – he, of all men, would be capable of saying "Well now, that's a different way of looking at things. Yes, I admit that that's – perhaps – what did – or did not – happen."

Anthony Mockler
Moulin d'Andé
May 1994

Prologue

A Sort of Death

All Fools Day 1991

It was a sort of death. That was the title he would have given it. He had done better, he reflected wryly, for his own characters. Major Jones would not have been proud of him; nor Scobie nor Pinkie nor that other sinful hero, the Stranger, the Hollow Man, the Priest. He looked out of the antiseptic room over the sterile Swiss sky. No vultures gazed back with either interest or hollow indifference. Vevey didn't have vultures these days; nor guerrillas; nor firing squads; nor much in the way of excitement at all except death itself. Not even a bomb party, he thought with regret: he'd go out without as much of a bang as that other very rich, very old reprobate of his, Dr Fischer. Well, maybe a little bomb, or at least a bombshell of sorts, in the will. He grinned. A last little bit of mischief. And now it was time to send for Leopoldo. If he was going to die conventionally, of old age and wasting leukaemia, in a hospital bed, rather than shot or drowned or in an air-crash as he had always prophesied and half-expected, then he might as well die fortified, as they used to say, by the rites of Our Holy Mother the Church. Unlike Scobie or Pinkie or even his poor anguished Priest whom he had so ruthlessly and dramatically and successfully barred from the Last Sacraments. Besides, it would give such pleasure to Leopoldo, who was one of the kindest men he knew, and the most loyal of friends. And, come to that, also, he supposed he owed it in a sort of way to Vivienne...

* * *

Graham Greene died quietly in the Hôpital de la Providence on the shores of Lake Geneva on Wednesday, April 3rd 1991. He was buried quietly the following Monday in the nearby cemetery of Corseaux, not far from Charlie Chaplin's grave. Richard Burton is buried there too. So he lies in congenial company.

Father Leopoldo Duran, who had flown to Switzerland from Spain, told the funeral congregation that they should know that it was Graham who had taken the initiative in sending for him.

"Graham Greene was a real Catholic believer. He had been ill for about 15 months. I told him most directly, 'Graham, God is waiting for you just now – pray for us where you will be for ever in God's blessing. I now give the last absolution'.

'This I did. He passed away in the most beautiful way, in the most patient way, and with immense calm. With a gesture he fell asleep. My faith tells me he is now with God or on the way there.'

Vivienne his widow, 85 years old, did come to the funeral. She had not seen her husband for some six years, and then for only a few hours. "When my daughter Caroline telephoned with the news of his death, I thought 'He's got another dawn than ours.' Do you know the poem? I can't remember who wrote it. There's a great gap really" Nevertheless she came; a substantial figure in black; and, as was fitting, was the first to sprinkle holy water over her husband's grave. But she may not have agreed with Father Leopoldo's nuanced *pronunciamento*. She had – has – a sharper and in her old age a less sentimental mind.

Was Graham really a Catholic, she had, in the interval between his death and his funeral, been asked.

'I don't think so, she replied. "You see, we Catholics pray for final perseverance. To slog on when you are disappointed or depressed. I don't think he could ever have done that. He discovered certain glimpses but the final perseverance would have been too much of a trial for him."

Vivienne had varied feelings about her husband. She always had had, but it was only after his death that she expressed them at all publicly; and then pithily. For much of their married life, she believed, Greene was a "cold, unhappy man". "In some ways he was a very cold person. He said, 'I put myself into my books, what's left over is nothing. There's nothing left over for life and people.' "

That was on reflection, a year or so after his death. Immediately after it she had analysed him rather differently, but just as interestingly.

"I think he was much happier than people believed," she said then. "He wanted danger. He wanted adventure. He wanted travel. He wanted money – not in a greedy way but the space that it gives you – and women, of course. And he had all those things."

Not bad for the abandoned wife of forty years. A generous and perceptive comment. Not vindictive; and not, when considered carefully, contradictory either.

* * *

Two months after his death, on Thursday, June 6th 1991, a Memorial Requiem Mass was celebrated for Graham Greene in Westminster Cathedral. This was a solemn, somewhat pompous affair, almost the official recuperation of a distinguished but erring son of Holy Mother Church; and it had its ironies. The Cardinal Archbishop of Westminster, Cardinal Hume, lurked in the wings unable totally to condone by presiding, unwilling totally to condemn by being absent. Father Leopoldo was permitted to concelebrate; but not to speak. The Reverend

Dr Roderick Strange, who delivered the Homily, hardly knew Graham personally; told the assembled multitude – the long aisles were filled on both sides – that: "Graham was not perfect" (which many present must have thought to be a bathetic understatement in the circumstances) but concluded that he was confident that Graham would be greeted on his arrival at the Pearly Gates "like doubting Thomas with the words 'Peace be with you'." His wife sat on one side of the aisle, his mistress on the other, with straight and solemn faces. Graham, who had a caustic sense of humour, would have been tickled pink.

Next morning the *Daily Telegraph* published a list of those attending, which is reproduced here below.

REQUIEM MASS

Mr Graham Greene

The Queen was represented by Prof Owen Chadwick at the memorial requiem Mass for Mr Graham Greene in Westminster Cathedral yesterday.

The Cardinal Archbishop of Westminster was present.

Mgr Patrick O'Donoghue was the principal celebrant and the concelebrants were Father Leopoldo Duran, Father Albert Huerta, SJ, Father Michael Seed and Father Roderick Strange, who gave the homily. Mr Ronald Challoner read the lesson and tributes to Mr Greene were paid by Miss Louise Dennys (niece), Mrs Muriel Spark and Sir Alec Guinness.

Father Daniel Cronin and Father Terence Phipps were robed.

The Prime Minister of Belize was represented by the High Commissioner for Belize. The congregation also included: Mrs Greene (widow), Mr and Mrs Francis Greene (son and daughter-in-law), Mrs Caroline Bourget (daughter), Mr Jonathan Bourget (grandson), Mr and Mrs R O Dennys (brother-in-law and sister), Mrs Raymond Greene (sister-in-law), Mme Yvonne Cloetta, Mr Nicholas Dennys, Mr and Mrs Graham C. Greene, Mr Alexander Greene, Mr Timothy Greene, Mr Christopher Greene, Lady (Elaine) Greene, Lady (Sarah) Greene, Mr and Mrs Oliver Greene, Mr and Mrs Charles Gooch, Miss S Gooch, Countess Barbara Strachwitz, Graf Rupert Strachwitz, Grafin Ilona La Rosee, Mrs Ave Barham, Mrs Daphne Barham, Mr M Barham, Mr and Mrs John Barham, Mr and Mrs John Walker, Mr David Walker, Miss M Walker.

The Ambassador of Cuba, the Ambassador of Nicaragua, Signor Stefano Ronca, representing the Ambassador of Italy, M. Christian Faessler, representing the Ambassador of Switzerland, Mr Milan Glozar, representing the Ambassador of Czechoslovakia, Senor Don Fernando Serrano Suner, representing the Ambassador of Spain.

The Duke of Norfolk, Lord Hunt of Tamworth, Lord Fitt, the Hon Julia Stonor, the Hon Geraldine Stonor, Sir Harold Hood, Lady Guiness, Sir Edward Ford, Secretary and Registrar of the Order of Merit, Sir Richard and Lady Attenborough, Lady Sloman, Mr Harold Pinter and Lady Antonia Fraser, Contessa Laetitia Cerio.

Mr George Bull, Royal Society of Literature, Mr Paul Scherer, President, Publishers Association, and Mrs Scherer, Mr and Mrs Max Reinhardt, Mr Auberon Waugh, Editor, the Literary Review, and many other friends.

Who were all these people? A man's life can be summed up, in a sense, by studying the list of those who are present at his funeral or his memorial service.

In the first place came, convention dictates, his family: *Mrs Greene (widow)* – his widow, his wedded wife since October 15th 1927, over half a century earlier; his only wife, from whom he had never divorced, who always, meticulously, had continued to style herself Mrs Graham Greene. The Requiem Memorial Mass, chanted in Latin, was very much her service, the day her day, the event itself, in a sense, her final triumph.

Mr Francis Greene was their only son. He lived, with his wife, in Devon. They had no children. He and his father were thought to have been on distant terms, though there were rumours of a death-bed rapprochement. *Mrs Caroline Bourget* was their daughter, the elder of their two children. She had married a French Canadian in 1961; they had had three sons (one of whom had died very young), Graham's only grandchildren, and had since divorced. Caroline lived in Switzerland, above Vevey and Lake Geneva. Her father had often joined her and his grandsons there for Christmas in his old age; as he had done for the last months of his life. *Jonathan* was present; Caroline's other surviving son, Andrew, had attended the funeral in Corseaux.

Graham himself had been one of six children: the third son of four boys and two girls. He had outlived all his siblings but one – *Elizabeth*, his favourite and younger sister. It was she who had introduced him into the Secret Service during the war. Her husband, *Rodney Dennys* whom she had met and married in Cairo in 1944, had also been in Section V of SIS; retiring in early middle age to become Herald of the College of Arms. It was their daughter *Louise*, tall, beautiful, owner of her own publishing firm in Canada, who gave by far the best of the three 'tributes' at the Requiem Mass. Graham, she said, was *not* a family man. He upheld the virtue of disloyalty; enjoyed being argumentative and upsetting (particularly to publishers). But he was loyal and devoted to individuals, to the people he loved and liked. This had heads nodding in agreement throughout the Cathedral.

Raymond had been the second son, Graham's elder brother, their parents' favourite, a school prefect and head of the house, of whom Graham had been very jealous as a schoolboy. *Mrs Raymond Greene (sister-in-law)* was his second, American, wife; by whom he had had two children: *Oliver Greene*, further down the list, and *Annabel*, who had married *Charles Gooch* and produced all the little Gooches. Raymond had been a famous mountaineer, and successful doctor. He and Graham, though reconciled at Oxford, had never really been close. Graham had liked his second wife, Eleanor Craven Gamble more than his first, an English rose named Charlotte – though he had once dreamt he was married to Charlotte and had, rather unwisely, before their own marriage, told Vivienne of his dream.

Mme Yvonne Cloetta alone in that first formal paragraph was a Greene neither by birth nor blood nor marriage. It was a tribute to the family's tact that she was placed among them at all. And her careful positioning, after the immediate family and the elder generation of Greenes but before the younger generation, may be put down to Vivienne's meticulous sense of precedence. For it is, after all, a moot point: what recognition, if any, does one give to the mistress at the great man's funeral? Yvonne was no ordinary mistress, she had been Graham's *maîtresse-en-titre* certainly since he had moved to France, to Antibes, on January 1st 1966; and very possibly for five or six years before that. As Graham used to say, they had been together for longer than most marriages last. Yvonne had been his emotional *point fixe* during the last quarter of a century of his life; and, being, in her very different way, as strong a character as Vivienne, but less resigned to Original Sin, had allowed him during her long reign no other affairs at all.

She was white-haired now, and in her sixties; but still *petite*, elegant and attractive. Max Reinhardt, Graham's contemporary, old friend, and final publisher, escorted her. In the Cathedral, and leaving it, she was the cynosure of neighbouring eyes. Little wonder that the Cardinal Archbishop felt reticences; and that Her Majesty the Queen was present only in the attenuated form of another aged but more reverend signior, Owen Chadwick, also, like Graham Greene, a member of her own personal Order of Merit.

Mr Nicholas Dennys, Nick, Graham's nephew, Louise's brother, had been running a bookshop in Gloucester Road since 1983. Graham was tickled pink that a member of his family had fulfilled a long-held ambition of his own: to be a second-hand bookseller.

Next on the list comes a whole further spate of Graham's nephews: *Graham, James, Christopher* and *Timothy* plus their respective wives and offspring: the strongest numerical contingent of Greenes present. These are the four sons of Graham's favourite brother, Hugh – "baby Hugh" as he was called in the family at Berkhamsted. Hugh, unlike Graham, was a uxorious man. He married four times: first a Guinness (which may account for the presence of a *Lady Guinness* among the aristocracy listed lower down) and lastly at the age of 75, an Australian script supervisor, thirty years his junior, *Lady (Sarah) Greene*. Hugh and Graham had always remained close, often collaborated, always corresponded; and Hugh's death in 1987 had shocked Graham greatly. He had loved Hugh, and Elizabeth, more than any other members of his family.

His affection however did not necessarily extend to his nephew, Graham Carleton Greene, Hugh's eldest son. One of Graham senior's last great public rows – rows which he always so much enjoyed – had involved denouncing Graham junior and his partner Tom Maschler, joint managing directors of the publishers Jonathan Cape, for selling out to the Americans, to Random House. This had all blown up just after Hugh's death; and though Graham junior had made a fortune from the sale, he had lost face, he was, faced with Graham senior's invective, lost for words, and shortly afterwards he lost his job. "A scarcely avuncular act", it was labelled. Nonetheless Graham junior attended both the funeral in Switzerland and the Requiem Mass in London. Perhaps they had made it up. Graham Greene was always extremely courteous in person, however ferocious his lambastings on paper might be.

Countess Barbara Strachwitz, present with her son *Graf Rupert* and her daughter *Grafin Ilona*, was Barbara Greene by birth, one of the "rich Greenes" who lived up at The Hall in Berkhamsted while the "intellectual Greenes" lived down at the School. She, her brothers and sisters, had been brought up with Graham, his brothers and sisters; twelve junior Greenes in all, a close-knit clan. Barbara, like so many of these twelve talented Greenes, merits a biography of her own. As a young woman she went with Graham on his first real adventure, their walk through Liberia in 1935; and wrote a book about it too, a better book than his. During the War, a most extraordinary thing for an Englishwoman, she married, in Germany, on March 27th 1943, not long after El Alamein and the invasion of North Africa, a German aristocrat, Graf Rudolf Alfred Strachwitz von Grose Zauche und Camminetz. Her uncle, old Sir Graham Greene, though in his late eighties – the Greenes were a long-lived clan – was very worried about it, and made anxious enquiries at the Foreign Office about his favourite niece's status and plans. They were filed, and fobbed off. Perhaps because another Strachwitz was at SIS Headquarters in North Africa at that time (under the assumed name of 'Adrian Hunter'). Was there any link? What with Elizabeth in Cairo, and Graham working for Philby in Ryder Street, who knows? The Graf was perhaps lucky to survive the July 1944 plot against Hitler, and its bloody aftermath.

Mrs Ave Barham, beautiful still in her very old age, was Barbara's elder sister, Ave Greene, the eldest daughter of Graham's Uncle Eppy. She was born a year and a half before Graham; and he had fallen in love with her and courted her when he was in his teens. But then so had Graham's eldest brother Herbert, who was notoriously handsome, much more suitable for Ave in age; and had not yet become the black sheep of the family. It was noticeable that Ave did not marry John Barham till rather late in life for a Greene – aged 25; and then only after Herbert had safely married, the year before and to Graham's amazement, a very nice girl: he couldn't see, he told Vivienne, what she saw in the cad!

So much for the Barhams. As for the *Walkers*, they were the children and grandchildren of Graham's eldest sister Molly, who was eight years older than Graham, who tried to keep him in order and whom he didn't much like as a child. But as a young man he had become very fond of John, his first-born nephew, *Mr John Walker*, for whom he had organised paperchases over the Sussex Downs.

Ambassadors, the world's tribute to England's greatest writer, were not as thick on the floor of the Cathedral as they might have been. No American Ambassador, no French Ambassador, no Russian Ambassador – and yet Graham Greene's novels had been both popular bestsellers and critically acclaimed in all their countries. Greene of course had been barred from one, condemned in the courts of another, and backed the wrong political horse in the third: the Visa affair of 1952, the 'J'Accuse' affair of 1982, the Gorbatchev affair of 1988. One can imagine scratchings of heads in the various Chancelleries as the pros and cons of sending a representative to the Cathedral were debated, and the old files dug up. Greene had become, in his forty-odd years of fame, something of an international loose cannon politically.

The Duke of Norfolk came out of a sense of duty: England's leading Catholic layman paying tribute to England's leading Catholic novelist. As Graham Greene so hated to be called; but, in worldwide reputation at least, rightly or wrongly, still was – *pace* Burgess, Lodge, *et al. Lord Fitts* came out of a sense of friendship: he and Graham had had a memorable drinking session together when Graham had visited Belfast, in June 1976, for four frightening days, and for the first and the last time. *The Hon. Julia and Georgina* (not Geraldine) *Stonor* were daughters of one of the oldest Catholic families in the land: Graham had been taken up by their parents, Lord and Lady Camoys, Sherman and Jeanne, in his fifties; and had spent the Christmas of 1960 with the family at Stonor Park. Jeanne Camoys was a beautiful, wilful woman; but Graham was always adamant that she had not been one of his mistresses. She had died; but another striking and charming aristocrat, over whom no such suspicion had ever been cast, had come from Italy, both to the funeral and the Requiem Mass. This was *Contessa Laetitia Cerio*. As a young girl she had become Graham's friend in December 1948, his *annus mirabilis*, when he had first come to Capri. With her father's help he had bought a villa there, Villa Rosaio in Anacapri; for the next forty years his favourite retreat. They had stayed very good friends, respecting each other and each other's privacy, ever since.

Richard Attenborough had shot to fame as Pinkie in the postwar film of *Brighton Rock. Young Scarface* they had retitled it for America; and Graham Greene had thought that Attenborough with his evil baby face was by far the best thing they had had in the film.

And finally *"Mr Auberon Waugh, Editor, the Literary Review"* was of course the eldest son, the successor in many ways, of Graham's contemporary Evelyn Waugh; who had been at Oxford with him (but their paths had not crossed); who had converted to Catholicism like him (but for very different reasons); who became, in later life, Graham's friend and a generous admirer of his versatility as a writer, though not always of his theology; and whose name is so often and so understandably coupled with Graham Greene's in literary studies, literary biography and literary criticism.

One difference between them, though, is that Graham Greene outlived Evelyn Waugh by twenty-five years. Another is that he had a more complicated life, both personal and public, than Evelyn, or indeed than most men; as this Prologue has perhaps, with all its welter of names and events, begun to indicate.

Chapter I

Greene Blood

It is the morning of Wednesday, October 5th in the year of grace 1904, third of the Reign of Edward VII, King and Emperor. Britannia rules the waves and, via the waves, most of the globe; and the Conservatives, for the next year or two at any rate, rule Britain.

In the Carlton Club three Greenes are sitting over their morning brandies and morning papers. All three are Conservative MPs, wealthy, powerful, successful. Greenes as a clan worship worldly success; and despise failure. Not all members of the clan, however, can be as successful as this trio. They stand at its pinnacle, an example to the rest. All three own town houses and country estates. They hunt and they yacht and in their own solid way (for none are particularly brilliant) they run the country and the Empire. One is a baronet, the first titled Greene. The second is a Lancers captain, a decorated hero of the Boer War. The third is heir to a vast Greene fortune that stretches half-way around the globe. They are proud of their position – three Members of Parliament from the same family! They are proud of their family: what a clan the Greenes are, to be sure! They welcome additions to it, even to the less substantial, less successful members of it, those who will have little or nothing to inherit but who are still generically Greenes with all that that implies.

They glance over the long columns of *Births*, *Marriages*, and *Deaths* carried on the front page of *The Times*. Their own name catches their eye. They point out to each other therefore with a certain pride the following curt entry under the heading of *Births*.

> "Greene. On the 2nd October at St. John's Berkhamsted, the wife of Charles H. Greene, of a son."

Thus anonymously and in the meticulous genitive case did the baby who was to become the most celebrated of all the Greenes make his first appearance in print.

The most successful too – he was a true Greene, through and through, bitterly though he would sometimes deny it.

* * *

The new-born infant began his long life in a small town, a large family and a complicated genealogical position. He had twice as much Greene blood in his veins as most members of his clan: for his mother, Marion Greene by marriage, was also Marion Greene by birth, eldest child of the Reverend Carleton Greene and a descendant, like both her husband and her father, of Benjamin Greene, the brewer of Bury St Edmunds, who had founded the family fortunes there a century earlier.

Large families play havoc with generation gaps. The Reverend Carleton Greene, Graham's grandfather, was first cousin to Charles Greene, Second Master at Berkhamsted School, his own son-in-law, Graham's father. Thus Marion Greene was, like her own children, a great-grandchild of Benjamin the Brewer. Or, to put it another way, Graham was both the great-grandson and at the same time the great-great grandson of Benjamin, the clan founder.

The infant boy was baptized Henry Graham Greene in the School Chapel at Berkhamsted on November 13th; but not by his only surviving grandparent, the Reverend Carleton, neither present nor invited. Yet his mother Marion, tall, severely beautiful, ram-rod straight, had – it was natural in view of her background and position as 'Miss Greene'* of the Rectory, Great Barford – a marked sense of rectitude and duty. She appears in later life to have suppressed her emotions, to have been, at least towards the younger generation, cold and aloof. She had suffered tragedies in her life: the loss of her beloved brother Herbert at the age of 21 and of her mother Jane (Graham's grandmother) not long after Graham's conception. But that in itself can hardly account for her treatment of her own father, the Reverend Carleton, who had been prostrate with grief at the death of his beloved wife. Not to invite the widower to his own grandson's christening was on the face of it a most brutal snub. Clearly there were greater complications in the newborn baby's family background than at first sight met the enquiring eye.

All Marion's children were to grow up tall and good-looking, like their mother; unlike their short, rather squat, somewhat unprepossessing father, Charles Greene. He was a busy, bustling, kindly man, rather shy, with a tendency towards pomposity and – in perhaps deliberate antithesis to his trio of cousins, the Conservative MPs – a convinced Liberal. In 1910, when Graham was six, Charles Greene became Headmaster of Berkhamsted School; and the family transferred *en masse* from St John's in Castle Street where Graham was born, to School House, at the centre of Berkhamsted's Victorian buildings – Graham's home till his marriage. There Graham shared a room with baby Hugh and his bed with many

* By the convention of the day (and indeed it still exists in the rare cases where servants continue to serve the landed families of England) the eldest daughter of the Reverend Carleton was known as 'Miss Greene' to the domestics and parishioners whereas the two younger daughters, Graham's aunts, both unmarried, were 'Miss Maud' and 'Miss Nora' respectively.

soft animals. He was a shy little boy, small and slight till his adolescence, with big ears, a triangular-shaped face and odd-looking, light-coloured, slightly protruding eyes. Like many shy little boys, Graham lived in a world of imaginative adventure, where he most loved playing soldiers. This love of soldiers – or rather of military adventure and military adventurers, preferably in far-off romantic settings – was to stay with him all his life. In many ways Graham Greene missed his vocation: he would have made an excellent general, meticulous as a planner, ruthless and formidable – but in time of war, not of peace; and in an unorthodox army: a conquistador's or a condottiere's.

Herbert, his eldest brother, whom at the time he hero-worshipped, organized all the young Greenes of Berkhamsted* into warlike teams; French versus English in the gardens, lights-out catch-as-catch-can with tense nerves in the dark hall and, most ambitious of all, day-long manoeuvres, scouting and fighting, equipped with provisions, in the fields and lawns behind The Hall.

Every summer there was the annual visit to Uncle Graham at beautiful Harston, a few miles outside Cambridge. Harston, despite the three maiden aunts,† was a magical place, especially for an imaginative boy, with its dark leafy walks, its lake, its secret island, and its faint air of scent and creaky mystery. It was there at Harston one summer that Graham read his first book – *Dixon Brett, Detective*. *Coral Island* followed, and *The Children of the New Forest*. Beatrix Potter too, Andrew Lang's *Fairy Tales*, then *The Enchanted Castle* and other books by E. Nesbit. But these were the preliminaries for his real delight: in war, battle and the roll of drums. Rows of Henty lined the Nursery shelves, tale after tale of Britain's imperial heroes and fighting regiments. From the toy shop in the High Street came boxes of lead soldiers – Redcoats, Sepoys, Zulus and the rest – to guard or attack his favourite Christmas present, a wooden fort.

* There were no fewer than a dozen of them all told: six of the junior 'intellectual Greenes', son of the Headmaster and Marion; and six more of the junior 'rich Greenes', their first cousins, the children of Uncle Eppy; who had made a fortune in Brazil; had married in São Paolo a German wife, Aunt Eva; and had come back to England to settle at Berkhamsted close to his elder brother, Charles, at The Hall. Here, for the record, are the roll-calls of the two bands of cousins. First the 'intellectual Greenes': Molly; Herbert, the most handsome; Raymond, the most conventionally successful; Graham; 'Baby Hugh'; and eventually born on the eve of the Great War, Elizabeth. Secondly the 'rich Greenes': Ben, Ave, Tooter (Graham's contemporary – christened Edward Reginald but always known as Tooter), Felix, Barbara and Kate. Every Christmas Eve the 'intellectual Greenes' were invited by the 'rich Greenes' to The Hall for carols sung in German round the Christmas Tree. As Graham was to put it many years later: "At Berkhamsted the Greenes represented practically 1% of the population. We were self-sufficient. We didn't need anyone else". It was to remain true in essence all their lives.

† Who 'looked after' their distinguished bachelor brother. Graham had little or no affection for them, by contrast to his love for his mother's two unmarried sisters, Aunt Maud and the family's favourite, the high-spirited Aunt Nora, known to all her nephews and nieces as Aunt Nono.

More exotic adventure stories followed: Captain Gilson's *The Pirate Aeroplane*, tale of a lost city in the Sahara – and, above all, unforgettable, Rider Haggard's legendary *King Solomon's Mines*. He read Anthony Hope's books too – not only the Ruritanian stories with the red-bearded Rudolf Rassendyl but also the lesser-known *Sophy of Kravonia*. And on his first trip to Brighton, with Aunt Maud, he had a special seven year-old's treat. She took him to see the film of the story. The accompanying pianist strummed out the thunder of Queen Sophy's guns – and the memory of that sound in that film theatre stuck in Graham's mind till his old age.

★★★

In August 1914 Graham was nearly ten and the young Greenes were summering at Harston in Uncle Graham's absence. From his desk at the Admiralty Sir Graham Greene forwarded sealed orders to Admiral Jellicoe appointing him Commander-in-Chief of the Grand Fleet. At Harston his nephews learnt with delight the news that the great Belgian fortress of Namur had fallen to the Huns. Had it held out, the war might be over too soon, they were afraid, for them to join in. Herbert marched proudly off to enlist in the Honourable Artillery Company, while in the school holidays Graham and Hugh played day-long and even week-long war games with lead soldiers on the big wooden tables in the dining-hall. Cousin St. George Lake sent the thrilled Graham a spiked and bloodstained Uhlan helmet. When Cousin St George was killed on the Western Front, Graham's emotions were more deeply stirred by this heroic death in action than they were to be by any other death in the course of his own long life. For Graham, as for many other militaristic schoolboys, the Great War was an epoch not of horror but of glory, peril and vicarious excitement.

Years later when Graham Greene was exchanging almost daily letters with his fiancée Vivienne, she quizzed him as to which historical event he would most have preferred to be present at. His answer was: at the attack on Zeebrugge. This was a heroic episode if ever there was one. It came in the dark spring of 1918 at the moment when even a thirteen year-old schoolboy must have been aware, from the attitude of his elders, that England was losing the war. The catastrophic retreat from the Somme had begun on March 21st. "The thing is over," proclaimed Hindenburg.

In early April, after a brief pause, the German Army attacked again in Flanders. But on April 23rd, Saint George's Day, Admiral Keyes sent out his signal to the cruiser *Vindictive*: "St. George for England", and, as the North Sea fog lifted, through chopped seas and minefields five obsolete cruisers filled with concrete, escorted by a storming party from *Vindictive*, were launched as blockships to close the harbour at Zeebrugge. It was an old-fashioned tale of individual heroism and self-sacrifice, of storming parties and gangways, flamethrowers and howitzers, surprise, sirens and sudden death. Though 188 sailors and marines (including two RN Commanders) lost their lives in the assault and the destroyer *North Star* was sunk, the daring exploit was a tremendous (and comprehensible) success. As the official historian noted: "In an hour of sorrow and despair it put new spirit and determination into the Nation's heart". But it must somewhat have amazed the future Mrs Greene (though she was herself fiercely patriotic) to have realized that the sentimental, occasionally cynical Balliol poet and aspirant novelist was still, underneath a layer or two of tortured convolution, a romantic schoolboy dreaming of heroic adventures in the service of England and to save the Empire. It was a side of Graham Greene that never – even more tortured though the overlaying convolutions whether by design or necessity became – totally disappeared.

The Great War ended; and with it the most placid period of Graham Greene's whole life. Looked at objectively, it had been a golden childhood: plenty of toys, treats, brothers and sisters and cousins to play with, interesting grown-ups to visit, and, finally, plenty of vicarious excitements and battles followed by a splendidly satisfying victory for England and the Empire.

So why did Graham Greene come in later life to portray, so convincingly, his childhood as unhappy and solitary, Berkhamsted as gruesome, and himself as justifiably suicidal? How did it all go wrong?

There *is* a conundrum here. Sean O'Faolain puts it down to "some deep unhealed traumatic wound".* Of this, however, as such, no evidence exists. A lack of affection? Distant parents were nothing unusual in Edwardian households; and the plethora of servants in the Greene household – nurses, cooks, maids, gardeners – ensured that the children had plenty of human contact and human warmth. A third question needs, therefore, to be put: were there any extraordinarily unusual features at all in Graham's otherwise pleasant, ordered and cosseted childhood? If they can be found, if they can be linked, therein, logically, must lie the explanation.

And there were indeed two absolutely extraordinary aspects that marked his childhood out as different from that of other children of his background and epoch. The first is an event; a most unusual happening. What happened was this: at the age of sixteen he was removed from school for a whole six months, no less, and sent up to London, to live in a psychoanalyst's house – an extraordinary thing in that epoch. The second is in the nature of an absence, and is even more

* Sean O'Faolain stopped by chance in the Fifties at a little town in Hertfordshire set in pastoral country within a crescent of the Chiltern Hills. "Halting at one of the pubs for a drink," he later wrote, "and observing a couple of men who were obviously schoolmasters chatting amicably over a beer, I remembered this was the hideous town (Berkhamsted) anathematized in the opening pages of *The Lawless Roads*." He concludes that Graham Greene describes his birthplace in the manner that James Joyce describes the Dublin slums: "figuratively, not realistically"; indeed with a "lacerated imagination".

extraordinary. It is this: that it is quite clear that Graham Greene never, ever so much as set eyes on his own grandfather, the Reverend Carleton Greene, though the Reverend Carleton, alone of all his grandparents, was alive at the time of his birth, alive during his childhood, alive indeed for the first twenty years of his grandson Graham's life. Why? Why was the grandfather kept from his grandson, the grandson kept from his grandfather? In between, barring the contact between the generations, stood Marion Greene, the dutiful daughter, the dutiful mother; whom we may dimly perceive at this distance in time as a tragic figure, trapped in some sort of insoluble conflict of duties and responsibilities – Marion Greene who, alone of the Reverend Carleton's children, had risked marrying and having children herself. Did she feel, particularly in the case of that odd, sensitive little boy, her third son, that it was a risk she should never have taken?

* * *

Up to the age of thirteen Graham had been living at home, as a day boy, a very protected existence. At thirteen he had to return to St. John's, the house where he was born – but this time as a boarder. He hated it. He makes much of his discovery of evil, of entering "a savage land of strange customs and inexplicable cruelties"; but in fact Berkhamsted was, as public schools of the period went, extraordinarily mild, with virtually no beatings, little bullying, absolutely no (at least according to Graham Greene himself) homosexuality, and a generally liberal régime. He makes much too of the difficulties of being the Headmaster's son: "I was like the son of a quisling in a country under occupation". He was certainly unhappy. But it seems far more likely that he was unhappy because he was overshadowed, in every way, by his elder brother Raymond.

Of all the Greene brothers Herbert, the eldest, had the least brains. Among the 'rich Greenes' (with whom Herbert was popular for his easy-going ways and his adventurous charm as well as for his looks) this might have been no great disadvantage. But it was extremely unfortunate that the eldest son and heir of the 'intellectual Greenes' should be a dunce. His parents sent him to Marlborough – presumably fearing that a Headmaster's son at the bottom of the lowest form would be unbearably teased had he stayed at Berkhamsted. He hated Marlborough too, even though he was so good a cricketer. Herbert, if anybody, suffered a trauma of sorts in his childhood, the trauma of rejection, particularly painful, one imagines, coming from his younger brothers who had once hero-worshipped him for his cricketing ability and gradually came to despise him and with casual cruelty mock at him for his lack of brains and of success.

But Raymond was quite different. Raymond was almost as good-looking as Herbert but much more quick-witted and successful. He was to become both a school prefect and head of the house – all, quite obviously, on merit. Raymond was an extrovert; and he appears to have had no complex whatsoever about divided loyalties or being the Headmaster's son. Charles Greene was extremely proud of this fine tall and popular offspring of his, no fool intellectually either; the *beau ideal* of the public schoolboy.

Graham, though, was, like most introverts, unpopular at school; and, being neither particularly brilliant in the classroom nor at all prominent in any other aspect of school life nor even particularly wicked or outrageous, and a nullity on the sports field to boot, lived throughout the next years, even when Raymond had departed to Oxford and a still more shining career there, in the shadow of Raymond's popular success.

But it was a book that seems to have done for him.

On one point, and perhaps only on one point, do Graham Greene's accounts of his own life carry the ring of utter truth, and that is when they deal with the books and the authors that influenced him. It is as though this, and this alone, is too important not to be entirely accurate. All the rest may when necessary be twisted and turned, dramatized, edited out, cut, exaggerated, run together or, as the case may be, respected in order to make a better or at least a more coherent story. But books – the centre after all, of any writer's life – are sacred.

And so it is absolutely credible that of all the books that influenced Graham Greene, the one that influenced him most was the one he first took down from the library shelf when he became a boarder, *The Viper of Milan. The Viper of Milan* differed from the previous books which had caught the boy's imagination in one most striking characteristic: its central figure was not a hero and an Englishman with, in counterpoint, a villain and a foreigner. Its central figure was precisely the villain and the foreigner himself, Gian Galeazzo Visconti, Duke of Milan. "From that moment," wrote Graham Greene, "I began to write... It was as if I had been supplied once and for all with a subject."

And that is probably true. He had discovered, above all, the presence and the attraction of evil. The trouble was, that at the age of fourteen, he immediately began to see evil and treachery all around him, in the basically placid surroundings of Berkhamsted. "As for Visconti, with his beauty, his patience and his genius for evil, I had watched him pass by many a time in his Sunday suit smelling of mothballs. His name was Carter. He exercised terror from a distance like a snowcloud over the young fields... I read all this in *The Viper of Milan* and I looked around and saw that it was so." The schoolboy Graham not only read melodrama, he lived melodrama. And he rewrote his life as melodrama. From a later less high-flown account it appears that Carter, an older boy in the same house, was in no way a physical bully but inflicted 'mental torture'; with 'sneering nicknames'. Compared to the very real bullying and literal torture which was then common, and accepted almost as character-forming in so many English public schools*, this was hardly Evil in the Visconti sense. His behaviour became furtive, indeed almost paranoiac. He hated

* Cp indeed the account of Bedales in *The Old School* edited by Graham Greene.

returning to school at the end of the holidays. His parents, both of them, watched his unhappiness and indeed oddness grow with increasing anxiety.

On the last day of one summer's holiday Graham decided he could stand it no longer. He made up his mind to run away and hide out on Berkhamsted Common (criss-crossed with trenches since the Great War) until his parents agreed that he should never again have to return as a boarder to St. John's. He wrote a note for them after breakfast, planned his campaign, and took to the heather like a Buchan or a Stevenson* hero. The escape collapsed ignominiously when he was caught by his elder sister, Molly, surrendered tamely, and was escorted home after only a couple of hours.

Droves of unhappy public-schoolboys, then as now, ran away from school or refused to go back. The phenomenon was not exceptional. But in the case of Graham Greene the treatment most certainly was. Marion and Charles Greene were not fanciful nor flighty nor unconventional parents. On the contrary their ethos was the ethos of their class; of duty and to some extent of rigour. It would have been normal for a runaway public schoolboy to have received, especially in those days, a stern talking-to from his father and a consolatory, but equally firm, heart-to-heart from his mother; and to have been sent straight back to school. In exceptional cases the parents might, reluctantly, have given way, and allowed their son to become a day boy, living at home, rather than force him to continue as a boarder. What they would never, ever, have done was to remove their son from school and home totally and send him away for six months to London to be psychoanalyzed. Yet that is exactly what the Greenes did in Graham's case. The inescapable conclusion is this: if the parents were not utterly exceptional, (which in the Greenes' case they were not) then the circumstances must have been. Only that could have justified so panicky a measure.

It is here that the question-mark hanging over the adolescent boy's grandfather becomes a crucial part of the conundrum. The Reverend Carleton Greene had always been subject to 'illnesses'. His wife Jane had nursed him devotedly. When she had died, suddenly, of a stroke, at the age of only 56, her husband had been left disconsolate. He had published the following year, the year of Graham's birth, a little book, an anthology, in memory of her and printed at his own expense, entitled *Death as Sleep* – a melancholy little work. Then no more is heard of him. His unmarried daughters depart, Maud to Berkhamsted, to live near her sister and nieces and nephews; Nora, Aunt Nono, to London. Who looks after their father? Yet till the eve of the Great War the Reverend Carleton remains, in name at least,

* If Graham Greene had a streak of the literary Celt in his veins, then it can be traced back to Robert Louis Stevenson, with whom he shared a common ancestor: the Reverend Lewis Balfour, D.D., Minister of Colinton near Edinburgh. His eldest daughter, Marion Balfour, was Graham Greene's mother's grandmother. Her younger sister, Margarite, was RLS's mother. Jane, the Reverend Carleton's wife, was RLS's first cousin. Graham therefore was Robert Louis Stevenson's first cousin twice removed.

Vicar of Great Barford; though at Great Barford the oldest parishioner most remembers, even nowadays, his 'absences'. From 1913 till his death in 1924 his whereabouts are a total mystery. But the indications are that he was by nature a manic-depressive; that he became gradually more and more unhinged after the death of his wife, and that he had at some stage been put away quietly in an asylum. If this was indeed the case, then Marion Greene lived with the fear that symptoms of their grandfather's "illnesses" might reappear in her own children; she may have been in agonies of guilt over the very fact that she, alone of her siblings, had married and had children at all. Indeed it takes no great imagination to see, in the strain such a situation and its concealment would inevitably have imposed, the root cause of Marion's own apparently cold and withdrawn personality. So Graham's distraught parents took the drastic step of removing their disturbed son from school and packing him off to a specialist; for fear that, unless he was promptly treated, he too might end up, like that non-person in his life, his wretched grandfather, locked away in a loony bin.

* * *

Graham Greene did not in fact go mad, then or later. For a writer he remained quite remarkably sane all his life, much more consistently so indeed than such contemporaries (and fellow-converts) as Evelyn Waugh and Antonia White. Towards the end of his life he perhaps came unwittingly to share the Reverend Carleton's views; in one of the few interviews where he allowed himself to be almost cornered, he admitted that, as an 'agnostic Catholic' he did not believe in Hell, or angels, or God as a disembodied spirit or even, very much, in Heaven. Somewhat obsessed with death, like his clergyman grandfather before him, he seems to have accepted the view of 'Death as Sleep' – though there is no knowing that he had ever read, or even heard of, the Reverend Carleton's little anthology.

* * *

Those six months in London did Graham the schoolboy a power of good, though not exactly in the way his parents had imagined. What he had been suffering from, though, was not incipient lunacy but a lack of attention. And attention during his stay at Lancaster Gate he received in abundance; from the first moment of the day when a housemaid would bring him his breakfast upstairs on a tray to his bedroom. After breakfast he would arise and walk through the Park to Kensington Gardens with a notebook, sit down and there write an account of his previous night's dreams. When the nearby church tower struck eleven, he would gather up his notes and go back to the house where his psychoanalyst and host Kenneth Richmond would be sitting in his study, stop-watch in hand. The boy would read out his dreams, the man would ask him for his associations.

In the months that followed, in over 150 morning sessions, the boy, hesitantly at first, then with increasing fluency and confidence, talked out his childhood, and in particular the last two lonely and miserable years in a way that few boys ever have the opportunity to do. This period, those sessions, account for the fact that, all his life, his memories of childhood were to remain so vivid and so highly charged with emotion. These unique six months – not some 'deep unhealed traumatic wound' – with all their talk, all their associations, all their churning through of his life so far, were the source from which the future writer was almost bottomlessly to draw – in all his memories of childhood, autobiographical, fictionalised or dramatized. That was their long-term significance.*

Straining rather, he managed to find horror and evil even in his London months. He was approached one morning by an elderly Old Etonian in the Park who asked him 'Do they cane at your school?' and then moved away; a non-event later memorably transmuted into "the small human viciousness of the thin distinguished military grey head in Kensington Gardens with the soft lips and the eye which dwelt with dull lustre on girls and boys of a certain age," – all this and a whole paragraph more. But in general it was an extremely relaxed six months, with visits to the theatre, literary dinner-parties, and, inevitably, romance, – for Graham was after all sixteen at the time, well past puberty, tall and gangly, and highly conscious, all the more so because of the new theories which he was eagerly imbibing every morning†, of his repressed sexual urges.

His first fancy was for a ballet student, Isola, who visited the house and whom Kenneth Richmond took him to see dance. Then Ave arrived in London, during the Christmas holidays, Uncle Eppy's eldest daughter. The 16-year-old boy took his 18-year-old cousin to the theatre; but at that stage – at least according to his own account – wondered only when beautiful Ave would transfer her own emotions to Kenneth Richmond.

That summer, back at Berkhamsted but still officially 'convalescing', he went as usual, with most of the junior Greenes, to Harston; and Aunt Eva took him on his first trip ever out of England. They sailed to Lisbon, to meet Uncle Eppy, due to dock there on his way back from Brazil, calling in at Coruña (where Graham

* Take for instance a minor example: his detestation of children's parties as demonstrated in the short story – one of so many he wrote about the displeasures of childhood – 'The End of the Party'. It is one of his earliest and one of his best, written in 1929. It ends melodramatically with one child literally frightening his brother to death in the dark at the end of a game they had been forced, unwillingly, to play. The conclusion apart though, the portrait of 'Mrs Hope-Smithie', the fat hearty bullying hostess, and the picture of the whole detestable atmosphere is so obviously drawn from Graham Greene's own remembered emotions that he must surely have relived the whole scene, and his own fears, in his psychiatrist's study – to reproduce it, vividly but horribly, years later.

† When the boy temporarily ran dry, Kenneth Richmond would explain the general theory of psychoanalysis along Freudian lines, though he was himself not particularly orthodox in his psychoanalytic approach: more of a Jungian, with elements of Adler thrown in. He was by all accounts

insisted on visiting the grave of Sir John Moore – "Not a drum was heard, not a funeral note, as his corpse to the ramparts they carried" – whom he was later, inaccurately but romantically, to claim as a relative); and Vigo.

"The lights of Vigo,; orchards, Harston apples," *he* wrote in a subsequent poem. "A dance or two, some sentimental tunes."

Aunt Eva took her daughter Ave along too, and in all likelihood it was that summer that Graham, who admits to falling in love with Ave 'later', first began to do so.

★ ★ ★

In his final year, no longer a boarder, now in the Sixth Form, and filled with a new-found self-confidence, Graham Greene found it much easier to make friends at school, particularly with other day boys, like Claud Cockburn and Peter Quennell, who were interested in literature. The two were already a contrast. Cockburn, who lived at neighbouring Tring and more glamorously at Budapest, was an ugly witty rumbustious boy, able because of his chess-playing ability to twist the Headmaster, Graham's father, always a keen chess-player, round his little finger. Quennell, a year their junior, was already famous for his good looks and his sophistication. His poem, *The Masque of Three Beasts*, was to make a big splash in Richard Hughes' anthology of *Public School Verse*. Together Graham and young Quennell would read aloud to each other with solemn glee semi-censored books like *Madame Bovary* or *The Yellow Book*. "His talk," wrote Quennell of Graham, "had an exuberantly sceptical and blithely pessimistic turn; and his contemplation of the horrors of human life appeared to cause him unaffected pleasure." If this is an exact observation – and there seems no reason why it should not be – then Graham Greene's basic human attitudes were, in his seventeenth year, already permanently set.

There was burgeoning interest, stimulated by Browning, in the lascivious; a clumsy kiss or two with Elizabeth and Hugh's Nurse, an attempted assignation with the golden-haired O'Grady girl.

an unorthodox man in every way – later to give up psychoanalysis for a business career; and spiritualism.

He certainly succeeded in convincing Graham of the importance of dreams. Dreams became with Graham Greene a persistent life-long obsession (though he was not above getting together with Ave to invent particularly significant dreams in order to enliven their mid-morning sessions). Part of his continuing treatment was to keep a dream-diary during his convalescence, with on one side of his notebook an account of his dreams, on the other his own analysis of them. Once a week he would send his diary notes up to Kenneth Richmond, and once a month go up to London to discuss both the dreams and their analysis with him. At home over the breakfast table he would mischievously egg on his unwitting parents to describe their dreams of the previous night in ever greater detail. "It's amazing," he once told Claud Cockburn, "what those dreams disclose. It's startling – simply startling"; and at the thought gave a low whistle.

But above all in that final year there was Ave, Ave playing tennis in the twilight, Ave who, next year, was sent away by her mother to Germany but from there sent Graham a postcard which he carefully preserved. Ave who however was probably in love with Herbert, three years her elder and just out of the Army, admittedly without a career as yet but very much a man-of-the-world.*

★ ★ ★

Meanwhile with increasing confidence and the whole-hearted encouragement of his parents Graham was writing. In the final months of his schooldays he had three of his short stories published – two, admittedly, only in the school magazine, *The Berkhamstedian*, but the third much more satisfyingly in *The Weekly Westminster Gazette*.

That was on May 6th 1922. By then his schooldays were drawing towards their end. Oxford lay ahead – and the beginnings of Graham's active and impassioned life. For at Oxford Graham Greene was to become involved in the most extraordinary set of incidents and adventures. His university career, beginning slowly, was to gather pace and end in a tremendous burst of unhappy love and bad literature.

Oxford, far more than his childhood, moulded the finished man.

*Graham Greene hints in his autobiography that Aunt Eva was seriously worried about the possibility of another marriage between first cousins in the Greene family: "which would," Greene adds, "have been a disaster". The thinking behind this throwaway subordinate clause is very obscure. Why would it have been a disaster? Marriage between cousins was, at that period, not unusual in English society; and the marriage between Charles and Marion Greene, first cousins once removed, was anything but disastrous.

In any case there could have been no question, whatever Graham implies, of Ave marrying him. Age alone would have ruled that out. Aunt Eva must have been worried about the possibility of Ave marrying Herbert. Indeed perhaps that is why Uncle Eppy found Herbert a job in Brazil – precisely in order to keep his lively daughter and her handsome first cousin apart. Which is not to say that Ave was not very fond of Graham but as one is fond of a younger cousin to whom one has grown close.

Chapter II

Balliol Man

"Balliol made me, Balliol fed me,
Whatever I had she gave me again:
And the best of Balliol loved and led me.
God be with you, Balliol men."

Hilaire Belloc

Four boys from Berkhamsted School went up to Oxford in October 1922: FN Ratcliffe to Wadham College, ER Guest to Oriel, FC Cockburn to Keble and HG Greene to Balliol. Of this little group HG Greene was probably the luckiest. Since the great Jowett's time, Balliol men were everywhere. For brains and ability, poetry, high spirits and good looks, Balliol had become *the* college.

Seventy-two other freshmen came up to Balliol that term, no less than thirteen of whom were Old Etonians – Cyril Connolly and Alfred Duggan, Lord Curzon's stepson, among them. Into this collection of swans the gangly youth from Berkhamsted did not particularly fit. It was only natural for a minor public schoolboy with little money and no particular distinction to fall back for company on his old school friends: in HG Greene's case therefore on that very ugly duckling, FC Cockburn.

Claud and Graham remained very close, at least in their first term; for at its end, in the Christmas Vacation, the pair of them organized one of those elaborate practical jokes to which Graham Greene was to become so addicted. They hired a barrel-organ in Oxford, dressed up as tramps with funny hats, and reddened noses, slept out in an open frost-covered field one night, and descended on Berkhamsted. The joke fell rather flat when they were not recognized by any of their former schoolmasters.

★ ★ ★

In their second term the two freshmen began, modestly, to make their mark. "Mr FC Cockburn (Keble) showed himself a sound Liberal" – the report was of a Union debate. Claud went on to become Secretary of the Oxford University

Liberal Club. Graham, for the moment at least, kept himself remote from politics. With the publication in February 1923 of "The Trial of Pan" in the *Oxford Outlook* he was making his first mark in Oxford literature.

"The Trial of Pan" is a rather clever long/short story in which God sits in judgement on the pagan Pan, and finds the tables turned and himself overthrown. Like "The Improbable Tale of the Archbishop of Canterbridge", another God-dominated fantasy that 'HGG' published in *Cherwell* at the beginning of his final year, its main interest is the apparent obsession Graham Greene appears to have had, long before he ever dreamt of becoming a Catholic, with God. The tales are of course extravagantly irreverent and decorated with blasphemous conceits but they are fluent and fast-paced, they read well; and it is quite evident that even then Graham Greene enjoyed writing about God – though God was never again to appear as an actual character in any of his published works, except, arguably, in *The End of The Affair.* In the battle against Satan "the Curate of Stow in the Wold was killed last night in an attempt to storm the Regent Palace Hotel", and the Archbishop of Canterbridge, a traitor, shoots God in his morning bath. "'I made myself man,' murmured he was once God, as sleep crept into his toes. 'A miracle... Very rash... I have done better in my day'... And in a bubble of bloodstained laughter God died."

Those first two terms he was living out of college, in lodgings in North Oxford in Bloomfield Road. Before leaving school he had twice failed to win a Scholarship to Balliol; and this meant that he had done less well than Raymond. Indeed Raymond, now in his third year, had shown that to have been at a minor public school was no barrier at all to an undergraduate determined to shine. Raymond totally outshone Graham. He was President of the Mermaid Club and President of the Oxford University Mountaineering Club, "one of the most energetic clubs in Oxford". He and Molly, the eldest of the Greenes, were great adventurers. Every summer they would go climbing in the Lake District and two summers previously, climbing down a vertical chimney, Molly, with Raymond leading and Charles Holland bringing up the rear, had fallen. It had been a hundred-feet fall and she had been extraordinarily lucky to come out of it with minor cuts and bruises. Raymond blamed Charles Holland, for they could all have been killed and the tail man was the pivot. Herbert was later to describe with appealing modesty how he hated and feared these mountain climbs, for which he had no ability or taste. But Graham appears, despite his professed love for danger, never even to have attempted the sport.

Raymond meanwhile was moving in the smartest of Balliol circles, a great friend of the most dazzling of all Balliol undergraduates of the time, Peter Rodd. He does not seem to have deliberately ignored his younger brother. It was merely that they were very different, with different tastes, friends and interests, members of different colleges too, and with an age gap that, at the University, was almost as important as it had been at school. That Easter Vacation Raymond, urged on by

Rodd whose father was the British Ambassador in Rome, set off for Sicily on the most rocambolesque adventure. The objective was to shoot Aleister Crowley, the black magician, the 'Beast', responsible (so it was thought at Oxford) for the death of a former undergraduate and poet, Raoul Loveday, who had become the 'Beast's' secretary. It all seems to have been more serious than a prank but less serious than a real murder conspiracy. Raymond travelled out with a young don from Christ Church, Claud Bosanquet, while Rodd prepared a sailing-boat for the getaway after the shooting. But the villa where Crowley should have been at Palermo proved to be empty; Peter Quennell, still at Berkhamsted School, and his patron Richard Hughes arrived; they all ran out of money and had to be repatriated by HM's Consul at Palermo. It was an escapade, for both Raymond and indeed young Quennell, that certainly makes the barrel-organ 'adventure' seem very tame.

★ ★ ★

From Graham's point of view one thing improved, objectively, in the Trinity term: he was out of lodgings and in College, with rooms on Staircase 20, for he had been awarded a Domus Exhibition in Modern History, worth a useful £70 a year. Living in Balliol, Graham now began easily to make his own friends among inconspicuous undergraduates of his own college and his own year. Robert Scott, son of an Exeter doctor, had, like Graham, a penchant for ingenious practical jokes; and the pair of them organized a whole series of complicated and successful deceptions, with Robert Scott disguised as Kipling lecturing to the Navy League at Berkhamsted and Graham Greene in return giving a slide-show of his 'adventures' as an explorer in Mongolia at Scott's old school, Highgate. With Scott again, and with Robin Turton, one of the smarter Balliol undergraduates, an even more elaborate deception was practiced on nearby Wallingford involving marketplace artists, runaway clergymen's wives and bananas for tea at the rectory.

Inevitably less than hilarious in frigid summary, these practical jokes are significant not, perhaps, because of any very profound psychological meaning – practical joking was very much an accepted thing among undergraduate society of the period – but because these particular deceptions involved such a combination of meticulous preparation with role-playing and disguise. Graham Greene was a stickler for meticulous preparation, he was adept at role-playing. And it would not be going too far to say that he relished deception, as the next episode in his Oxford career, one of the most feckless, surely, that any eighteen year-old undergraduate was ever to attempt, was most strikingly to indicate.

★ ★ ★

This was a much more dangerous business than even Raymond's Sicilian excursion; indeed perhaps it was the most potentially lethal affair that Graham Greene was ever to involve himself in. Did Graham realise the risks he was running? Or was it just a callow escapade, undertaken pretty casually and without any real thought of the consequences? It began well, and it ended well. Possibly it is wrong to make heavy weather of it.

Naomi Royle-Smith edited the *Weekly Westminster Gazette*. Graham had met her, together with Walter de la Mare, at the Richmonds' house in London; and had plied her with many unpublishable fantasies, and some publishable poems, short stories and reviews. That June, at the beginning of his first Long Vacation, he persuaded her to send him to Ireland on assignment. The Irish Civil War that had begun a year earlier with the bombardment of the anti-Treaty Republicans in the Four Courts was over; De Valera had laid down his arms. But Ireland was in a tense, troubled state; as Graham well described it in his eventual article, full of "a constant fear at the heart that something terrible, unknown and unpreventable" was about to happen. It was no place, outside Dublin, for two young English undergraduates.

For Graham took Tooter with him (now up at Cambridge). They crossed from Holyhead to Waterford; and they hiked up – they were both great walkers, tall, thin and silent – through the Free State, encountering hostility, even at one village being stoned as Englishmen. Then they parted company, Graham to try a litle solitary reconnaissance near or across the Border.

This was where real danger lay. The journalistic trip had been risky enough in itself. But, amazingly, it was only 'cover'. Graham had written that previous term from Oxford to the Free State Government in Dublin offering his services as an Englishman and a Balliol undergraduate to cross the Border (on both sides of which armed forces were massing) and report, from Ulster, on the military dispositions there.

British journalists are sometimes discreetly asked, when on assignment abroad, to report back to the Foreign Office on what they may or may not have seen. It is against the ethics of the profession, and most refuse. But this was monstrously different. Graham Greene had not been asked to "keep his eyes open"; he had offered his services as a spy unasked. And above all, he had offered to spy not for his own country but, in effect, against it. Legalistically speaking, there was a pungent flavour of treason here.

Fortunately the Free State authorities appear to have suspected that this was only too obvious a plant, a rather amateurish attempt by the British or more probably by the Ulster government to feed false information about troop strength and movements back to them. They could hardly have guessed that it was the frustrated sense of adventure of a budding novelist who enjoyed role-playing, however unscrupulous, for its own sake – and who was, perhaps subconsciously, eager to undergo himself the experience of being a hunted man.

All therefore ended quietly and well, with the publication of an excellent article, Graham Greene's first foreign *reportage* ever, in the *Weekly Westminster*. "It is the poverty and expensiveness of Dublin that first impress visitors, "he wrote. "The houses are dilapidated, the roads unswept. The two principal thoroughfares, Grafton Street and Sackville Street, would disgrace an English country town… The specimens of the army which we saw in the capital were not encouraging. There seemed to be little discipline, only one in fifty condescended to salute an officer if he met him in the street… But the most impressive thing about Dublin is its expectant but apathetic air."

This was to be Graham Greene's style of *reportage* throughout his life; little or no political analysis, but plenty of atmosphere, an eye for the striking detail, the pen of the fairly beady-eyed observer. Already there is a touch of Greeneland; even in this earliest piece, the seedy is omnipresent, though the word itself as yet is not. A certain English superiority too; not quite Lord Curzon, but more than a touch of "lesser breeds without the law"; which became modified in the course of Graham Greene's life but never entirely disappeared.

What is most striking, however, is the tyro writer's mastery, already, of two different styles of writing; one would hardly recognise in this observant and comparatively restrained journalist the author of the extravagant fantasies published in the *Oxford Outlook*.

★ ★ ★

At the beginning of the next academic year, that autumn of 1923, Peter Quennell came up to Balliol. Quennell "sought out the staircase on which my school friend Graham Greene lived. Our reunion, however, was disappointing. Having taken up residence a year earlier, he had already formed his own circle, which rightly or wrongly, I considered rather tedious; and, after a week or two of sharing their honest fun, I wandered off into a different milieu. Why Graham at Oxford should have so carefully avoided notice is a question that I cannot answer."

This was hardly fair of Quennell. Compared to the glamorous aesthetes of Christ Church,[★] to Harold Acton and the notorious stammering Brian Howard,

★ This was the milieu into which Peter Quennell so rapidly "wandered", introduced to the Hypocrites Club, like Claud Cockburn before him, by that "little prancing fawn", Evelyn Waugh. "I had thought Brian Howard precocious," wrote Harold Acton, "until I met Peter Quennell." Skinny, narrow-chested, with a piping voice, high shoulders, a dancing gait, thin straw hair and moth eyebrows brushed upwards – so Acton described him, Acton himself being described by his fellow undergraduate at Christ Church, the poor Cornishman, AL Rowse, ("These public schoolboys – Etonians and Harrovians, Wykenhamists and Rugbeians, even Berkhamstedians and Lancingites – were all years ahead of me, so much more sophisticated") as confronting a gang of rowing men at Worcester with the cry: "We are so dec-a-dent, and they are so in-no-cent." But despite what Peter Quennell implies, Graham Greene came into close contact with that milieu: not via wealth, social ease or homosexuality certainly, but through literary interests and poetic ambitions.

Graham Greene and his beer-drinking cronies may have appeared tedious and in-no-cent. But in Graham's case at least the fun was a lot less honest that Peter Quennell suspected; and notoriety, not obscurity, was certainly an aim. Indeed in his second year at Oxford Graham Greene, like most undergraduates, settled into his stride; and one can almost palpably feel him growing in ability and self-confidence.

He became, at the beginning of the academic year, co-editor of *The Oxford Outlook* – in fact as his fellow co-editor, Scaife of St. John's was that term elected President of the Union, Graham virtually ran the magazine on his own.

The Oxford Outlook had been founded five years previously by Beverley Nichols, also of Balliol, as "A Literary and Political Review, Edited and Controlled by Oxford Undergraduates" whose kindly aim it was "to give Oxford's opinion to the other Universities of the Empire". Like most undergraduate magazines, it had not entirely fulfilled the ambitions of its founder. But all the same, was it right of Graham, as editor, to sell out, surreptitiously, to a local politician?

For that is what, almost literally, he did. With another General Election looming he approached the Liberal MP for Oxford, Frank Gray; and offered to bring out a special edition of the *Outlook*, heavily in favour of the Liberal Party, provided Frank Gray financed it. The MP stumped up £100, and the *Outlook* appeared on time, well before December 6th 1923, the date of the General Election, carrying a long piece by Claud Cockburn which was described by another Oxford magazine as "A Liberal Manifesto". It was £100 well spent. Frank Gray was re-elected; the last of the Greene MPs, Sir Walter Greene, Bart, lost his seat; and back in Berkhamsted Graham's father, who, Claud Cockburn wrote, "was in the widest as well as the party-political sense of the word a Liberal" and who "in the crack-up of Liberalism saw the mark of doom" must have been delighted – ignorant as he was of the rather dubious subsidy involved – at this combined effort by his favourite ex-pupil and his now successful third son, who had both imbibed such sound Liberal principles as the result of so sound a Liberal education.

Enterprising as an editor Graham certainly had become; business-like in matters of money (as he was to remain all his life); and with no more moral scruples as regards editorial independence than he had *re* the ethics of the foreign correspondent. Perhaps he felt that neither he nor small Oxford magazines could afford moral scruples. Perhaps he was simply by nature and inclination amoral. In his next venture, buoyed up as it was by his two previous successes, he pushed the boundaries of both editorial and journalistic integrity still further back. Hubris appeared to have overtaken him. But instead of the immediate or eventual Nemesis, a rather good novel – *The Name of Action* – alone eventually resulted.

This time it was to the German Embassy in London that Graham wrote. He explained that he co-edited a small but influential Oxford journal; and offered to go out to the Rhineland and write a report on the situation there – provided the German Embassy paid his expenses.

The response could not have been more encouraging; or surprising. He came back to his rooms late one afternoon – it was his second term as editor – to find the First Secretary of the German Embassy ensconced there and his only bottle of brandy almost empty.

This was the beginning of a long friendship. Count Albrecht Bernstorff was in his mid-thirties, fat, genial and witty, the sort of roué Graham always liked, the first of the kind Graham had met. He whisked his undergraduate up to London, wined him at the Abyssinian Club, and accepted his plan – indeed Graham's letter could hardly have come more appositely, for the Count, an Oxford man himself, one of the original Rhodes scholars, had been planning to influence Oxford opinion against the French. He agreed to pay Graham's expenses, and provided his man with a pile of introductions for his journey.

Graham persuaded Claud Cockburn to go with him. In Germany they were joined by Tooter, who was already there – Tooter who, like all Aunt Eva's children, half-German by birth, spoke German fluently. The three undergraduates had no over-melodramatic adventures. They went to 'occupied' Cologne, Essen, Bonn, Trier and Heidelberg. But Graham Greene in particular drank in the atmosphere of brooding menace and darkly-lit streets, of violence on the edge of breaking out, and of what he exaggeratedly called murder plots in romantic Heidelberg.

Back in Oxford he honourably discharged his dubious debt by publishing the following term a long article in the *Outlook* ironically entitled "The French Peace" – slanted admittedly, giving examples of Frency military repression and particularly of their use of 'blacks' as occupying troops: "a deliberate insult against a defenceless people" and an encouragement to rape; and a shorter more restrained piece in the *Oxford Chronicle*. Presumably there was a private and more detailed report to the German Embassy in London too.

And, had Graham Greene left it at that, there could be very little to be said. But he now embarked upon the second stage of his complex scheme. He wrote to Bernstorff offering his services not exactly as a spy but as a courier; offering, to be precise, to carry money and instructions from the German Government to its 'underground' agents in French-occupied Rhineland. He used the same argument as he had used to the Irish Free State Government. As a Balliol undergraduate, he suggested he would probably be able to pass through French border controls without arousing suspicion.

The Count refused that tricky offer. He suggested, instead, that Graham might like to return to the Rhineland, contact this time what from the German point of view were the 'collaborators', the French-backed Separatists; and write a report on them for the German Government.

It was a fascinating little spiel. Graham Greene was showing a natural aptitude for the role of spy. Very few undergraduates, after all, have had the oomph, or the sophistication, to write to foreign governments and foreign embassies proposing themselves for the job: most, traditionally, wait to be recruited. Very few of those very few can have learnt from their initial mistakes as quickly and intelligently as Graham had learnt; that one must proceed by stages, first offering one's services as a propagandist (but, from the outset, for money, a more reliable link from the agent-runner's viewpoint, than principle or, simply, the love of excitement); and then but only then, when a certain trust has been established, proposing oneself as an agent. The Germans were trying to manipulate Greene; but Greene at the same time was doing his best to exert leverage on the Germans.

The would-be spy now decided to equip himself with fresh journalistic 'cover'. With aplomb he contacted an extreme right-wing paper, *The Patriot*, owned by the Duke of Northumberland. This supported the French occupation of the Rhineland, and therefore the Separatists' cause of an independent Palatinate. He offered to write a report for them for no fee, provided that *The Patriot* accredited Mr Greene of Balliol College as their correspondent in the Rhineland. *The Patriot* agreed – provided he in his turn agreed to represent only their point of view.

This suited Graham very well. He would now be able to contact the Separatists as representative of a paper that was anti-German and on their side. It might have worried a lesser man that the trip would involve lies to his hosts, the Separatists, and continual deceit: for though his ostensible role would be that of a pro-French, pro-Separatist British journalist, in fact his real task would be to produce a secret report on the movement and its members for an anti-French, anti-Separatist foreign Embassy; with, very possibly, most unpleasant consequences for named individuals should Germany ever reabsorb the Rhineland.

To add to the web of complications he was weaving, Graham now proceeded to write to the French Ministry of Foreign Affairs in Paris, explaining that he was about to visit the Rhineland for the pro-French English paper, *The Patriot*, and asking them for written introductions to Separatist leaders; which, he says, they agreed to give him. There are indications that, if the mood had moved him, if that famous 'virtue of disloyalty' had come into play, he might have ended up double-crossing Count Bernstorff by selling a copy of his 'secret' report for the Germans to the French as well. In fact it was never to come to the test. France and Germany reached a compromise settlement before the summer; and as the possibility of an independent Palatinate Republic being set up faded away, so too did any interest in the Separatist leaders.

Meticulous prepartion and paperwork, complex role-playing, an almost innate love of the tortuous, plus careful attention to the cover story, careful consideration of the money involved, and no apparent account taken of the morality or immorality also involved – if these are the marks of the double agent, then that was Graham Greene's natural bent both at Oxford and indeed, it might be argued, throughout his whole life.

Alternatively, it was just another high-spirited undergraduate prank.

⋆ ⋆ ⋆

So ended, in a certain frustration, his second year at Oxford. That summer of 1924 he was forced by lack of money and the failure of his Rhineland plans to join the family for their summer holidays by the sea. Romantic longings and clumsy kisses apart, it seems likely that it was on this Long Vacation that he was first pricked by sharp physical lust. Hugh and Elizabeth had a governess now; and at Sheringham, on the Norfolk sands, Graham was mesmerized by her long pale naked legs. His upbringing had been puritanical and emotionally cold. All his life he was, in one sense, to find the sexual urge distasteful and its satisfaction repellent. Yet all his life too he was to be fascinated and driven by that same urge.

Boredom and frustration were enemies he was to learn to keep at bay by work. That Long Vacation Graham settled into the writing of his first novel. Its original title, – which changed several times as the ending, always the most difficult part for a tyro novelist to manage, was vamped and re-vamped – was *Anthony Sant.* It is a vigorous, lively manuscript, telling, unsurprisingly, the story of a young man, his birth, childhood, schooldays and subsequent picaresque adventures.

First novels are notoriously autobiographical and much of the fascination of reading the manuscript comes from spotting the incidents that have happened to Graham in life – running away across the Common, sawing at his knee with a penknife – and happen to Anthony in the story. There is a favourite aunt, Aunt Janet, who has – because of a ghastly family secret – never married; and Anthony becomes furiously jealous when he thinks, mistakenly, that he sees her with a man friend. It is interesting that for the purposes of the story Herbert is cut out; Anthony has one brother only, John, three years his senior, and one sister, Margaret, two years older than John – modelled, obviously, on Raymond and Molly respectively. Margaret is self-possessed, pushy and inquisitive. John the hero dislikes, and Margaret he is quite certain he loathes. Mr Sant, Anthony's father, a small man with bookish tastes⋆ seems equally unloved – till he, at one stage, dies. The hero is summoned home for a rather well-managed and affectionately described deathbed scene where father and son are reconciled. On the contrary against his mother, Mrs Sant, tall dark and domineering, Anthony directs an hysterical outburst of hatred. The family relationships are passionately felt; they have a genuine ring of stifled love and barely suppressed fury about them.

⋆ "Short himself and latterly a little stout, he had married a tall slender wife and begotten a family of tall children;" – thus Peter Quennell, describing with courteous elegance Mr Greene the Headmaster, and Mrs Greene – "and perhaps it was his own comparative shortness that had encouraged him to develop at school so majestic a persona." The Greenes were thus transcribed by their third son into the Sants.

But the novel deteriorates rapidly when the writer ceases to describe the world he knows and lets his imagination and his hero roam – Anthony escapes the constrictions of a stifling home life to join a travelling circus and is seduced by Rose, a horseback tumbler. Filled with self-loathing, he sees his noble passion for the beautiful, his equally noble passion for the physical, transformed into a beast-like coupling with a depraved and grimy woman on a dishonoured bed. God, God, God, he cries out in his disgust.

This is the writing of a young man both repelled and fascinated by the idea of the act of sex. Yet even when for Graham Greene the act of sex had become not a mere literary longing but an actual physical experience, he was to continue as a novelist to describe it in much the same terms as in this first passage ever, though with perhaps not quite such artificial harshness.

In the surviving manuscript version the novel fades away with, in an obviously superimposed 'Archbishop of Canterbridge'-style ending, God's face zooming in close to the earth before soaring away again into the immensities of the heavens as the hero tumbles out in self-disgust into the dark wood, there to be swallowed up amidst the putrefying odour of natural decay. And in a long dithyrambic sentence that continues for many woeful lines more *Anthony Sant* ends.

The novel, like so many first novels, is unarguably a mess. But it moves fast and despite an epigraph taken from Conrad does not, as Graham Greene's subsequent novels were to do, become hopelessly bogged down in reams of slow-moving langourous prose and tedious introspection. And Graham Greene even in his very first novel was not so poor a writer as simply to recount in fictional form his own life. Then, as always, he introduces a twist, and a very ingenious one at that. Anthony whimpers at one point that he is not a black sheep of the family. But in fact, almost literally, he is. It would be sinful, a great-aunt thunders at Aunt Janet, if any man were to be allowed even to think of marrying her. And then the dreadful truth comes out: she has shameful blood in her ancestry, negro blood. So the hero is born a throwback, a black child to white parents, a genuine nigger baby. This interesting conceit* makes in fact very little difference to the plot. Anthony is still brought up and sent to school as a normal English child and it is only sporadically that the author seems to remember, and use, the colour of his skin. The important point appears to be that Anthony is different.

Indeed, Anthony concludes, just as Robert Louis Stevenson was marked out by his consumption, just as Byron stood out from the throng with his gammy leg, just as the stutter of the poet Darley distinguished him from other men, so I too am set apart from the common herd.

There can be no mistaking the real hero of that striking flash of revelation.

* Which suggests that Graham had some inkling of the Reverend Carleton's "bad blood"; and also perhaps why he thought his favourite aunt, the lovely Aunt Nora, had never married. It was this autumn that the Reverend Carleton Greene died, on October 4th, two days after his grandson Graham's twentieth birthday.

Chapter III

Enter Vivienne, Softly

In the first term of their final year Graham Greene and Claud Cockburn joined the Communist Party of Great Britain – the CPGB. They kept very quiet about it at the time. It was not at all a frivolous thing to do. There was bitter hostility to the Party in those years on the part of the public, great fear too, and close surveillance by the police.

Why did they do it? It was an extraordinarily heated political atmosphere during the whole time Graham and Claud were up at Oxford, with no less than three General Elections in those three years: a thing never known before or since. By their final year the Liberal position was no longer tenable for generous-spirited young men. By its treachery the Liberal Party had caused the fall of Britain's first Labour Government which they, the Liberals, had put into power. But the Labour Party itself has been pusillanimous, failing to stand up, in the *Workers Weekly* case, for the total freedom of the press. The Workers Weekly, being prosecuted for sedition, was the journal of the CPGB. The whole election of October 1924 turned on this *cause célèbre*. The two undergraduate editors – Graham of the *Outlook*, Claud of *Isis* – almost certainly became Communists out of solidarity; and quite right too.

They both, in a sense, remained Communists for most of their lives; Claud actively as a truculent and indeed ruthless Party activist, Graham more passively as a proclaimed if intermittent sympathizer. It was therefore a momentous joining for both of them, that led, in both their cases, to a lifelong commitment. An historic personal moment, in fact. Yet both preferred, even years later, to draw a veil over their Oxford joining.

Indeed Claud in his memoirs makes no mention at all of belonging to the Communist Party at Oxford; an extraordinary thing as he describes in considerable detail how he later joined it in the early Thirties. Moreover his widow Patricia Cockburn had no recollection of his ever having mentioned, even in a casual aside, having been a member of the Party as an undergraduate. Yet it is not something that anyone usually forgets; and Claud was a very talkative man, a notable raconteur, without normally an ounce of reticence.

As for Graham, by nature a much more secretive person, he too kept very quiet indeed about his membership of the Party at Oxford. It only came out as a result of an indiscreet moment at a private dinner party in the post-war years. Graham was furious at the time. Once it was public knowledge, though, he never denied it; but he certainly attempted to play its importance down. The conclusion that must be drawn is this: had it not been for that indiscreet moment many years later, the fact that Graham Greene and Claud Cockburn joined the Communist Party at Oxford would have remained a well-kept secret; as they both had indeed wanted it, it seems obvious, to remain.

Where there is secrecy, where there is obfuscation, there is usually something to hide. There was certainly obfuscation surrounding Graham's next journey abroad, to Paris in January 1925. This trip Graham made alone, which was in itself unusual. He did not propose any articles on it to either the *Outlook* or the *Weekly Westminster*, which was highly unusual. He certainly would not have financed the journey himself. He went, almost certainly, as a 'fraternal delegate' from the Oxford Party cell of the CPGB to attend the meeting of the PCF, the *Parti Communiste Français*, at Menilmontant near Belleville.

In his autobiography he gives the wrong year, 1926, for the trip and, more significantly, the wrong Vacation, the Easter Vacation, emphasising his awakening sexual interest and the 'romantic' side always associated with Easter in Paris. But it was not at Easter. January in Paris is very different from April in Paris; and the proof that the visit was in January exists in his own handwriting on contemporary documents of the time.

He plays down the political connection; yet vividly describes how the *Garde Républicaine*, rifles and bayonets at the ready, lined the squares of Menilmontant, ready to suppress the potential insurgents. For the PCF was many times the size of the Communist Party of Great Britain, much more of a threat to the established order, much more militant and overtly revolutionary. All over Europe at that time established governments and the ruling classes lived in enormous fear of being overthrown not by war, not by the armed forces of the USSR, but by their own working classes, organised by Communist agitators and intellectuals, and supported by Moscow. In England that fear, though pervasive, was unrealistic: the CPGB was too small, and its public meetings (as caustically described by Graham in a later novel, *It's A Battlefield*) too chaotic. But in France the power of the Comintern, the Communist International, was starkly revealed.

To sum up: Graham Greene was a member of the Communist Party at Oxford. He tried to conceal this in later life. He went to France in the Christmas Vacation of his final year at Oxford and attended an impressive meeting of the French Communists. He was fascinated by spying at the time and had previously been prepared to act for foreign Embassies or for foreign Governments without overmuch scruple. The Comintern was certainly interested in recruiting agents; and, later on, in the Thirties, was to make a practice of doing so from sympathetic members of the British ruling class while they were undergraduates. The Paris meeting would have provided an ideal setting for approaching a young and somewhat isolated Englishman. These are facts. They lead to a possible, and fascinating, hypothesis, which readers may deduce for themselves. But the hypothesis is only that: a hypothesis. Is it supported or is it invalidated by the later events of Graham Greene's long life?

* * *

In any case it was poetry rather than politics that on his return to Oxford was to fascinate Graham. He was thrilled (and wrote Hugh, unbeknownst to them both a future Director General, an ecstatic description) when at the beginning of the Hilary term, his last but one, he and other Oxford poets, Harold Acton, Brian Howard and Patrick Monkhouse among them, were invited to come up to the BBC studios in London and read a selection of their poems over the airwaves. AL Rowse of Christ Church was among the group. In his memoirs he gives what appears to be the only actual physical description recorded of Graham as an undergraduate.

"What I remember," he writes, "is the extraordinary youthful appearance with the curly flax-gold hair and the odd strangulated voice, speaking from his adam's apple as if he had difficulty in producing the voice. Most of all one was struck by those staring china-blue eyes, wide open to the world."

February 1925 was a crowded month at the University. The versatile Robert Speaight, another Oxford poet, triumphed in the title role of *Peer Gynt* at the OUDS, warmly praised by a visiting Danish critic, Nordahl Grieg of the *Oslo Aftenuaw*. Harold Acton had his second book of poems *An Indian Ass* published in London by Duckworth's and welcomed with rapture everywhere except in the Cherwell where Robert Byron launched a ferocious attack on Speaight, Acton and the whole Oxford dramatic and literary scene. The new *Oxford Outlook* appeared; and sold out within 48 hours. 'FCC' – Claud Cockburn now in the *Isis* – was generously enthusiastic about the editor's poem. "Mr. Graham Greene has never been unintelligible but '*The Back Porch*' is something of a novelty in its manner, introducing as it does into its catchy syncopation a number of choruses from the most popular songs of the year" – a technique that Graham Greene was later to adopt and adapt in his early novels. But the Cherwell critic was sterner: "Mr Greene tries to be a Sitwell and does it thoroughly badly in '*The Back Porch*'." He added, however: "Mr Greene expresses good ideas on films."

* * *

One reader at least did not think so. Vivienne Dayrell was working in a cubby-hole of an office for Basil Blackwell at 49 The Broad. She was a shy girl, lacking self-confidence, but with very strong convictions. She dashed off a letter of protest to Mr Greene about his film criticism, hesitated and then finally posted it.

Mr Greene wrote back, politely, feelingly and apologetically, on embossed Balliol College writing paper, inviting Miss Dayrell to forgive him and to have tea with him. They had tea on March 17th and Graham fell, almost at once, passionately in love.

Later he told Vivienne that it was the second page of her fire-breathing letter that had attracted him. Bored with the amusements Oxford could provide, he made a vow to himself to suggest himself into love with her if she turned out to be at all pretty. She was small but shapely; inclined to think herself over-plump; with beautiful dark hair, fine white teeth, rounded arms and shoulders, a generous mouth and a perfect skin. Two months later he acknowledged, ruefully, that his arrogance had been rightly punished and that he was indeed desperately in love with her.

Though Vivienne was nineteen, only a year younger than Graham, her character had not hardened. She was childlike, malleable, eager to please, impressionable, eager to love; but sentimental, wary, easily scared. The dominant influence in her life was that of her mother, Muriel. Muriel was almost the caricature of a doting, possessive mother, and had probably been so "from the moment I saw your chubby pink face and heard your cheerful gurgle". Later, she certainly had reason to be. She had walked out of her marriage to their father Sidney Dayrell-Browning in the middle of the Great War, a bold thing to do in those days, taking with her her daughter Vivienne and the younger child, her son Patrick. "There was no compensation in my marriage," she was to tell her daughter years later, "but you and Pat, and your mind was my greatest. I gave you two good care because I cared for nothing else and was shut up and deliberately balked of every other interest by the narrow views and narrow pocket of a narrow little man. Whew! That awful caged feeling I had with S.B. like being in a small dark room furnished in bamboo. I've locked up the drawer in my mind where every memory of it is only too damn clear and try to start at October 30th, 1915 when I burst the door and left him."

Her husband disappeared, forever, traditionally enough to South America and Muriel, a strong-minded woman, settled in Hampstead, determined to do the best she could for her fatherless children. Her family supported her and the two grew up supported by a cocoon of sympathetic uncles and aunts and above all by Alfred and Amy Green-Armytage, their grandparents. Vivienne went to South Hampstead High School and in the holidays to Worthing in Sussex and to her grandparents in the prosperous Bristol suburb of Clifton. She was a romantic poetic child and from the age of thirteen she was writing poems: "To Mummy at Christmas", "To Mummy on her Birthday", "For Mummy Dear in remembrance of October 30th, 1915" "For my cousin Adrian Green-Armytage, at Downside", "For my cousin Doreen Green-Armytage"; "For my baby cousin Gerard, in heaven"; "To my darling grandmother Amy Green-Armytage", and touchingly, "To my grandfather Alfred Green-Armytage, who understands".

Her grandfather had taken her to the Cenotaph on the first anniversary of Armistice Day and there, at the Cenotaph, the passionate patriotic young girl wrote a poem: "To the soldier-clerks of London who fell in the Great War". Muriel was immensely proud of her talented daughter. She presented her to Walter de la Mare, for whom she wrote a poem, and to GK Chesterton, President of the Poetry Society, for whom she wrote another. She persuaded Basil Blackwell to publish a book of her daughter's poems and essays. GKC wrote a genial foreword: "I think the work very beautiful and still more promising" and her mother added a proud personal note: "All the work of my young daughter contained in this first volume of her Verse is original and has been written without aid of any kind... Vivienne's present age is 15½ years. Muriel Dayrell-Browning, January 1920." Vivienne dedicated the book, published a year later, "To Mummydar, Who Has Shown Me Beauty Everywhere". It is a charming volume, the verse ringing out with a Bellocian swing – "I'll meet my Fate in Devon – my land of heart's desire" – and one of the handful of essays beginning, delightfully: "Fourteen long years on earth! I sometimes think that when one has passed twelve, there is not much to live for".

Four long years later and Vivienne had been accepted by Basil Blackwell as an apprentice. He was a notoriously kind-hearted man and one can see Muriel pushing hard for her daughter's job. But he was no fool and he undoubtedly saw potential talent in the young woman whose schoolgirl poetry he had once published. Legend had it that Dorothy Sayers, his former secretary, used to perch on his knee. That was not Vivienne's role. She was not Mr. Blackwell's secretary or his personal assistant – she was more a general factotum, ready to turn her hand to anything, picking up meanwhile the elements of bookbinding and design and printing, happy to have the chance – unusual for a girl of her class, in her day – to be earning, however modestly, a living. She lived at the YWCA in Magdalen Street, right in the centre of Oxford, by the University Church of St Mary's, five minutes' walk from her work. The girls lodging there were allowed out till ten o'clock, but only on alternate nights. From Hampstead Muriel kept a careful watch on her daughter, demanding accounts of how she spent every minute, almost, of her spare time.

The Green-Armytages were a solid professional clan, not particularly established nor in any way distinguished. Their connections were with the Indian Army – Vivienne's Uncle Paul was a Major in the 117th Mahrattas and her godfather, her Uncle Vivian, a military gynaecologist in the Indian Medical Service, Calcutta. What little money there was to spare in the Hampstead household was set aside for Vivienne's brother Pat, for his training at Sandhurst and his future as an officer. Nor were the Green-Armytages an old Catholic family. On the contrary only a generation earlier, in 1890, AJ Green-Armytage had published a booklet entitled "Anglo-Catholicism the Safe Way; or 4 Reasons for Not Going over to Rome". Over to Rome, nevertheless, despite AJ's rearguard battle, they had gone, Vivienne (brought up a non-Catholic) with them; and in the traditional manner of converts were more papist than the Pope. Indeed what had induced her to write with such indignation to the Editor of the *Oxford Outlook* was his casual reference, in an article on films, to Roman Catholics "worshipping" the Virgin Mary. This, she pointed out, was simply inaccurate. Catholics revered the Virgin Mary but did not worship her. The correct theological term was hyperdulia.

Heavens knows what Vivienne made of the tall by now rather formidable third-year Balliol man with his sudden abrupt silences and highly developed sense of criticism who had invited her to tea. He dropped into the office a couple of times. As Editor of the *Oxford Outlook* he had business with its publisher, Mr Blackwell, but Vivienne was too shy in front of her colleagues at work to do more than scurry out and in for a brief glance. Then he wrote her a charming letter inviting her to the movies, to which, he explained, he went four times a week. They met, on the last night of term, outside The George and saw *Three Women.*

For Vivienne, Easter meant a welcome break in France; but for Graham the time of travels and escapades was most definitely over. Exams – his Finals – loomed frighteningly close and after exams the choice of a career. AL Rowse sent him a poem for the next issue of the *Oxford Outlook* and he wrote back from Berkhamsted with his usual meticulous courtesy to explain that he was giving up the *Outlook* and passing the reins – and the poem – on to his successor, Patrick Monkhouse. He later confessed to Vivienne that it had been a tremendous wrench. Perhaps the *Outlook* was never quite to fulfil all his ambitions as a springboard – he would not be able to boast as its first editor Beverley Nichols was shortly to do of himself: "has visited and candidly commented upon most of the countries of the world". But it had got him to the Rhineland, given him a taste of adventure and a taste of power; and he had been an excellent, innovative editor. Under his editorship, as one of the more staid magazines commented, the *Outlook* had put the O! back into Oxford.

Graham returned to Oxford as soon as he decently could; to work, and to see Vivienne. He invited her out to dinner and the theatre on April 17th exactly a month after their first meeting. She had been to a dance the night before and nearly refused. But she came. She wore – as it was an occasion for dressing up – a hat at dinner, and they sat at a little table by the window looking down at the passers-by in the street. They went to the Playhouse, saw "The Ship"; and it finished so late that they had to run back to the YWCA to get Vivienne safely in before the stroke of ten. Graham was back for his final term in north Oxford, living in digs at 29 Thorncliffe Road, a mile and a half away. That night he walked two miles past his digs, almost in ecstasy, wondering when he dare ask Vivienne out again. Macloed dropped by at Thorncliffe Road about midnight. Macloed was by way of being his closest friend at the time. Macloed had been at the Playhouse too, in the back seats. They talked about the play, and the *Outlook* and about Acton and about themselves. Suddenly Macloed asked: "Who was that strikingly beautiful girl you were with?" Graham made a casual reply; but inwardly he rejoiced.

* * *

Vivienne apart, another great excitement was looming, perhaps the greatest of Graham Greene's young life. His first book was about to be published. It was due to come out on the last day of April: *Babbling April* it was entitled, to be published by Basil Blackwell (Vivienne not far apart, therefore), a book of poems by Graham Greene, the tangible proof that he too, like Peter Quennell and Harold Acton, was a recognizable, a fully-fledged poet. The title was taken from Edna St. Vincent Millay.

> "It is not enough that yearly, down the hill, April
> Comes like an idiot, babbling and strewing flowers."

The poems had almost all been published before, in the *Oxford Outlook* and in the *Weekly Westminster* or elsewhere. There were 32 of them, a slim volume. *Isis*, now edited by Claud Cockburn – he unlike Graham had not abandoned university journalism to concentrate on exams – gave it a welcome puff on April 29th. "This is the attractive title of a book of Verse by Mr Graham Greene which will be published tomorrow by Blackwell. Mr Greene's work is well known in Oxford... It will be sold at 4/6d, we hope to a lot of people."

There is nothing like the glory of a first book published and the glow of fame and delight, however transient, surrounding such a happy event to stimulate romance. In the first days of May Graham swept Vivienne off her feet. Invitation after invitation showered upon her: to concerts at Balliol, to dinner at The Trout, persistently to come and see *St Joan* – on Monday, Tuesday, Wednesday, Thursday or Friday. She never did; but Graham went and the fine profile of St Joan in armour reminded him of Vivienne's. He chided her gently for still writing to him as "Dear Mr Graham Greene". They went out to Moreton-in-the-Marsh for a long walk in the Cotswolds and came back, extravagantly, by taxi. There was an even more extravagant and daring 'flip' one weekend up in an aeroplane. A snatched kiss – probably on the cheek – led to a stiff letter, Vivienne suggesting rather provokingly that Graham would be off with someone else in a fortnight. There was a splendid afternoon and evening in Eights Week at Headington. Vivienne persuaded Graham to come with her to Mass at the Catholic Church and he found it quite interesting even though he had only set foot in a church twice in the past three years. By May 25th they had agreed to write to each other every other day.

But there was a fly in the idyllic ointment of that month of May. Harold Acton had written, in *The Cherwell*, a full-length review of *Babbling April*, and it was damning. "A FRESH YOUNG ADVOCATE OF THE 'CENTRE' PARTY" it was headed; and after a long exordium ranging from Nietzsche to Mallarmé it turned to the subject in hand.

"Admitting that Mr Graham Greene belongs to the party in poetry which Mr Graves calls the centre-party, the genius of which is practical rather than adventurous, which advocates a poetry of bare statement rather than a poetry of incantation or august eloquence" – such as Harold Acton confessedly preferred – "we do not wish to be unfair to Mr Greene, who prefers a glass of clear sterilized water."

"For Mr. Greene has courted his metres well, and his command over the little comforts of life and nature is remarkable. The weather is always clear. The poet is always able to walk into the garden, play tennis during the summer and bridge during the winter, enjoy his tea (especially the scones, muffins, crumpets and tea-cake), and listen to the gramophone playing '*What I'll do*'. A girl's red lips are also in the neighbourhood. Thus happy, healthy, lucky, sane and extremely sentimental, Mr Graham Greene ought to impart much pleasure to reviewers. If he fails to delight them, it will be because they are envious of his material, if not of his spiritual welfare. *Babbling April* is a diary of average adolescent moods. Whatever we may think it is not a mere exhibition of snap-shot photographs of unrelated objects; the objects are related, and they have a pathological sequence."

"Mr Greene has chosen to write about fundamental themes; about love, and God, and death, and failure, and desire, and spring. Adolescent feelings ooze through these poems because he has accepted an adolescent way of taking life. Like Mr. Frost, he believes in leaning hard on facts, but the outlines are all blurred with lethargic sentiment. Occasionally he can control his sentiments, as in '*I shall be happy*', the best poem in the volume, where there is none of the strain and self-consciousness inherent in all the other poems, and where there is none of Mr. Graham Greene's repulsive modesty. This false modesty is often apt to crystallize into cowardice. '*How timorously*', Mr. Greene begins on page one, and on page thirty-two, Mr. Greene has to remind us that if he places the revolver to his head it will be with '*eyes blind and fingers trembling*'. The reader is tempted to throw down the book with disgust, to cry aloud 'For God's sake, be a man!'"*

* The first poem of *Babbling April* entitled *Sensations*, described *inter alia*

> "How we make our timorous advance to death by
> pulling the trigger of a revolver which we
> already know to be empty
> Even as I do now."

The last poem, *The Gamble*, takes up the same conceit, with the Poet this time slipping a charge into one chamber out of six and then, "eyes blind and fingers trembling", pulling the trigger.

> "Will it be mist and death?" he asks. Or will it not?
> "Either is gain," he concludes,
> "It is a gamble which I cannot lose."

What the poet's feelings must have been as he read on with horrified fascination, any author of any published book will be able, with a shudder of sympathy, to imagine.

"But Mr. Greene is at his worst in such a poem as '*Atmosphere*', where he has to depend on his effect by repeating the first line again at the end: '*I am homesick for old memories*', or in '*Small Talk*', where he repeats the lines: '*The price of butter's rising very high*', or in: '*If you were dead*', where the possibility (which, we are told, would not matter anyhow) is repeated in the first line of each verse, and in '*Old Age of a Georgian*', where the Georgian's son is made to say: '*Darling, come out. The wind is on the moor*', as an alternative to sitting with papa, a-reading Yeats, Davies and De la Mare. This last poem affected us in a most uncomfortable manner."

Controlling his urge to vomit, Harold Acton reached his peroration: – "If Mr. Graham Greene desires to achieve a thing of beauty, he must detach his personality from the wishes of his unsatisfied libido – a difficult process for him, if we are to judge by *Babbling April*. Otherwise he will continue to dint the contaminated dusk with the slender banjo-tunes of an adolescent hysteria."

Rarely can one undergraduate have inflicted on another such a damnably effective review. Shaft after shaft deserved to strike home, and struck. Never again in a long lifetime of reviews did Graham Green have to face such a devastating attack. Little wonder that he summoned his friends to Thorncliffe Road – Robert Scott, George Whitmore, Bill Coghlin, who edited and sailed, and Arthur Braine-Hartnell, who wrote very fair poetry – for a riotous consolatory lunch where they got gloriously drunk, staggered down to the river, hired a punt and smashed into every other boat they could see. They reached Balliol just in time for Hall, Graham to find two notes in his pigeonhole from Vivienne and a copy of the *Oxford Outlook* – which carried, meagre compensation, a full-page ad for *Babbling April* and a favourable though shortish review by Patrick Monkhouse. In any case Graham was too befogged to take it, or them, in. By the end of dinner he was, understandably, – a thing that was to happen almost never again in his life – alcoholically paralytic.

He riposted, naturally enough. The next issue of *The Cherwell* carried a long

Over twenty years later, taking these two poems as his starting-point Graham Greene published, in the *Saturday Book*, a short story entitled "The Revolver in the Corner Cupboard", describing how a bored adolescent flirted with death by playing Russian roulette six times – and 'winning'. Mischievously enough, Greene cast this piece of fiction in autobiographical form, with "I" – himself – as hero – no blind eyes or trembling fingers in the later account – and set the "incidents" on Berkhamsted Common and at Oxford. Though ignored at the time of its first publication, this tale, repeated, then embellished, was to become a notorious part of his own personal legend – Graham Greene at his most successfully mythopoeic. By the end he seems even to have convinced himself that the legend was true – he certainly convinced the general public (though never his closest friends).

letter from 29 Thorncliffe Road addressed to the Editor, a fairly groggy counter attack lambasting Mr. Acton as an Edwardian warbler.

Provoked, Harold Acton closed in for the final *hautain* kill.

"Dear Sir," he replied on May 23rd.

"Plainly Mr. Greene does not deserve a reply. I reviewed his *Babbling April* at some length, and was sorry not to be able to speak of it in more favourable terms. Even as the fruit of Mr. Greene's journalistic nib, it disappointed me, and I was obliged to say so. Easily I could have dismissed it in a paragraph, a few appropriate words, with the vast contempt I felt for Mr. Greene. I was too generous. And behold my generosity rewarded by a would-be provocative epistlet. With a personal knowledge of Mr. Greene's grim stolidity (since he has chosen to be crudely personal about myself) I have no doubt that he employed his whole week pondering a retort 'through the crumbling of some bread' (Hovis?) during high tea at his lodgings in Thorncliffe Road."

"This correspondence," ED.CHERWELL understandably enough ruled, "must now close". It was, to change the metaphor, game, set and match to Harold Acton, and a less acute critic than Graham Greene might never have forgiven him. But Graham Greene always combined an eagle eye for other writers' faults with the rare ability to admit to his own faults, however vilely pointed out by others. Only six months later he was writing to Vivienne, still in Oxford, to tell her how much he had enjoyed his feud with Harold Acton, and how much he missed and respected him. One might not have thought so at the time; there was a boisterous incident with fire-extinguishers being dropped on one another by Harold and Graham in Balliol, watched by a startled, or possibly an amused Dean – for the literary 'quarrel' must have reached even the ears of the dons.

What is extraordinarily significant, and makes the whole episode stand out as a parting of the ways in Graham Greene's career as a writer, is how the letter to Vivienne continues. Although, Graham writes, no-one else is to know but her, Harold by his criticism of *Babbling April* had been a most tremendous help.

Good for Graham Greene. Few writers would have been able to admit as much. Though there were poems still to come, and better ones, ("Casual Myrrh", for example, in the June issue of *The Outlook*), to all intents and purposes Acton's article in *The Cherwell* marked the end of Greene's career as a poet. The subsequent verses were occasional pieces, or private love poems. Graham Greene had been following a false trail; Harold Acton pointed it out to him; Graham Greene chose his correct path. It was shortsighted to call the *Cherwell* review damnably effective, it was in its end result a blessedly effective one.

Five hundred copies of *Babbling April* were printed by Basil Blackwell. Three hundred and two were bound; 12 copies were given to the author, and 40 review copies were sent out. The unbound copies were later withdrawn from stock and scrapped. At most therefore two hundred and fifty copies of *Babbling April* were sold.*

★ ★ ★

It was hardly surprising that in these gloomy circumstances, with exams and, worse still, departure from Oxford looming, the love affair between Graham and Vivienne began to go wrong. She wanted pleasant, lively company, and he was turning moody and serious. Worried about his future, she tried gently to urge him to concentrate on work for the last fortnight before his Finals, and he resented it. They went out for the day to Abingdon, and he was miserable because he had not said anything he had intended to. The only consolation was that Macloed was round again, even more unhappily in love and in a hysterical condition, so that Graham had to forget his own worries and calm his friend down. He described Macleod to Vivienne as funny, odd, stocky and looking nothing like a poet – though, he added with a touch of understandable venom, in fact his poetry put Acton's or Peter Quennell's to shame.

The next two days were even worse. Graham took Vivienne for two miserable walks down by the Wolvercote Canal. He finally got out what he wanted to say. He proposed marriage. She refused. She mentioned 'Hugh', who worked in the office with her and was in his late twenties, implying that that was a far more suitable age – if she had wanted to marry, which she did not. He was consumed by jealousy. He took her to tea at The Trout. Vivienne was soft-hearted. He took her to the cinema at Headington and they played 'rabbits' in the back row – a harmless little game it must have been, for he wanted to kiss her but dared not. He also longed to slay 'Hugh'.

On June 5th he went home for an unpleasant interview. Like so many undergraduates, he had got heavily into debt. He admitted a hundred pounds of this to his father, who was almost embarrassingly understanding. He arranged that Raymond should sell off his library, his five hundred books, and take, for his pains, half the profits. Schools – the Final exams – began on June 11th. On June 14th the history dons of Balliol gave a farewell dinner to the undergraduates going down. On June 16th he wrote a note to Vivienne thanking her for the roses she had sent prior to the following day's ordeal. By that Saturday the exams were more than half over – eighteen hours done. He invited Vivienne to the Elizabethan Singers. On June 20th term ended. On June 21st, outside Oxford, he and Vivienne said their sad farewells. With his remaining possessions he caught the train to Bletchley and Berkhamsted. Balliol was behind him. Oxford was over.

* And it is said that for many years afterwards Graham Greene tried to buy in those two hundred and fifty copies; for he was not proud of his *juvenilia*. Any still in private hands must have great rarity value.

★★★

Graham Greene left Oxford with more than a second-class degree in history and from Vivienne the first romantic kiss she had ever bestowed. He left with more than a côterie of friends, a bevy of acquaintances and the inevitable intellectual arrogance of a Balliol man. All his futures, though he did not know it, were already signposted: the journalist, the editor, the critic, the traveller, the spy – not to mention the most important future of all, the novelist. All his tastes were foreshadowed: for film-going, for the theatre, for provocations and practical jokes, for literary controversy, for convivial drinking, for long walks, for collecting books, for a certain frugality in his dwelling-places, for anonymity combined with fame, for left-wing politics, for the underdog, for letter-writing, for the love of women.

In his writings Oxford stimulated nothing – not a character, not a story, not even a setting.★ But, from the point of view of his life, Oxford set the pattern in the carpet, Oxford shaped the man.

★ Not entirely true. It stimulated one radio play, many years later. See pp152 & 160 below.

Chapter IV

Warily to Rome

Vivienne may have thought when Graham went down from Oxford, that she had seen the last of that particular young man. If so, she much underestimated him. For the next two years a perfect avalanche of letters descended upon her – at times of great emotion as many as three a day. They did not sweep her off her feet – she had other suitors and, despite that first kiss, she was not in love with Graham. But in the end, inevitably, they snowed her under.

They were long, they were literate, they were extraordinarily sentimental. They were Graham Greene's chief literary product over this period, considerably over a million words in all, the equivalent of a dozen of his later novels. On Vivienne the cumulative effect of that mountain of pages was both wearisome and yet most flattering. How could one ignore someone who wrote so constantly, swore such fidelity, would not be halted by snubs or silence? It was wooing by letter carried to extremes; and in the end, for better or for worse, it was to work.

First, though, there were many months of difficulty ahead, in particular the eight months between the young man's coming down from Oxford and his landing his first proper job. Graham kept Vivienne abreast in his letters of all his difficulties, of all his hesitations, dilemmas and equivocations, involving her most unfairly (but again rather flatteringly) in decisions that could only be his alone and tangling both himself and herself up in almost inextricable knots.*

Yet these are, of all his letters, the most informative and the most interesting. Tucked away amidst all the mush and gush are passages that reveal a highly ambitious young man, keen on fame and very conscious of money too, with an acute eye for his own foibles and a nice line in descriptions of his fellow human-beings.

* In early July Graham applied for a trainee post with the British American Tobacco Company that would have taken him out to China at the end of September. He started work at the BATS office at Millbank in August, hating it, finding book-keeping nonsensical, but attracted by the money and the adventure. Should he go on or should he give up? Letter after anguished letter descended on Vivienne at Oxford. It all depended on her, on her allowing him just a ray of hope of marriage. This was most unfair. It placed an enormous weight of responsibility on her plump and pretty shoulders which she had neither asked for nor deserved. The poor girl, too soft-hearted to say no, too sensible to say yes, was in misery.

Before beginning at BATs he had seen Vivienne twice. On July 23rd he had made it up with her – the Thunder Night and the Thunder Star they christened it. (She, frightened, had apparently for the first time given him a kiss rather than the other way round. She christened their kisses 'stars' and 'Wuff' – Graham – tactfully accepted the romantic term, adding badly-drawn stars to his letters and rejoicing when, in letters or in life, they came to him in 'clusters'.) August 5th was Degree Day at Oxford. On its eve he wrote her a poem "Lord Love". In the evening, after the ceremony, they went happily to the cinema together, Graham staying (as he was often to do) at his old digs in Thorncliffe Road. Next morning, with a touch of self-dramatization, he read Conrad's *Youth* in the early train up to London and to his first day at the BATs office.

Vivienne was warm-hearted and affectionate by nature, she felt 'responsible', she had agreed to answer his letters and she religiously did so – he became very petulant if there was any failure in this – but, as she made it clear again and again, she was not 'in love'. Graham was not an easy person to be in love with, he was not conventional, he had not for instance, invited her – any girl at Oxford's dream – to a Commem. Ball, and she did not approve of his friends, such as Claud Cockburn. Moreover he was too intense and, when with her, too 'serious'; unlike 'Hugh', who was always witty and urbane. On the other hand he was prepared to do almost anything she suggested: he readily accepted that she would never consider, even remotely, marrying anyone who was not a Catholic – that would be to marry outside the Church, and a mortal sin, besides being no true marriage – and he seemed to have drawn the logical conclusion that he would therefore have to become a Catholic.

Even so, Vivienne was perfectly sincere in her desire not to marry. She was a romantic, she almost certainly considered, like many devout Catholic girls, renouncing the world, the flesh and the devil by taking the veil, and she felt an utter repugnance towards the 'physical' side of marriage. She was in a sense a child rather than a woman, living in a cocoon of cosiness symbolized by her dolls and her cat 'William', hating everything that was violent and 'dingy'. Yet warm cosy natures love affection and human contact. Vivienne was torn two ways. But what she certainly made quite clear to Graham from the start was her ideal of celibacy. And Graham accepted it. He wrote proposing a different style of marriage to the normal, with companionship and companionship only.

Back at Berkhamsted, in high good humour at his release from BATs – his business career had lasted precisely ten days – he wrote offering her a choice of glittering futures; with the Right Honourable Graham Greene, Prime Minister (but, he specified, Conservative Prime Minister: Vivienne was – and is – staunchly Conservative, and he was not about to upset her with radical views); or with Graham Greene, the great novelist, O.M.; or with Sir Graham Greene, War Correspondent of *The Times* (and secret adviser to the King of Afghanistan). All she had to do was to choose! Who knows what her choice was? For Graham apparently destroyed all *her* letters. But one cannot help wondering if, when sixty years later Graham Greene the great novelist did receive his O.M., he remembered that letter of his exuberant youth and spared a thought for long-discarded Vivienne.

Nervously Graham went to tea at Hampstead, met Vivienne's mother and Vivienne's cat; and liked them both, he assured Vivienne, a lot. She in turn had to face a much more nerve-wracking family occasion, Graham's twenty-first birthday party in the West End, complete with dinner, the theatre, Mr and Mrs Greene, Aunt Nora, Raymond, Hugh and a gangly Elizabeth. It all went extraordinarily well. As they left the restaurant, Raymond whispered "A.1" to Graham with genuine warmth.

★ ★ ★

Graham settled for the future knighthood. It proved, however, far more difficult to get a start in journalism than the Balliol graduate had anticipated. In the end he had to accept a totally unpaid post as a trainee sub-editor on what he considered to be a third-rate provincial paper, the *Nottingham Journal*. He consoled himself by calculating that this was bound to lead to better things.

Graham arrived in Nottingham by train on Sunday, November 1st 1925. He found the journey, the weather, the city, his digs, and the company there peculiarly depressing. Next day he wrote to Vivienne to ask for advice. How should he set about becoming a Catholic? Should he just call at a priest's home? Did any of her Oxford priests know any nice ones at Nottingham? But Vivienne was incensed.★ She did not answer any of his questions. So Graham went to Mass – he didn't think much of the pale young priest who seemed to have a very limited intellect – and, not having heard from Vivienne, decided simply to drop a note in at the Cathedral asking for instruction.

The first wary face-to-face encounter between Graham Greene and an official representative of that One Holy Catholic and Apostolic Church of which he was to become so dubious an ornament took place on the afternoon of Friday

★ Thoroughly incensed. Very rashly Graham had left for Vivienne to read at Oxford the completed chapters of his new (Conrad-inspired, historical romantic-revolutionary) novel, *The Episode*. Vivienne had spotted a scene based directly on the occasion late that July at Wolvercote by the canal when she had turned down his proposal of marriage. Furthermore at Oxford Graham had often used the pen-name of 'Hilary Trench' for his more romantic and sentimental published poems. And here was 'Hilary' being turned down in the novel! It was all too much! Graham's frantic replies and denials make hilarious and in the end (for in his final letter he admitted it all and asked humbly for her forgiveness) touching reading. There is a moral to the episode, though; whenever Graham Greene has denied that a story or character of his was based on real life (as he did, with such a wealth of circumstantial and convincing detail to Vivienne and as he was often to do in the future) it is a fair bet that exactly the opposite is the truth.

November 13th. Graham found Father Trollope gross in appearance. A very trashy novel from the Boots lending library lay in his room. Nonetheless they arranged times for instruction.

Fortunately the Bishop, whose Visitation he attended the following Sunday, looked the part and, unlike Father Trollope, inspired Graham with respect. The Bishop had a face both wily and holy, spoke simply of duties and statistics, his own tasks as a Bishop, the numbers of conversions and such like; thus impressing Graham with the thoroughly businesslike methods of the Catholic Church.

Father George Trollope was number two to the Bishop, the Administrator of the Cathedral, himself a convert, and a much shrewder man than the rather disdainful Balliol graduate had at first suspected. He had averaged, in his ten years at the Cathedral, fifteen adult converts a year, and he had, besides Graham Greene, a dozen other people under instruction at the time. In other words he had vast experience of how to handle all types of person, the simple and the complex, and he certainly handled Graham Greene extraordinarily well. Father Trollope, before his conversion, had been a professional Shakespearean actor and perhaps that training gave him a feeling for other people's character that most priests lack.

At his first instruction, that Monday, he carefully avoided anything other than hard facts; and Graham changed his mind about him immediately and completely. It is almost as if Father Trollope had been granted a miraculous view of Graham Greene's praise, in his previous letter, of the Bishop's matter-of-fact account of his own role and duties and had adapted his tone accordingly. It helped that, when Trollope was himself a former schoolboy at Merchant Taylors, his own father's greatest friend had been Dr. Fry, Graham's father's predecessor as headmaster of Berkhamsted. No doubt Father Trollope had realized that Graham Greene would be reassured if he felt that the priest instructing him was on his own social level; and in casting around conversationally had hooked this extremely fortunate connection.

Graham and his instructor fixed their next session for ten o'clock the following morning. By its end Graham felt obliged to concede that, granted the divinity of Christ, logic dictated that the Catholic Church was the only possible choice.

This was a very different tone to that which he had previously used in his letters to Vivienne where he had tended to stress, no doubt much to the poor girl's embarrassment, that if Catholicism could produce as wonderful a creature as herself, then it must be true. He was becoming interested intellectually; and, that, as he himself said, was half the battle. But there is another side to it. Graham Greene always felt a pull, throughout his long life, to structured working organizations and showed great loyalty to those to which he had belonged: to take three examples, Balliol College, MI6, and the Bodley Head. Ineffective structures, however, like the Church of England, the Liberal Party or the Society of Authors, he tended to reject; as he did purely social structures such as London clubs or, indeed, marriage. But on the larger scale he felt at home with the Catholic

Church, the British Empire and the established marxist-leninist structure of the USSR – all three at the time efficient working organizations with a clear chain of command, a certain intellectual justification, and a sternly practical approach to the problems of organized existence.

★ ★ ★

Graham went home for ten days at Christmas and on Christmas Day attended what he thought might well be his last ordinary Anglican service ever. He found the sermon appallingly sentimental. To Vivienne he wrote that what appealed to him most in the Catholic Church was the tough but stimulating belief in Hell. On Boxing Day he went hunting with Raymond and his cousins Tooter and Felix (but on foot; and they saw more of the fox than the mounted followers). Herbert resurfaced not in person but by a letter which Graham received with foreboding and an amazingly violent disgust. Herbert had led a rickety life – "I have been in dance halls and cabarets," he was to write a few years later, "in Paris and Lourenco Marques, in Santos and Buenos Aires, in Rio and London". Uncle Eppy had found him various jobs (Santos was Uncle Eppy's Brazilian base) but Herbert had held none of them down, and when yet another job folded, a telegram would come to Berkhamsted requesting funds.

Herbert and Graham had, at least up to this point, been linked by a curious complicity. Certainly it was Herbert who had introduced Graham to low life in London. He was an habitué of the pub in Poland Street where the most notorious of the Brighton racecourse gangs, the Sabini gang, had their headquarters. And he was always confiding in Graham by letter, which put Graham in an awkward spot when the confidences had to be kept hidden from his 'people'. But this time Graham felt Herbert had gone too far. More money troubles were looming; and if he had had any sense of decency, he would have taken the honourable way out – and shot himself.

This was an idea that Graham was to repeat time and again to Vivienne, softening it only by pointing out that, as Herbert was not a Catholic, self-destruction in his case could not be considered a mortal sin. Such rancour worried Vivienne.★ She was uneasy about Graham's friends and in particular about Claud Cockburn whom she suspected, much to his annoyance, of involving

★ Who always had a soft spot for Herbert. Whatever his faults, he was, as she years later put it, the only one of the four Greene brothers to have had a successful marriage.

Exactly why the relationship between the two brothers should have deteriorated this far is not clear. Admittedly Herbert's continual shiftless demands for money caused enormous worry to his parents. But Graham himself was not yet self-supporting – and had to rely on an allowance he knew his father could ill afford. Did the rivalry over Ave account for at least a part of Graham's bitterness? Shortly after this Ave herself fell dangerously ill with measles; and Graham confessed rather rashly to Vivienne that he had had a dream in which he had behaved improperly with, of all people, Ave.

him in 'grime'. She was uneasy about his determination to take up journalism as a career, though Graham pointed out that he couldn't expect his father to go on supporting him indefinitely and that journalism offered a better start and better prospects financially than, for instance, the Home Civil Service. He had three ambitions in life, he wrote to her charmingly, to make a fortune, to become editor of *The Spectator*, and to marry Vivienne.

It was the third ambition that made her uneasiest of all. Graham seemed to be taking it for granted that they would be getting married that year. Nottingham from her point of view had been a welcome relief, a means of postponing all decisions. But Nottingham was drawing to a close, Graham would be expecting to see her much more often – and, meanwhile, there was 'Hugh' promising to write her "long and luminous and deeply amorous letters" in a much more relaxed style than Graham. On the other hand Graham was becoming for her sake, but with evident seriousness and determination, a Catholic.

Graham always said in later life that he became a Catholic to please, or rather to satisfy, Vivienne; she, with evident exasperation, denied that she had forced his hand. But it is certainly true that she desperately wanted it and was almost over-anxious in her concern with Graham's going to Mass and to Benediction and to Instruction. Any sign of back-sliding hurt her, and he did not want to hurt her. Yet Graham could be severe enough with Vivienne on occasions. Before Christmas he rejected, not scornfully or sarcastically, but with total firmness a 'Special Letter' from Vivienne suggesting that her mother should adopt him and that they should live together as brother and sister under her mother's roof. Yet despite his critical intelligence he put up no opposition at all to a pro-Catholic pressure that could have exasperated a much more tolerant man.

For the Church of England Graham had had neither respect nor even that mocking affection which so many of his class have felt; and in the person and teachings of Christ not the slightest interest. Very clearly he was not (like so many converts of the time) attracted to the Catholic Church by the glories of its historic traditions, by its aesthetic appeal, or even by the sentiment that here was a Church that spread (unlike his own insular Church) throughout the whole world. His conversion was not a gesture in favour of the underdog, either: there is not the slightest hint of that in any of his letters. Why did he become a Catholic then? Partly to please, and to win, Vivienne; partly, no doubt, to *épater les bourgeois* and in particular his own family (though, if they were horrified – as well they may have been – they managed to conceal it very well); mainly because he was much more interested in the concept of God than he was ever openly to admit.

By mid-January Graham and Father Trollope had done Papal Infallibility and were proceeding next time to the five cases where Protestants argued that the Pope had shown fallibility. Graham felt able to report that he had a foundation of Catholicism, now, and was sure of the result.

Vivienne at this news panicked a little. She was so uneasy about the terms of the marriage, of the proposed brother/sister relationship that she consulted Basil Blackwell, who had an avuncular relationship with his young staff, and, though not so directly, 'Hugh' too. They both thought the idea was ridiculous, and Basil Blackwell even referred to it as a blasphemy, which upset Graham immensely. If B.B. made physical consummation (the first time Graham had actually used a phrase that was not a circumlocution) an absolute necessity to a man, then, Graham pointed out, he would have to admit that in a few years time he would cease to love Mrs B.B. and probably didn't even do so by now. He argued which such fierce sincerity that he seems to have convinced Vivienne and, indeed, himself.

Basil Blackwell was right of course; and it was understandable that 'Hugh', with the benefit of almost a decade's more experience, should have declared that Graham was either a knave or a fool. But Graham and Vivienne were not to blame for what, with hindsight, appears a damnable approach to matrimony, and one bound to lead to tension and unhappiness. If blame there is, it must be attached to Vivienne's mother who had brought her up to feel repugnance and horror for the 'physical' side of things; and perhaps not even to Muriel so much as to her husband whose approaches she had found so distasteful that she had never enjoyed what would now seem to be a normal sexual married life. Indeed enjoyment is very definitely not the *mot juste*. Muriel, she told her daughter, could not altogether blame a man of that sort for going to seek elsewhere the pleasures that she was unable to grant him without a shudder. It was for Vivienne a tragic and bewildering heritage.

* * *

In these last weeks at Nottingham the pace of Graham's instruction hotted up. By mid-January he had done Beatification and Canonization. The following week he did The Saints and told Father Trollope he would be leaving Nottingham. Father Trollope thought the rest of the Instructions could be crammed into a month, though it would mean ten a week. But Graham was not even sure that he had a month. He had his first meatless Friday on January 22nd but forgot to tell his landlady and most reluctantly had to give his mongrel Paddy the bacon part of his breakfast bacon and eggs. He found he was enjoying his Instructions so much that he was afraid he might miss them badly when they were over. That Sunday he went out to tea with an extraordinary old lady, Mrs Laws, who was a friend of his people's and lived in the nearby countryside. It turned out that she would have become a Catholic herself had it not been for fear of wounding her husband too deeply. She recommended Bruges to Graham for its Catholic atmosphere and the little medieval village of Eze perched above Monte Carlo for a visit. Graham's thoughts turned, exultantly, to honeymoons.

Then, at the beginning of February, blow after blow fell. He had never, despite his Balliol superiority, graduated from sub-editing to leader-writing on the *Nottingham Journal*, as he had initially expected. His hopes of a job on various London newspapers all collapsed; and the *Weekly Westminster*, his literary lifeline, ceased publication. He might as well throw in the towel, he decided – and advised Vivienne to follow her mother's advice (he had come to dislike Muriel very much) and flirt hard at Oxford. All that was left to him was a 'career' in the provincial press – or abroad.

In his instruction he had reached Mortal and Venial Sin; and perhaps Father Trollope helped him – now that he had no choice but to stay till at any rate the end of the month and the end of his instruction – out of the slough of Despair. At any rate within ten days he had recovered his spirits and with great determination was firing off letters to the *Manchester Guardian* and to the *Yorkshire Post*, to Kenneth Richmond to ask for an introduction to the *Daily Telegraph* and, rather curiously, to Count Bernstorff at the German Embassy to ask for an introduction to *The Morning Post*. Failing all of which he decided to get a tutorship till October; and if nothing had come up by then to try for the Colonial Service. West Africa, he mentioned, had always attracted him because of Llewellyn Powys' stories. The screw was moderate, there was leave every eighteen months, and retirement with a pension at about forty. Entry only at twenty-two – hence October – but easy with Public School, University and a medical. It would probably, he added, be easier to say goodbye now.

Vivienne was having none of this. She cannot have helped admiring Graham's determination and now felt that she ought to match it with at least a little determination of her own. Braving parental disapproval she came up for a weekend to Nottingham, having meanwhile quarrelled quite badly with 'Hugh'. It was a lovely weekend, spring was in the air, almost, and they seem to have made up their differences and their minds.

The last lap of those extraordinarily formative four months in Nottingham loomed ahead. Graham was quite frightened, he explained, about his looming First Confession; for in three years at Oxford, when he'd really only thought about his own pleasure, a certain amount of 'grime' had accumulated. Vivienne sent him a missal to encourage him, and had his grey flannel trousers specially cleaned, pressed and repaired for the occasion. It was not till the Saturday that he learnt that the 'ceremony' would take place at 3 o'clock the following day. The Instructions were – just – finished in time, though Father Trollope sent Vivienne a message that she would have to instruct Graham herself in the Rosary and its use. Charles Greene also sent a letter – a very unusual occurrence – wishing his third and now almost Romanized son every happiness.

Graham wrote on Sunday February 28th, his last day in Nottingham, feeling very nervous as if he were going to the dentist's! He was encouraged at Mass by a tremendously fierce and splendid sermon attacking the Church of England. But he was discouraged and embarrassed by the fact that he would have to make his

General Confession not to Father Trollope but to his wretched colleague, a man for whom he had no respect. And he would also have to make it not at a confessional box, shielded, but face to face in the priest's room. Then there would be the public recitation of the Creed, and he had always found it embarrassing to have to read aloud.

Nevertheless he triumphed over all these obstacles. He was conditionally baptised that Sunday afternoon. The Cathedral Register records the baptism as being of "Henricus Graham Green" omitting the "e".* The two witnesses were Stewart H. Wallis and Father George Trollope. Graham Greene was now, like Vivienne, a fully-fledged member of the Catholic Church – a soul in a state of grace, a new Adam, sloughing off – at least in theory – the old.

* The Catholic Church recognizes other Christian baptisms as valid; but in case the formalities have not been correctly performed, advises "conditional baptism" – in effect a repeat, possibly superfluous – in the case of adult converts.

It is not necessary or indeed usual for conditionally baptized adult converts to take another name; and in the first published account of his conditional baptism Graham Greene said that he could think of none that he wanted and kept his old name. However, years later, both in his autobiography and in many interviews, he made a great point of insisting that he deliberately took the name of Thomas, after St. Thomas the Doubter: Doubting Thomas.

There is no record of this in the Register; as there should have been had that in fact been the case. The choice, however, did become part of his 'legend' – as the referring to it in the Homily at his Memorial Service (and indeed, previously to that, by Father Leopold at his funeral) indicates.

Chapter V

Adam and Eve

From this point onwards for the next twenty months Graham and Vivienne marched, almost in step, towards the most disastrous and irreversible event of their lives, their marriage. This is a harsh verdict. It reeks of hindsight. It makes no allowance for the undoubted periods of happiness, for the comradeship and the achievements. Yet it is difficult to believe that in their heart of hearts, looking back on their lives, the two protagonists could have done anything else but agree. Marriage was to bring them some heartsease but far more heartache.

All the other apparent difficulties – youth, lack of money, mother-in-law problems – pale into insignificance beside the one major fact: that they were simply not in character compatible. Two such different people, one feels, should never even have considered getting married. Vivienne was basically conventional and conservative, easily shocked and easily upset. Graham was a would-be adventurer, both mentally and physically, with a highly developed critical sense and a decided penchant for the shocking. From time to time they seem to have realized how ill-matched they were. Indeed hardly was Nottingham a fortnight behind them than Vivienne was telling Graham how tactless he was and how he revelled in repellent horror, and Graham was concluding, quite rightly, that they were temperamentally different and, so far from being "mental twins", as Muriel had once remarked, were in fact mental opposites. But then these wise conclusions were swept away in a wave of sentimentality, optimism and undoubted physical attraction. What basically seems to have happened is that Vivienne who before had been so undecided and rightly wary, had made up her mind during that weekend at Nottingham to give way to Graham's arguments and insistence, and, as so often happens in similar cases, Graham, feeling the battle won, began more and more to wonder whether after all this was the right woman for him. Certainly his letters to Vivienne became less frequent, less long, more critical and more matter-of-fact. But they remain affectionate, passionate and sentimental. For he had so committed himself to Vivienne in the year he had known her that he could not decently or honourably pull back now that, at last, he had won her over. Willy-nilly too the march of events, external pressures, swept them both along. It was becoming an understood thing, among their contemporaries and their elders, that they would get married as soon as they could decently afford to do so. And within a week of leaving Nottingham this suddenly seemed to be no longer a mere pipedream but a practical possibility.

For Graham landed a job. To his own amazement he had in fact landed three possible jobs. He had gone straight from Nottingham to London, to digs in Battersea. His letters had brought results. In came offers of sub-editorships from the *Daily News*, the *Daily Telegraph* and finally – his grail –, complete with an interview with Geoffrey Dawson, the Editor, from *The Times*.

Vivienne was worried, with almost wifely concern, that a sub-editing job, even on *The Times*, might be a professional blind alley; and, as things were to turn out, she was perfectly right. But Graham swept her worries aside. Dawson had explained to him that sub-editing would give the technical expertise which he could combine with writing in his spare time: then he would be in the running for an editorship elsewhere.

He began work that very Wednesday, finding the conditions at Printing House Square much pleasanter than in Nottingham. At five the sub-editors could telephone down for tea and cakes to be brought up; at eight there was a break for dinner either in the Mess or, with the workers in the Canteen where the fullest of meals would cost only 1/3d. Working hours were from five to eleven at night, and soon a five-day working week was to be introduced. But the greatest joy was to be surrounded, in contrast to his time of purgatory in the sub-editors' room at Nottingham, with University men.

Meanwhile he was fulfilling his new religious duties carefully. Father Trollope had given him a letter to Father Christie at The Oratory in Knightsbridge; and he went through the Passion Week service with Father Christie, was pleased to hear that Father Trollope was in line for a bishopric, and worried about how to begin his first private confession. Were there any formulae, he wondered? He was screwing up his courage to go. But the truth of the matter was that though he fulfilled the formal obligations of Mass on Sundays and Holidays of Obligation, fish on Fridays and occasional Confession – all under a certain mild pressure from Vivienne – his observance was superficial only. When he had left Nottingham Cathedral after his reception, he had wondered whether he might perhaps have a vocation for the priesthood; and indeed many of his friends were to see Graham Greene as a priest *manqué*. But he himself quite rightly pointed out that he could never have respected the vow of celibacy. In London, though intellectually convinced of the claims of the Catholic Church, he took the actual rules and regulations regarding behaviour no more seriously than he had done the rules of school or of college. And in particular, inevitably, in those twenty months he experimented with sex.

Most of these experiments took place during his first few months in London. There are times when he could not see Vivienne, he who at Nottingham was often counting the minutes till their next meeting. He criticizes quite harshly, though always with politeness, her mother's attitude towards sex and the lack of physical enjoyment in her parents' marriage. Indeed the whole tone of his love letters changes. During those months he had for the first time in his life plenty of money, comparatively speaking, in his pocket – and money earned by himself that he could feel free to spend exactly as he liked.

Moreover he had his friends – young men in their early twenties like himself, on the loose for the first time in their lives: Whitmore, Guest, Macloed with a sleek Talbot two-seater, Scott, Braine-Hartnell and his second cousin Christopher Isherwood, met by chance in the Strand. But the friend who first introduced him to brothels was Claud Cockburn, famous throughout his life for his roving eye and at that time, with his experience of life in Budapest, by far the most sophisticated sexually of the group.

There were a couple of tentative experiences that went off at half-cock with tarts picked up after a film at the Empire in Leicester Square – to be found in the Leicester Lounge at £1 a time. The Savile Row brothel, though five times as expensive and therefore a rare treat, was much more fun because it was more of a ritual – and happened to be next door to the Alpine Club where Raymond was a member, which added to the spice of the thing. The girls had to be summoned by telephone, and so a sort of market code was used down the lines to indicate preferences, as if ordering sides of beef. The brothel was kept by a traditionally blowsy warm-hearted Madame and the door was opened (on appointment only) by a maid properly dressed in cap and apron. To add to the general feeling of an Oxford prank Graham's introduction came from 'Major Grant'* and he himself chose his traditional pseudonym, embellished however by a military handle too: 'Captain Trench'. In France, of course, Graham and his contemporaries would years before have been taken in hand by older women or else introduced to similar establishments by their fathers or uncles. There could have been no question at the time in either country of "going the whole hog" with girls of the sort whom they might one day expect to marry. England was less well-organized, more puritanical, more furtive. Graham was in a particularly frustrating position with a proposed marriage ahead, one of whose still-agreed conditions was celibacy by mutual consent; and even his Guardian Angel must, one feels, have turned a sympathetic though not condoning eye on the young man's lusts.†

Vivienne intuitively recognized that Graham was changing, and that the terms of their marriage too would have to be changed. For Graham's language was

* Claud Cockburn? Not a man averse to aliases, either, though rarely military ones. In the Thirties 'Frank Pitcairn', the notorious Communist journalist and agitator, was in fact Claud, writing and agitating under a different name.

† Graham made a few real friends among the brothel-girls; one of them suggested that he help by making a blue film. He did not take up the girl's offer. He was to use it, however, many years later as the basis for a touching short story.

changing. But Graham protested that he ought to be allowed to use words like 'incelibate' naturally and without a 'scolding' from her. He protested furthermore, though perhaps over-strongly, that he had no desire at all to change their proposed arrangement. One of the advantages they had both worked out was that if the marriage was not satisfactory then, as it would not have been consummated, under Canon Law an annulment could without difficulty be obtained. Let Vivienne rest easy in her mind, Graham declared. There could not only be an annulment but he would make a financial settlement as well. But by that autumn as inevitably they became, with Graham's newly-roused experience, a touch more physically infatuated with one another, they realized that they were both play-acting and that by the third and final act the dénouement would be other than planned.

One potential threat to Vivienne and Graham's future marriage faded. 'Hugh,' presumably having decided that with Vivienne he was batting on a losing wicket, swiftly upped and married another girl. Vivienne was not so feeble as to sit around moping or waiting for Graham to amuse her. She went, that June, to Trinity College Commem. Ball. Girls had their rituals too and she marked down with the little pencil attached to a blue ribbon on her engagement card her twenty-six dances, mainly foxtrots and waltzes, with 'Louis', with Patrick Monkhouse, Graham's successor as editor of the *Oxford Outlook* and with 'Harman'.

But as fast as one threat faded, another arose. Stella Weaver came to work at Blackwells, a woman older than Vivienne but sympathetic to her, born an Acton, (a Catholic therefore and in practise a most rigid one), married to a tall distinguished-looking but wayward don, a Fellow (and future President) of Trinity College, Reggie. Stella took Vivienne under her wing and persuaded her to leave the YWCA and come and live at 10 Holywell, even closer to Blackwells, a fine family home in a picturesque street just opposite the Porter's Lodge at New College.

Stella had expelled, temporarily, her husband from the house (and, it seems, more than temporarily from a shared bedroom) on what to Graham, when he learnt about it, appeared to be the most ridiculously old-fashioned Victorian principles.

She was obviously a domineering character, she appears to have disapproved of Graham even before meeting him, she had no intention of allowing Vivienne and Graham to see each other unchaperoned if she could possibly help it, and Graham was naturally infuriated to find Vivienne parroting the opinions and prejudices that Stella proceeded, at every available opportunity, to drum into her. That said, Stella and Reggie too (whom Graham rather despised for his pusillanimity) proved to be very true friends to Vivienne; and they had an adopted daughter Loulie Gurney-Martin who took a great shine to the new lodger and brightened everyone's lives in what cannot, otherwise, have been a very comfortable household to live in.

Vivienne sent the expectant novelist* that Christmas a fountain pen, red lacquer, and a portrait. He sent her, most romantically, a large blank book, grey covered, marked inside (with a wild flower attached): "For Vivienne. A Private Book which will never have an end. All the verses, indiscriminate of value, which you caused." He had copied out twelve poems on twelve separate pages. Vivienne kept the book for many years, adding to it a score or so of poems, mostly by her husband after their marriage but including a poem from her to him, on his first post-marriage birthday, entitled rather delightfully "Ode to G. on a State Occasion". Vivienne may not have been Graham's intellectual equal, or ever have wanted to be, but she was certainly no fool, had a nice sense of wit and Graham, who did not joke with his critical acumen, thought one of the few poems she ever showed him, *The Bride*, to be extraordinarily good, almost up to Wordsworth's or Shelley's standard. Marion Greene wrote to her affectionately: "My dear Vivienne" and then "My Dearest Vivienne"; and Loulie, at the Weavers, who had an adolescent crush on her, wrote a little poem that is worth citing for the transparent honesty of the picture it paints:

You are never angry or cross
But always calm
To see you there
Is soothing balm
Curled cat-like in your chair
Deep buried in a Magic book
Your face, your eyes
Your Hair
Comfort me at a glance.

Vivienne inspired affection. Graham had no intention of losing her. Though, indeed, his determination to marry that coming year, 1926, was undoubtedly reinforced by the news that Herbert was going to pip him to the post. Herbert's long-suffering fiancée Aubrey Nutting had been amazingly loyal to someone she

* Graham was no slouch when it came to getting his novels published. He sent his first novel *Anthony Sant* to the newly-established literary agent AD Peters even before leaving Oxford. Peters was most enthusiastic about it, and Graham had responded to his constructive criticisms with sporadic bursts of rewriting, conscious that Conrad's first great success had been *The Nigger of the Narcissus* and hoping perhaps – Conrad was less than a year in his grave at the time – for a similar success for *Anthony Sant*. Those aspirations failed. Nothing daunted, Graham completed his second novel *The Episode* in the summer of 1926, borrowed a fiver from his mother (meticulously repaid) to have it typed out – and sent the corrected typescript to AD Peters; where, unlike his first novel, it met with swift rejection. That did daunt him, momentarily. Reviving, he set about revising it thoroughly, was thrilled when Kenneth Richmond sent him four pages of close criticism ("My hat, Graham, what a heroine!"), less thrilled when Vivienne, also consulted suggested that the said heroine, Elise – modelled on Conrad's Donna Rita, the *femme fatale* of *Arrow of Gold* – was "amoral". His plan was to submit the revised *Episode* directly to Conrad's publishers, Heinemann's.

could not, in Graham's eyes, possibly respect and whom in any case she had not seen for over a year. But Herbert's job crisis had eased, thanks to Uncle Eppy's intervention, and Aubrey was sailing out at the end of February to South America to marry him in Buenos Aires in March.

Graham reported with a touch of amazement to Vivienne that the lucky couple had cleared over £300 worth of cheques in wedding presents; added mischievously that he'd asked Aubrey, should she run across a Mr Dayrell-Browning in South America, to inform him that her brother-in-law-to-be was marrying his daughter, and pressed Vivienne to announce their own engagement officially in *The Times*. By the beginning of March he let it be known, with panache, that he had started another novel.

The novel that was eventually to emerge, *The Man Within*, is, like *The Episode*, a historical novel – a tale of smugglers, gaugers, revenue officers and the Lewes Assizes – set in the eighteenth century. Andrews, the hero, on the run, takes refuge in the remote cottage of Elizabeth, the heroine. To foil his pursuers he has to pretend, and to remember to pretend, that Elizabeth is his sister. Yet under the name of Elizabeth the traits are those, unmistakably, of Vivienne – dark hair, pale face, calm eyes, a lovely voice with "the peace of God" most noticeable about her – an Elizabeth/Vivienne aged nineteen, (as she had been when he had first met her) with the power to infuriate – "'God, you're respectable,' he said with resentful amusement" – but also to shame the twisted, tormented, depraved but basically decent Andrews /Graham.

For they had found, thanks to Muriel but only after tremendous tussles with her over other possible flats, a home; a self-contained flat in Hampstead Garden Suburb, reasonably far away – from Graham's point of view – from his future mother-in-law.

On March 17th Graham signed the lease and two weeks later he left Battersea and moved in, all by himself, living on pub lunches and, in the evening, kippers and syrup rolls. He dealt with surprising aplomb with gas men, paper hangers, delivery vans, and an old deaf carpenter. He had the Vampire Vacuum Cleaner personally demonstrated. He asked Raymond and Charlotte for a Staines coffee set, sent off a cheque for £6.5s.0d to Canada Life Insurance and informed Vivienne that his mother had noticed a hugh selection of gate-legged tables in the secondhand department of Maples.

He went dutifully down to Berkhamsted for his father's last Founder's Day, Dean Incent's Day, celebrated in the rain and reported by himself (anonymously) in *The Times*. His parents had found a house for their retirement at Crowborough in Sussex. They named it Incent's, and Graham went down there too, that summer, inspecting with particular interest the spare room.

The wedding date was set for mid-October, shortly after Graham's twenty-third birthday. The wedding was to be held in Hampstead, in a charming little church set in a tiny backwater, Holly Place, the first Catholic Church to be built in London since the Reformation. Graham fixed up reservations for the honeymoon with the Per Mundum Travel agency in Battersea, planning to splash out on it an extravagant £40 to £50 as the wedding presents began rolling in – cheques for two pounds or two guineas from each of the Harston aunts, twenty pounds from his mother, most infuriatingly nothing at all till the wedding day itself from Reggie and Stella, ten shillings from younger brother Hugh, and, to his joy, a longed-for fifty pounds from Uncle Eppy. "You shall have the car to take you to Victoria," Uncle Eppy wrote, "a very appropriate name for a young man who has secured a bride like Vivienne, far too good for him. No man is good enough for a good bride on his wedding day – he can only hope to become so one day."

Graham was doing his best. He went to Confession, to a 'penance mass' at the Cathedral (his usual penance had been Five Our Fathers and Five Hail Marys, once rising to six of each) saw about Confirmation (which he had been promising but delaying) and the wedding banns, and learnt the "Hail Holy Queen" by heart. Vivienne by now had left Blackwells and Stella's baleful influence and had moved to her mother's flat in central Hampstead. Graham fought hard against attempts by Muriel to 'manage' the wedding – probably a losing battle. The list of invitations rose to nearly two hundred with, oddly enough as he pointed out to Vivienne, only about half-a-dozen Catholics among them. On Graham's side there were, apart from the massed ranks of the Greene clan, Sir Graham Balfour, Stevenson's* second cousin and biographer and his wife, and from Oxford days Braine-Hartnell, Cockburn, Coghlin, de Laszlo, Guest, Kincaid, Macloed, Monkhouse, Scott and Whitmore – with, as an afterthought, Cockburn's great friend Harding, whom Vivienne did not much care for, and from Cambridge, Christopher Isherwood.

Graham warned Vivienne that he would not be an easy husband to be married to. But how can she have believed it when he could write so enchantingly beforehand comparing October 15th to the marriage feast at Cana in Galilee?

A fortnight before the wedding Graham bought spats. He had never imagined himself in spats…

"The marriage took place on Saturday," announced *The Times* of Monday, October 17th 1927, "at St. Mary's Catholic Church, Holly Place, Hampstead of Mr.Graham Greene, third son of Mr. CH Greene, formerly Headmaster of Berkhamsted School, and Vivienne, only daughter of Mrs Dayrell-Browning, of Hampstead."

* Graham Balfour had stayed for a year with Robert Louis Stevenson in the South Seas; his *Life* of his, and Graham's, cousin was published in 1901. Had RLS lived to the same ripe old age as Graham Greene, the lives of these two great and, related, storytellers would have overlapped; and perhaps Stevenson too, then aged 77, would have been at Graham's wedding; which would certainly have added lustre to the occasion.

The Marriage service began at 11 am. Stella had forbidden Loulie, much to Graham's fury, to be a bridesmaid, though she and Elizabeth would have made – except for Elizabeth's unusual height – a good pair. Raymond was best man. In the Marriage Register Muriel Amabilis, *Mother*, was described as the daughter of Alfred Green-Armytage; who gave Vivienne away. Sidney Roderick Dayrell-Browning, *Father*, was optimistically but inaccurately described as "the late". Father John Philip Valentine, *Vicarius Cooperativus*, married them. The wedding march was by Lohengrin, played by Whitaker Wilson.

Vivienne carefully preserved the wrapping-paper, with a jokey inscription, of the groom's wedding present to her. The reception was held at 8 Holly Place, formerly the Presbytery. There is no record, formal or informal of Raymond or Grandfather Alfred's speeches. Mrs Laws, the old lady living near Nottingham, was invited to the wedding; but for all that the happy couple did not go to Eze. They travelled out via Paris and Marseilles to Cavalière, spent ten days there, came back via Avignon and Paris where on the way back Graham showed Vivienne round, and by Sunday October 30th were back in their little flat in London which they had nicknamed 'the Basket'.

Chapter VI

Novelist!

Everyone will say, Graham had warned Vivienne gleefully, that we are marrying too young. Everyone was right. Indeed three of the four Greene brothers can be said with hindsight to have married too young – Raymond at 24, Graham at 23 and eventually Hugh at 24 – and their marriages did not last. Herbert waited till he was almost 30, and of the four brothers his and Aubrey's was the only marriage happily to survive.

Graham was not sure whether it would. Three weeks before their own marriage he had told Vivienne he was all against Aubrey and Herbert having a baby immediately; indeed he was totally opposed to having babies at all... For over a year, though sporadically, he had been making his attitude towards children clear. What he wanted, he had explained to Vivienne chillily enough fifteen months earlier, was more money in hand, and less responsibilities. At the time Vivienne may not have taken him seriously. But there could be no misunderstanding with a letter written at a date so close to their marriage. It posed, obviously, a tremendous problem. Graham may have thought that they were marrying young; but from Vivienne's point of view her own age was a perfectly suitable one for marriage; and the normal thing, the expected thing, indeed the Sacramental thing, would be to proceed to have children.

Graham's refusal to have children can almost be said, therefore, to have undermined right from the start any chance of their leading a normal happily married life. It was, from his point of view – and it is this that makes the whole thing tragic – absolutely understandable. He simply could not afford children. Indeed he had wanted to postpone the marriage for another year until he was earning ten guineas a week, with perhaps an extra two or three from reviewing – he aimed for six hundred pounds a year. The young couple's financial situation was undoubtedly tight and their entertainments would be limited.

But the physical side of their married life would be more limited still. For if no children could be risked, their intercourse would have to be confined to the 'safe' period; and even that, Graham must have known, was by no means foolproof. So self-restraint was the rule; and, lest self-restraint break down, the 'Basket' had in effect to be divided by a curtained alcove into two bedrooms. This was to impose, evidently, an almost impossible strain on a highly emotional and very loving young couple; and particularly on a young man as highly sexed as the new husband.

* * *

To Graham in the period following his marriage it looked as if his own career had stalled while his contemporaries and wedding-guests were forging ahead. Claud Cockburn, after a shaky start,* had managed with cheek and determination to wheedle his way onto *The Times* as right-hand-man to the Foreign Correspondent of *The Times* in Berlin, Norman Ebbutt. This was a considerable success. Christopher Isherwood had published *All the Conspirators* and Macloed *Beauty and the Beast.* That too was success. But Heinemann's had rejected *The Episode.* That was failure – fortunately, though, not for long.

Charles Evans had sat on it for eight long months. Evans' politeness softened the blow. Apologetic for the delay, he asked whether he might see the author's next work.

Thus encouraged, Graham continued with *The Man Within* at the rate of 500 words a day, his normal daily maximum. This meant, roughly, that he could produced a novel in a year. *The Man Within* was ready for the typist within a year of his wedding day. It was published by Heinemann's † on June 13th 1929, a red-letter date in Graham Greene's life and, arguably, in English letters, the first of a long long series of novels whose publication would stretch out over the next half-century and more.

* Shortly before Graham and Vivienne's wedding Claud had been forced to fill in as a temporary schoolmaster at Berkhamsted – an ominous thing, to judge by the precedent of Charles Greene who had done the same in his day but had stayed on for ever.

As Claud was entering schoolmastering, his cousin Evelyn Waugh had been leaving it. Sacked, Graham had written with a certain *schadenfreude* to Vivienne, for drunkenness – the first recorded written comment by either of these great novelists on the other. But 'E.W.' was about to put that experience, alcohol included, to only too successful a use, by bringing out, in 1928, a first novel, *Decline and Fall*, the apotheosis of 'Captain Grimes', that would make its author both famous and fashionable.

† Charles Evans appears to have been as excited by the novel's prospects, pre-publication, as Graham most obviously was by its acceptance. Cecil Roberts, a Heinemann bestseller and a former Editor of *The Nottingham Journal*, whom Graham had long shamelessly and successfully badgered for an introduction to Heinemann's, dropped round at their offices in Great Russell Street and was handed a proof copy by his publisher. "I believe we've got a winner," cried Evans. Cecil Roberts read it and wrote back enthusiastically: "Do you think one Heinemann author led to another? After all, the old paper has started off Barrie, myself and now young Greene."

At the same time Charles Evans found Graham a new agent, sending him down to the American Book Agency in the Strand, Albert Curtis Brown's. "The bearer of this note," read David Higham, the Agency's General Manager, Books, "is a young author whose first novel I have just taken and who has, I believe, a considerable future. He ought to have an agent, and I should like that agent to be you."

First novels by unknown writers are often not reviewed at all, and sink without trace. But *The Man Within* was from that point of view amazingly successful. In the week following publication it was reviewed in swift succession by, on the Thursday, *The Times Literary Supplement*, on the Friday by *The Times* itself, on the Saturday by *The Spectator* and on the Sunday by *The Sunday Times*; and the reviews were favourable, verging indeed in the case of the *T.L.S.* on the qualified ecstatic. *The Man Within* sold so well that it was reprinted no less than four times in 1929. It was priced at 7/6d, divided into three parts and eleven chapters, was three hundred and fifty-four pages long; and sold, in all, over eight thousand copies; bringing to Heinemann's therefore some three thousand pounds and to its happy author roughly fifteen per cent of the sum – in any case well over four hundred pounds. But this was the British and Empire market alone. It was published simultaneously by Heinemanns' American owners, Doubleday Doran, and did well, though not equally well, in the United States.

The plot is weakly melodramatic, the characters unreal and the dialogue at times acutely embarrassing. What may have attracted the readers – for something must have done – is the passionate portrait of what was then a most unusual hero: "neurotic and cowardly and nerve-racked with a touch of sensuality and the sort of idealism that's turned upside down" plus, to boot, "an unnaturally strong craving for the physical". So Graham Greene had, from the outset, planned 'Andrews', and so he was faithfully portrayed. But the reader who must, of them all, have felt the greatest interest in the portrayal was Vivienne.

Vivienne was highly sensitive, as the furore over *The Episode* had shown, to portrayals in her husband's fiction of herself and in particular of herself and Graham and their emotional life. On that count she must have read the first part of *The Man Within* with almost unmitigated relief. The book (in its original edition) is dedicated "For Vivienne My Wife – in Wonder", followed by a quotation from Thomas Hardy ending with the (in the context most flattering) line: "The sweetest image outside Paradise." She herself, 'Elizabeth', is portrayed as a pure calm and totally admirable creature; and the setting is such that there can be no actual parallels with real-life incidents, as in the sad affair of the Wolvercote canal. Andrews, on the other hand, who courts her and by the end of Part One is admitting to himself that he is in love with her – the whole of Part One is an almost uninterrupted duet between the pair of them – is most disappointingly atheistical, full of sneers at religion and her high sentiments. Let that pass, however. Andrews is clearly not an exact portrait of Graham, though he has many of Graham's mannerisms and uses many of Graham's expressions.

But in Part Two Andrews is seduced by a certain Lucy. No wife could possibly read that scene, written by her husband, without an extraordinary sinking feeling of distress. It cannot have helped that Lucy is described as "slim, long-legged with small firm breasts". This could be, perhaps, passed over as merely conventional male fantasy, though unflattering to Vivienne. But the dialogue between Andrews and Lucy is so very obviously not the product of imagination that even the most innocent of wives must have recognized it for what it was: the realistic portrayal of a situation which the writer – in this case Graham – and a tart, 'Lucy', had shared.

"You are a funny boy," says Lucy. "No, not tonight, I'm sleepy. Not inclined," says Lucy. "You can have me – tomorrow night, if you'll pay for me," says Lucy. "You are so young, I am sure that there are still things I can show you," says Lucy. "You know what you are missing don't you?" says Lucy. The pretence, never very satisfactorily maintained, of early nineteenth century dialogue is totally dropped. "Have you enjoyed yourself?" asks Lucy. "I've wallowed," replies the hero, "if that's what you mean." Andrews "damns himself for a swine" when he thinks about Elizabeth, but cannot hold back "the animal in him". His lips grow dry with excitement, he knows that he can make her wriggle, he feels the touch and shape of her thigh, his flesh rises to her whisper, he buries his mouth between her breasts – and then he feels utterly disgusted. But as she points out – speaking here, one feels, not for Lucy as such but for the world, the flesh and the devil in general – "For a day we are disgusted and disappointed and disillusioned and feel dirty all over. But we are clean again in a very short time, clean enough to go back and soil ourselves all over again."

The Man Within can largely be read – and it is a fascinating exercise for any reader to read it from this point of view – as a bitter self-analysis, as a confession to Vivienne, and as a plea for her understanding and forgiveness – in one sense most astutely handled, for the writer exaggerates his own faults and indeed wickedness to the point where his beating of the breast and the repetition of *mea maxima culpa* must have softened any woman's heart, particularly as soft-hearted a woman's as Vivienne. But what can she have made of the following passage with its terrifyingly precise implication?

"He felt no fear of death, but a terror of life, of going on soiling himself and repenting and soiling himself again… For certain exalted moments he had dreamed of taking Elizabeth to London, of gaining her love and marrying her, but now he saw that even if he gained that high desire, it would be only to soil her and not cleanse himself. When I had been married to her for a month, he thought, I would be creeping out of the house on the sly to visit prostitutes… He was hot with shame and self-loathing."

It is doubtful whether anything in the long run would have saved Graham and Vivienne's marriage. But he would certainly have done better for both their peace of mind to have kept certain secrets utterly secret, or at least to have avoided thus arousing, as he must have done, his wife's suspicions and mistrust. Yet what life loses, literature, even in the case of so bad a book comparatively speaking as *The Man Within*, may gain.

* * *

It was very pleasant to be not merely a published novelist but a successful novelist; and pleasant too, whatever the private worries, to be a successful novelist's wife. The young couple's social life expanded. They were taken up in a mild way by two formidable hostesses, Hilaire Belloc's sister, Mrs.Belloc Lowndes, an author herself of over fifty crime novels, and the famous Lady Ottoline Morrell of Gower Street and Garsington Manor. To their younger literary contemporaries the Greenes seemed at the time comparatively well-matched. Vivienne was not Graham's intellectual equal; but she was intelligent, well-read, pretty and very feminine. However the main impression they made was of being a colourless couple, hard-up, living in a cramped flat in north London and always having to catch a tube home Cinderella-like, before midnight.

Graham's next move therefore was a bold attempt to improve his position: to demand a three-year contract from his publishers. He demanded it; and, rather amazingly, he obtained it. Three-year contracts were usually reserved for the more successful authors, like Aldous Huxley, whose new novels, as they appeared in swift succession during Graham Greene's Oxford days, had immediately provoked a rush to the bookshops. In *Chrome Yellow*, at the beginning of the Twenties, he had cruelly portrayed Lady Ottoline Morrell as "Priscilla Wimbush". In *Point Counter Point* he caricatured Middleton Murry as "Burlap". Middleton Murry was so upset that he nearly challenged Aldous Huxley to a duel. This sort of excitement, rumours of which inevitably spread, increased sales: and Huxley's American publishers, Doubleday Doran, were delighted.

So Graham Greene's demand came at a very favourable moment. Doubledays were doing well with Huxley: and Heinemanns were doing extraordinarily well with JP Priestley's *The Good Companions* that would sell in due course half a million hardback copies. So Charles Evans for Heinemanns, and Nelson Doubleday, for Doubleday Doran, agreed each to guarantee Graham Greene an income of three hundred pounds a year for a period of three years running from September 1st 1929 to September 1st 1932 – his long-desired six hundred pounds per annum was thereby at last achieved. Graham Greene for his part contracted to produce in return one novel a year. Three novels in all, therefore, each to be ready by the middle of the year; in other words in mid-1930, in mid-1931 and in mid-1932.

It was just as well that he had signed up when he did. Eight weeks later, on Thursday October 24th, 'Black Thursday', Wall Street fell with a sickening crash, and the Great Depression began. Had Graham Greene delayed his demand for a three-year contract it is most unlikely that he would have obtained it. As it was, Nelson Doubleday had to sell Heinemanns lock stock and barrel.*

* Charles Evans and his fellow directors bought Heinemanns back from Nelson Doubleday for £200,000. It was a baronial business complete with its own printers, its own country estate, and indeed with Rupert Hart-Davis, soon to be married to Peggy Ashcroft and soon to become a great friend of Graham's – and, justifiably, a great enemy of Priestley's; of which more later.

Graham took a momentous decision. He decided to resign from *The Times*.* His fatherly immediate superiors tried to discourage him. It was in any case extremely difficult to fix an interview with the editor, because, as Claud had found, "Mr. Geoffrey Dawson had perfected a technique for not telling people anything much and yet appearing all the time both approachable and communicative."

Graham found it as difficult as Claud. When he finally did succeed in cornering Geoffrey Dawson, he was told in paternal tones that there was no objection at all to his continuing to write novels on *The Times*; indeed both the art critic, Charles Marriott, and the drama critic, Charles Morgan (one of Greene's *bêtes noires*) had done so successfully. But if his mind were really made up, it could only be condemned, said the Editor, as "a rash and unfortunate decision".

So indeed it was; and Graham was bitterly to regret it. He was surrendering a certain income for one equally high but of very limited duration. The obvious thing would have been to have stayed on *The Times*, written his three contracted novels in the daytime, worked in the evenings, and thereby have doubled his income without, in effect, doubling his work – for he was already writing every morning. He and Vivienne would then have been, with well over one thousand pounds a year, comparatively prosperous instead of comparatively poor.

The Name of Action was well under way when Graham signed his three-year-contract in September 1929. It was published, by Heinemann and by Doubleday, eleven months later. It is the first of Graham Greene's European thrillers, and a far far better book than *The Man Within*.†

Evelyn Waugh, before leaving England for Abyssinia (where as Special Correspondent for *The Times* he was due to cover the coronation of His Imperial Majesty Haile Selassie I, Negus Negusti, King of Kings) found time to review in

* By March 1929, when Graham had begun his new novel *The Name of Action*, he had been on *The Times* exactly three years. He was earning ten guineas a week and was reasonably happy. But he was no nearer becoming a leader-writer or a foreign correspondent that when he had first started. Candidates, Claud Cockburn wrote, if they survived a trial on some provincial newspaper – exactly Graham's case – "did a spell in the Home Room of *The Times* occupied with domestic reporting and were then – assuming that worthiness was maintained – transferred to the Foreign Room." Claud himself had managed, thanks to a splendid scoop at Dresden, to bypass the traditional hurdles and, in that spring of 1929, move directly to the Foreign Editorial Room, by his account a most entertaining place, which he enlivened by inventing the now-legendary caption "Small Earthquake in Chile: Not Many Dead". But Graham was still stuck in the Home News Room, occasionally deputising – his main excitement – for the Correspondence Editor.

† Graham Greene himself divided his novels into 'Entertainments' and the rest, a division (often arbitrary and on occasions contradictory) that has puzzled critics. Arguably a more logical division would be between his 'European thrillers', mainly pre-war; and the rest.

It is the greatest of shames that he forbade The Name of Action to be reprinted in his lifetime and that therefore it is extremely difficult to get hold of a copy. Perhaps his Literary Executors will reverse this decision?

The Graphic (but so hastily that he got the title completely wrong, which must have seriously spoilt its author's pleasure) "Mr. Greene's new book, *The Name of Reason*."

"I can foresee his early elevation to the position of a respectable, romantic best-seller," wrote Evelyn Waugh.* "He has a real sense of the importance of plot and the structure of narrative."

"His plot this time is the expedition of a wealthy, quixotic Englishman to a city state in the Palatinate to help free it from a fairly benevolent dictatorship. The revolutionaries prove rather disappointing; the dictator's wife is irresistible; political events tumble and mingle with the events of the hero's romance in the most agreeable way possible."

"I think," concluded Waugh, "he ought to repeat and augment his success with this book."

But he did not. *The Name of Action* was not reviewed widely, it was not much liked where it was reviewed, and it did not sell well.

It is not, admittedly, a first-class novel. It is not even a first-class thriller. Trier, the setting, lacks that sense of brooding political menace that had so impressed Graham and his companions in real life. But it is full of felicities. Conrad's influence is noticeable: Mr Crane, the American arms dealer, with his small eyes and baggy trousers, might have stepped out of the pages of any of the Lingard novels; and Kurtz the arch-revolutionary echoes, in name at least, the central figure of *The Heart of Darkness*. But Greene did not suffer from Conrad's unbounded hatred and contempt for revolutionaries. Rather the contrary indeed; and though there are echoes of the ineffectiveness of the anarchists meeting in Mr Verloc's bookshop, there are none of the exaggerated physical deformities that symbolise in *The Secret Agent* their moral turpitude. And to the characters he had found in literature Greene this time added characters obviously discovered by himself, drawn from the life of the streets and river-banks and *gasthauses* of Trier, convincingly portrayed – massive German landladies and *hausfraus*, government officials, barge owners, and inevitably the ubiquitous police.

There are three points of particular interest in *The Name of Action*, signposts to the future. First (as indeed throughout Europe), the level of political violence in Graham Greene's novels is beginning to rise. Struber, Paul Demassener's friend, has been assassinated before the story opens – indeed Struber's funeral offers Demassener the puritanical tyrant the occasion to seize power; and the dictator himself is, as the story ends, rather ridiculously wounded. But, much more

* Evelyn Waugh had already been married (Harold Acton was his best man) and, with bitterness, divorced. Just before going to Abyssinia he was received into the Catholic Church; unlike Graham, with great publicity and panache, by the famous society Jesuit Father D'Arcy at Farm Street. The *Daily Express* published a full centre-page spread, with pictures, entitled '"Converted to Rome – Why It Happened to Me" by Mr Evelyn Waugh'.

significantly, a policeman is shot and killed 'on stage' by the revolutionary Kapper – the first of a long long series of murders, 'accidents' and violent deaths that from this time onwards will tend to limit very severely the expectation that any character in a Graham Greene thriller may have of surviving successfully from its beginning through to its end.

Secondly, a newspaperman for the first time puts in an appearance. It is only a cameo sketch but it is very well handled indeed – of, interestingly, a *Chicago Tribune* reporter, with his "Christ, what a scoop!" as he spots, by chance, the fleeing dictator in the last chapter. Claud Cockburn had become, on the last day of 1929, the new Washington Correspondent of *The Times* after having lived, journalistically, through the scoop-crowded days of the Crash of '29 in New York. Did he write to Graham, in his wonderfully vivid way, descriptions of his new 'colleagues' in the newspaper world? Did Graham draw on Claud's letters for this, and possibly for subsequent, portraits?

Thirdly, and very noticeably, Jews here first enter a Graham Greene novel. They enter almost all his European thrillers and they play an increasingly large role in them till suddenly, as at the wave of a magician's wand, the very word 'Jew' disappears entirely, as a descriptive term, from his vocabulary. From *The Heart of the Matter* onwards a phrase such as: "said the Jew", so common in *The Name of Action*, becomes absolutely unimaginable. There is nothing blatantly anti-semitic in this. Indeed the revolutionary poet Joseph Kapper, "a thin Jew", is portrayed as a far more effective and heroic figure than the rich idealistic Englishman, Oliver Chant. But it was an accepted literary convention among English middlebrow thriller writers of the pre-World War II years, ranging from 'Sapper' up via Agatha Christie to Graham Greene, that Jews were referred to as Jews; and this of course reflected a social reality, that Jews were perceived by the English middle classes as being different – different in race, different in appearance and different in behaviour. As novelists both Graham Greene and Agatha Christie appear to have reflected, almost instinctively, certainly uncritically, the social conventions of the period. Pre-war it was socially permissible to refer to Jews openly in novels, adding a few racial characteristics; and they did so. Post-war it became socially a gaffe; and Jews, as such, vanished from the pages of the English novel, or at least from the cast-list of the English thriller.

Chapter VII

Enter Annette, Secretly

Barely had Graham delivered his first contracted novel than he had to start thinking about his second one; and this is where his troubles really began and the pitfalls of the three-book contract system yawned wide before him. He began this next novel a month before *The Name of Action* was published. But he had run out of inspiration. So, like all authors in a similar predicament, he leafed back, literally or metaphorically, through what he had already written, searching for that missing but necessary ingredient.

Predictably but unfortunately he found it in his unpublished novel, *The Episode*. There could be no question, however, of simply rehashing *The Episode*, for Charles Evans had seen it and rejected it and would of course remember it; he would be unlikely to take kindly to the same dish being served up again under a new title. But there was a theme – Spain and the Carlist Wars – and a setting. Rashly confident, after Trier, that he could now handle foreigners and foreign parts, Graham Greene decided to set his new novel fairly and squarely in Spain rather than, as *The Episode* had been, in London with Spain as a mere distant background. But there was in actual fact this enormous difference: that whereas he knew Trier and the Rhineland pretty well, he had never – apart from that day visit with Aunt Eva ten years earlier – set foot in Spain. At any rate he re-read *Arrow of Gold*, drew up plans for a heroine, Eulelia Monti, on the lines of Conrad's Donna Rita, drew from *The Man Within* a Christian name for one of his twin heroes, Francis (Andrews had been Francis) and from *The Name of Action* a surname for the second of his two heroes Crane and set to work.

But then came the publication of *The Name of Action* and with it Graham's realization that *The Man Within* had been his second false dawn – followed, obviously, by depression and a lack of confidence in his future as a novelist. He decided to turn his hand to something quite different. It was to be a biography; and by mid-November 1930 he was hard at work in the British Museum researching for his '*magnum opus*', the book that he had quite decided would restore, definitively, his reputation and ensure his future position in the literary world.

This meant that he now had two books to write. One, the new novel – due to be finished within the next few months – was important only because it would keep the staff of life, the six hundred pounds a year, flowing in. But the other, the major project, the biography, would take longer and would need a great deal of research. To write a novel while working in the afternoons and evenings on a newspaper is possible and Graham had proved that he could do it. But to write both a novel and a biography while holding down a full-time job is almost impossible. And that is why it seems likely that it was this projected biography rather than instinct or a simple desire for change which finally induced Graham to opt for cheap living in the country and to resign from *The Times*. Certainly the dates fit: mid-November a major new project is under way; December the full-time job is abandoned; and sometime between February 4th and March 2nd – dates of the last letter from Hampstead and of the first letter from Gloucestershire – Vivienne and Graham move house to Chipping Campden.

⋆⋆⋆

Nobody in their senses chooses to write a biography of a person with whom they have nothing at all in common. Graham chose as the subject of his *magnum opus* a poet, Rochester. Part of the charm of the choice was that so many of Rochester's erotic poems were to be found only on the "Reserved Shelves" of the British Museum and the Bodleian. When John Hayward had in 1926 organised an edition of Rochester's Poems, there had been no question of such a book going on public sale. It was printed for private distribution only; and even then the copies sent across the Atlantic were seized and destroyed by U.S. Customs as pornographic material.

Graham wrote to John Hayward. John Hayward enlivened their first meeting by reciting Rochester's "Imperfect Engagement" out loud. He was an intelligent wicked, caustic and gossipy man of letters, a year younger than Graham, for most of his life totally confined to a wheelchair by muscular dystrophy, with one arm half-paralysed, a powerful head and a long string of lady friends. He was to become Graham's preferred bawdy companion.

As *Rochester: A Restoration Portrait* developed, the correspondence between Graham Greene and John Hayward (who was, among other things, a most meticulous scholar) grew. So did Graham Greene's researches among aristocratic archives and muniment rooms – Lord Dillon's, Lord Listowel's, Lord Sandwich's and Lord Sackville's.⋆ What appealed to Graham, however, was not the aristocratic contacts that his aristocratic subject-matter necessarily involved (for Rochester the poet was also Rochester the second Earl) – he was never a social snob, rather the contrary – but Rochester's rackety character, his love-affairs with

⋆ At Knole: which had passed in 1928 to Edward Sackville-West's father. There Edward Sackville-West and Graham renewed an acquaintance that was minor or non-existent at Oxford but which was also to develop into a lifelong literary and social friendship.

actresses, his passion for brothels, his "cursed bawdy talk", his delight in disguises and practical jokes, all tastes that Graham shared or was to share. Furthermore Rochester had died young, aged 33, and Graham was intuitively (but oh how wrongly!) convinced that he himself would die at 32. It seemed the ideal subject for a sympathetic and therefore successful biography. There was also a most important, apparently paradoxical, and therefore most attractive aspect: that Christianity, as Greene was to point out, had dominated Rochester's thoughts, one way or another, all his short and crowded life.

Just as *The Man Within* had begun with Andrews coming over the top of the Sussex Downs as the last light fades, so *Rochester* begins with Henry Wilmot, his Cavalier father, harrying Essex' flank over the final ridge of the Cotswolds to Chipping Norton.

Deeper into the Cotswolds, in Chipping Campden, Graham and Vivienne rented a cottage, Little Orchard, up Hoo Lane, picturesque but primitive, without electricity, with rats, for £1 a week. Graham wrote to Lady Ottoline Morrell that, though they missed her Thursday teas in Gower Street, his writing was going extremely well, for there was nothing to do in the country except read, write and walk. For the first time in his married life he had his own study. Thus set up, he managed to write 24,000 words – almost one third of the new novel – in a month.

This was the first and last time Graham Greene lived in the country. The Cotswolds were splendid hunting, shooting and fishing country, splendid ratting, bird-watching and gardening country. All this left him cold. Splendid walking country too, with splendid scenery – and that he much enjoyed, going with Vivienne for long country walks and taking off, with any of his family whom he could persuade to come along, for walking tours that might stretch up to a week in length.

Vivienne's main task, apart from providing her husband with meals and attending to his creature comforts (once she was away for the night at Stratford-on-Avon and poor Graham for the first time in his life had to cook his own bacon and eggs) was to listen as he read out to her sections of his new novel, and to make intelligent comments and suggestions. She was good at this, and enjoyed it, and Graham respected his wife's views on the technical problems of novel-writing far more than he did those of his agent or publisher.

It was not a bad life for Vivienne. They had a maid, a skivvy, Nellie Greenall; and a part-time gardener; and she gradually made many local friends. The greatest of these was Fred Hart, a confirmed bachelor, a thoroughly honest, totally upright man who appears to have become for Vivienne the father-figure that she had never known. Indeed in the post-war years and right up till his death at the age of ninety-two he was the person to whom Vivienne turned and on whom she could utterly rely in a crisis. Graham became more and more convinced that Fred Hart was in love with his wife. The situation interested him, did not worry him.

Charles Wade of nearby Snowshill Manor was Fred Hart's inseparable friend and companion. At Snowshill the young couple drank rhubarb wine which succeeded, Graham thought, in softening the vulgarity of a fellow guest, an oily young publisher named Allen Lane. Their host kept a list of visitors under different headings with one warily entitled, "Literary Coves". (This included, besides Graham himself, Edward Sackville-West and Anthony Asquith, plus Virginia Woolf and John Masefield). Vivienne adored Snowshill, which had the most extraordinary collection of handicraft objects. What particularly fascinated her were the dolls and the dolls' houses; for Vivienne was to become herself probably the greatest collector of, and expert on, dolls' houses in England.

In such an atmosphere Graham was peculiarily out of place. He never had an interest in objects or possessions, other than books. As Vivienne's social life broadened, his own level of boredom dramatically increased.

Raymond was off on the British Himalayan Expedition, sailing from Venice via Port-Said to Bombay with his photo in *The Times* and three months of adventure, conquering Mount Kamet on the Empire's edge, ahead of him. That was life as it should be lived, full of excitement and travel and adventure. Walks in Gloucestershire were hardly a consolation.

Graham clearly suffered from claustrophobia, repressed physical energy and frustration. This, added to the lack of a regular office routine and outside contacts, was not good for his marriage. He caught a bus to Oxford now and again, to visit Hugh who had founded – also reported in the columns of *The Times* – the Oxford University Film Society, and to see a good film with him. But the occasional day trip or over-night trip to London was the highlight of his country life; and there, almost certainly in that early autumn of 1931, he met Annette.

★ ★ ★

It may have been Herbert, back from South America, who introduced Graham to the enchanting Annette. Annette was a high-class prostitute living in Warren Street; and either Herbert or Graham was in Soho looking for another prostitute when Annette opened the door and he – whichever 'he' it was – immediately thought: – "This is the one for me." If it was Herbert (the evidence is ambiguous) he fell in love with Annette and later introduced Graham to her. If not, it was Graham himself to whom Annette opened the door; and Graham who fell for her like a rainbow. Certainly for the next year and a half she was the sun that shone over Graham's dulled country life and lent colour and sparkle to his visits to town.

★ ★ ★

This was a pretty miserable period for Graham as a writer. He had finished his second contracted novel, *Rumour at Nightfall*, in the early spring, shortly after arriving at Chipping Campden, in that first great surge of writing; and it was due out in the autumn. When it came out, *The Spectator* gave it, deservedly, only two dismissive sentences: "Mr Greene is one of those authors who have something to say but whose turgidity prevents them saying it. The theme is the interplay of one Spanish and two English characters in the Spain of the Carlist wars."

The Times Literary Supplement remained silent; and the *Sunday Times*, which had praised his first book and reviewed his second, ignored his third. Understandably depressed, Graham wrote to Lady Ottoline to thank her for her comfort. Writing books, he concluded, was bad enough in itself; but having them published was pure torment.

Even worse was to follow. *Rumour at Nightfall* had come out on November 1931; and by December he had finished his biography of Rochester, was sending it off to his old tutor at Balliol to be vetted for historical faults; and was looking forward, he told Lady Ottoline, to publication in April and to being reviewed by a totally different set of critics.

The outcome was far more disastrous than he can ever have anticipated. He was certainly well aware that he had rushed the writing of *Rochester*, cramming it all into six months' hard slog without a break. But Evelyn Waugh's very first book had been a biography, *Rossetti*; had been considered publishable, and had indeed been published* to a certain critical acclaim. Unlike Evelyn Waugh then, Graham now had three published novels behind him, and was therefore, comparatively speaking, far better established.

Yet *Rochester*, the *magnum opus*, was turned down flat. No record survives, at least in public, of Graham's reaction to this disastrous turn of events. But it must have been despairing; and he must have felt absolutely desperate. His novel was a failure – only twelve hundred copies were sold and in the United States under a thousand – and now, almost unbelievably, the work on which he had been counting to restore his reputation, the great biography, a year's solid work (the writing included) with its carefully prepared presentations of notes and portraits, a book on which he had done so much research and into which he had poured so much of himself, a serious book, a book all his family and friends knew about – basely rejected! And this by publishers whom he had believed to be his friends! He was so discouraged by Heinemann's reaction that he did not submit the rejected manuscript to any other publisher.†

By the beginning of 1932 therefore Graham was in a fairly desperate position.

* In June 1928 by Duckworth's, largely thanks to a young graduate editor there, Anthony Powell, Graham's junior by a year at Balliol, and his future post-war colleague in the publishing world.

† So for years and years the manuscript of *Rochester* slumbered half forgotten, among Greene's other papers until, over four decades later, it was re-discovered and published after all – in 1974, under the title of *Lord Rochester's Monkey*, as a coffee-table book.

In the absence of a contract Charles Evans was justified, if harsh, in rejecting it. *Rochester* never was unpublishable; but it is a dull book; and, coming from the pen of a minor novelist, it would probably have sunk without trace. Even the general reviews in 1974 were more baffled and

His contract with both Heinemann and Doubleday Doran was due to end on August 31st, and after that, unless they renewed it, he would be both penniless and jobless. It shows both his determination and his desperation that he began writing his next novel, the third and last of the contracted trio, promptly, on the second day of the New Year.

One thing buoyed him up. Before January ended he had, at long last, had an article published in *The Spectator*. Derek Verschoyle,* a 21 year-old Anglo-Irishman, had just been appointed its Literary Editor by Wilson Harris, *The Spectator's* new (and politically Liberal) Editor; and from this time onwards Verschoyle was to send down by train to Little Orchard an increasing stream of books for review on which Graham could sharpen his wits and, on occasion, his teeth.

Graham Greene was to become an excellent literary critic. He enjoyed reading books on almost any subject. Fiction and non-fiction alike were grist to his critical mill; and he enjoyed writing about what he had read. His reviews were acute, intelligent and highly literate. But he had an analytic mind and a biting turn of phrase. He was more inclined to find fault than to dish out compliments. He did not suffer literary fools gladly. He did not even suffer himself gladly.

This last is an extremely important point. Anyone reading Graham Greene's literary criticism, particularly his longer pieces, cannot help noticing how, under the guise of reviewing other people's books, he is in fact commenting upon his own. One of his major critics, Professor Stratford, makes this point very strongly, in particular as regards Robert Louis Stevenson's influence.

"Although," the Professor writes, "he has never directly acknowledged this influence, Greene has written several articles on Stevenson and has referred admiringly to him in a dozen others… Whenever he took up Stevenson's cause in the margin of his early literary criticism, Greene was really pleading his own."

Being given the opportunity to write reviews for *The Spectator* boosted Graham Greene's confidence enormously, at a time when it needed boosting. But it also boosted, at a time when these were even more obviously needed, his own powers of self-criticism. By late spring he was three-quarters of the way through his new novel. As he was writing it, he was also simultaneously keeping up a running fire of commentary in the columns of *The Spectator* ostensibly on other people's books but in fact very largely on writing techniques in general and on his own past

respectful than enthusiastic. For Graham Greene was no biographer, and he was never, though tempted, to try his hand at the genre again.

What is extraordinary is that Graham Greene was to succeed at so many different kinds of writing; not that he should have failed in some.

* Exactly where and when the two men first met is unclear. But for the next eight years, from 1932 to 1940, Derek Verschoyle was to remain Literary Editor of *The Spectator* until he was succeeded briefly – the closest he ever got to achieving that particular one of his three ambitions – by Graham Greene.

deficiencies in particular. He was being forced to think, and think hard, about how to write novels well just at the moment when he was himself engaged in writing one.

These thoughts, these forced reflections, obviously affected his own writing. His previous novels had failed. His career as a novelist was on the rocks. Clearly his only hope was to change technique. He was forced to think about technique. He thought about it carefully and analytically. And he changed it.

That at least, with nuances, is Professor Stratford's explanation* of the "mystery of Opus IV"; and indeed, with variations, Graham Greene's own explanation too.

The mystery is, basically, this: that Greene's fourth novel, the one he wrote so rapidly in 1932 between January and July, is so totally unlike any of the previous three that it is hard to believe that it comes from the pen of the same author.

Greene himself attributed the extraordinary change in his technique not to his reviewing but rather to one particularly scathing review of *Rumour at Nightfall* that made him utterly abandon Conrad. "It made no difference to me," he wrote, "that the review which had opened my eyes was by an author, Frank Swinnerton, for whom I had little respect – I knew the truth when I read it. There was nothing for me to do but dismantle all that elaborate scaffolding built from an older writer's blueprint... and start again at the beginning. Never again, I swore, would I read a novel of Conrad's – a vow I kept for more than a quarter of a century... until I found myself with *Heart of Darkness* in a small paddle boat travelling up a Congo estuary in 1959 from one leper colony to another. I had to begin again naked, and perhaps it was for that reason I chose an adventure story..."

This explanation would be more convincing if in fact Greene had not re-read *Heart of Darkness* on June 26, 1932 and indeed *The Secret Agent* two days later, that is to say while he was writing the 'adventure story'. This is perhaps an unimportant inaccuracy. But what is totally unconvincing is the importance given by Greene to Frank Swinnerton's review. Ronald Matthews, Greene's friend, noticed this. He dug out a copy of Swinnerton's review – when, years later, he was discussing the matter with Greene.

"Read it out to me," said Graham.

Matthews read it out. Swinnerton was a perfectly respectable literary figure who had published six novels and written critical studies of Gissing and Robert Louis Stevenson. Every week he produced a Book Page for a popular London evening daily, the *Evening Times* – not the sort of paper that Greene would *a priori* (unless the review was exceptionally perceptive) tend to be influenced by. On the evening of November 20th, 1931, Swinnerton had reviewed five new novels, two

* Professor Stratford's excellent book is entitled *Faith and Fiction*. Four pages (pp 116-119) comment, in detail, on Greene's early *Spectator* criticism as it can be applied – and per the Professor was in fact to be applied – to his own writings.

favourably, two with moderate enthusiasm; and finally, in three paragraphs, Mr Graham Greene's new book, *Rumour at Nightfall.*

Greene listened to Matthews reading out the three paragraphs.

"It's hard to see," he said, "why that review made such a strong impression on me. Swinnerton wasn't really vicious."

On the contrary it is a perfectly ordinary, slightly baffled review, much less harsh than either the *New Statesman*'s or the *Spectator*'s, complaining simply that Mr Greene's characters talk an incongruous language that seems to belong to another planet. Far from saying that Greene is too influenced by Conrad, Swinnerton points out that Conrad's depth of vision comes from an insight into the complexities of human nature which Greene appears to be confusing with the complexities of artificial (and lethargic) dialogue. "Not one of his characters," writes Swinnerton, "can give a simple answer to a simple question." Yet the basic story, in the critic's opinion, "could have been told with verve and passionate excitement by a writer of the romantic school" like Greene – if only he had cut out the psychology. Read with any attention at all, Swinnerton's mild and thoughtful criticsm, far from suggesting that Greene is on the wrong track or should abandon Conrad, emphasises the virtues of the romantic as opposed to the realistic school, and simply suggests that Greene should cut down on the introspection and improve the dialogue. From there to "beginning again naked" is a very long step indeed. Ronald Matthews was not satisfied with Greene's explanation; and nor can we be.

For, as Matthews points out, the new novel, *Stamboul Train*, was to represent a complete and utter break with the past, to be the first which any reader can recognise as being, from start to finish, an authentic Graham Greene. The beginning is no longer slow and laborious. The background is no mere imaginary confection but realistic and essential. The principal characters are quickly and concisely established. A brief exchange of platitudes tells us more about their personalities than two and a half pages of introspection or ruminative dialogue had done in any of the preceding books. And the characters themselves come to life. As Matthews puts it, all of them have a living to earn; none of them crumble away into dust when touched; one can practically guess their incomes and resources. As for the action, it is fast-moving, finely handled, cutting from scene to scene and from place to place with great ease and control.

Greene swiftly offered Matthews another, and much better, explanation, "It's very simple," he said. "The book was written to make money" and was much influenced by films and by film technique. This is most certainly true.

But though Matthews recognized the truth of the cinema technique explanation, it did not satisfy him either. For, as he most perspicaciously observed, the revolution in the novelist's technique was only half the thing. What had changed even more significantly was the attitude of the author towards his characters. The change in the moral climate, he told Graham, was extraordinarily striking: "What intrigues me is this: that all your characters in the first novels are alone, and empty, but that from *Stamboul Train* onwards a feeling of tenderness surrounds them as if, quite apart from the plot, there is somebody there who loves them."

Graham evaded his friend's implied question, evaded the suggestion that, though God is nowhere explicitly mentioned in *Stamboul Train*, He is there waiting in the wings and that Graham was experiencing a second and more real conversion.

"I wish I could help you more," Graham said, when Matthews ruefully admitted that he would have, he feared, to give up his attempt to discover "the shock I'm looking for, that sent you along this new route."

Even Professor Stratford reaches, by different means, the same conclusion and puts, implicitly, the same question: "It is through their inadequacies" (he is concluding his analysis of *Stamboul Train*) "that characters come to life, through their unhappiness that we find a means of sympathizing with them. They have all been hurt by life, and this is an experience one feels that Greene himself, for all his precocious 'terror of life', must have first felt deeply some time after the writing of *Rumour at Nightfall*."

Some time after the writing of *Rumour at Nightfall* – and it is the only obvious 'experience' that Greene had – he met Annette. If he fell in love with her, passionately and hopelessly in love with her, that would have been "the shock" for which Ronald Matthews was looking and which Graham Greene, with his great personal reticence, could not possibly admit to his friend. Matthews, also a convert, had himself experienced a 'second conversion' and so was naturally inclined towards that theory. But it may have been the experience of human love, not divine love, that diffused the aura of tenderness over the characters of *Stamboul Train* so rightly noted by Matthews, . One rather hopes that it was, and that Graham had found, for the first time joined together, sexual and romantic contentment.*

* Annette disappeared from Graham's life as suddenly as she entered it. If she is alive now, she will almost certainly be in her late seventies; and only she could confirm, or deny, the truth or falsehood of the attachment of a young man she may not have known as Graham Greene but as Hilary (or perhaps Captain) Trench. The only evidence supporting the theory stated above is the evidence of chronology; for Graham Greene's diary, now at Texas, begins abruptly enough on June 3rd 1932; and the diary for the proceeding months has been either destroyed or kept private. And this later diary has itself been 'weeded', with half or even three-quarter pages torn out here or there, and sentences heavily marked out; but so carelessly (deliberately or sub-consciously) that the various scattered references to "A", or even "Annette", are unmistakable.

Chapter VIII

One Thousand Seven Hundred and Thirty Eight Pounds, Three Shillings and Eight Pence

One of the minor mysteries with *Stamboul Train* is: who helped Graham to find his characters?

Hardly Vivienne; and hardly Chipping Campden in general, for the two most thoroughly memorable characters are Mabel Warren, the tweedy gin-soaked unscrupulous reporter for the *Clarion*, covering Central Europe, and the uneasy rich young London Jew, Carleton Myatt, a commodity trader. Both woo the heroine, Coral Musker. Mabel Warren wins her, Carleton Myatt abandons her for the (half-Jewish, sleek, sophisticated) Janet Pardoe who has been Mabel Warren's 'companion' in Vienna.

The real fascination of the novelist is clearly with the Jew Myatt, a rounded closely-observed character; and his real success is with Mabel Warren. Mabel, with her lugubrious sentimentality and maudlin pathos, steps out of the pages of *Stamboul Train*, a monster of vitality, a memorable creation. But where did Graham draw her and Myatt from – the Lesbian and the Jew? From life? From Annette's acquaintances and anecdotes? Or from literature? From the pages of other writers' books? Both are possible. Neither is certain. But what is certain is that the pair of them did not spring, fully-armed, from his own head; and even less so from Vivienne's.

★★★

In those first months of the year 1932 Graham's main worry was money. He kept a careful note of what he earned by reviewing – just over £2 in January, just over £1.16.0d in February, just over £16 in six months. Then in July came a totally unexpected income tax demand for £60. Ruin stared the young couple in the face.

The only consolation was that it was a really marvellous summer in the countryside. Uncle Eppy owned a farm at Litle Wittenham in the Thames Valley; and the rich Greenes summered there, inviting Graham and Vivienne over for tennis and riding. Barbara fetched them – Barbara, Ave's younger sister, now in her early twenties, a lively and energetic girl, very thick with Hugh.

The most interesting visitor of all was Rupert Hart-Davis, tall, fair-haired, pleasant-looking, blond, whom Graham decided he liked immensely. Hart-Davis was no longer an editor at Heinemann's. He had resigned, and was Secretary of the Book Society, rather an influential post; for every month the Book Society selected a new book as its Book Society Choice. He was staying in the nearby village of Blockley, far more beautiful than its name, with Colonel and Mrs. Turner and their daughter Comfort – she too far more beautiful than hers.

Stamboul Train, completed on July 17th, typed out in two weeks, was sent off to Heinemann's on August 4th; and tension mounted. By August 18th, with Heinemann's verdict expected any moment, Graham was in a state of enormous tension. When he went down for breakfast the following morning, he found the long-awaited letter on the breakfast table. He took it upstairs and opened it with trembling fingers.

It was, Charles Evans wrote and Graham read, "the best book you have written so far". He had found the story quite enthralling, "I wish you could have found a way of bringing that scoundrel Grumlich to justice," he added. "This may seem a naive remark for a blasé old novel reader such as I but it will show you that your people have got hold of me."

Graham could hardly believe the sentences before his eyes. They were, he thought, too good to be true. He hurried to the nearby Catholic Church, got on his knees, and thanked God.

But next morning reaction set in; next month even more so after a dismal meeting with Charles Evans and Mary Pritchett, Doubleday's representative in London, where they had renewed his contract for a year but only on condition that past losses on his past books were to be made up out of the profits, if any, on future books – thereby reducing him, Graham realised, to a sort of indentured literary serf. He was almost in tears. He wandered miserably down Bond Street looking at the whores; and wrote to Braine-Hartnell, in Siam, about a possible job at the University of Chulakundra.

Ratcliffe, one of the four Old Berkhamstedians who had gone up to Oxford in Graham's year, paid a visit, bringing with him a young Norwegian poet, Nordahl Grieg;* who charmed Graham and Vivienne with his courteous manners, his delicious accent, his delightful accounts of his cottage in Lapland and of the beauties of the Norwegian forest. He suggested (there had as yet been no reply from the Rector of Chulakundra) that Graham apply instead for a post as a

* He who as a drama critic had reviewed Robert Speaight in *Peer Gynt* (See page 25 above). There was another connection. Nordahl's brother Harold Grieg, was publishing *The Man Within* in Oslo; the first of many Scandinavian editions of Graham Greene's books. At the time these foreign translations brought in only a few pounds.

lecturer in Norway. Everyone else seemed to be travelling and going abroad; Evelyn Waugh had been to Abyssinia, Peter Quennell to Japan, Claud Cockburn was now back in Central Europe, Raymond was about to go off again on an even more ambitious mountaineering project, the Everest Expedition* – and all Graham had to look forward to was a walk with Vivienne to Burnt Norton; and then, while she stayed with the Turners at Blockley, a four-day walking tour with Hugh over the Cotswolds. The brothers doubled back along the Ridgeway past the White Horse at Uffington in the pale autumn sunlight with the fields being harrowed and the ploughmen singing as the horses disappeared over the swell of the Downs, back to a house dispiritingly empty in Vivienne's absence.

Graham went up to London to visit Wormwood Scrubs† – thanks to an introduction from Colonel Turner to the prison governor. He cabled Annette to expect him at 6.15 in the evening. Back in his hotel he found a telegram in the rack from Rupert Hart-Davis. The first word was "Congratulations". *Stamboul Train* had been selected as the Book Society Choice for December. This was marvellous and unexpected news. This meant money. Keep your eye open for *Stamboul Train* on December 1st, Graham told Hugh. But three days before publication date came a wire from Charles Evans asking Graham to telephone him immediately. Crisis. JB Priestley, Heinemann's most sucessful author, was threatening to bring a libel action if the book were published.

The portrait of "Mr Savory" in *Stamboul Train*, author of *The Great Gay Round* (half a million words, two hundred characters) with his pipe, his jolly cheerfulness, his mock humility, and his habit of dropping his aitches whenever he can remember to is a small but wicked masterpiece of satire. Savory is one of the six main characters travelling on the Orient Express, and he appears, from almost one end of the book to the other, ridiculous as a novelist and absurd, though occasionally pathetically touching, as a human being.

In later life Graham Green was always to deny that he had modelled Savory on JB Priestley, and Priestley himself denied that there had been any threat of a lawsuit.‡ Priestley's denial was rubbish: he had learnt only too well the lesson of his then friend Hugh Walpole who had been made the laughing-stock of the

* It failed.

† Graham had had, on August 18th, a new idea for a novel based on the class struggle and the murder of a policeman. Should the murderer be hanged or pardoned? Its eventual title was to be *It's A Battlefield*.

‡ See *The Times* Diary of August 31st 1971; headed "Greene Fingers". This came a month before publication of Graham Greene's autobiography *A Sort of Life* in which he writes, of the portrait of Savory, "J.S. Thomas, the politician, was in my mind when I gave him a touch of Cockney, Baldwin when I gave him a pipe." John Atkins, Graham Greene's most perspicacious critic, rightly pours scorn on Greene's contention that he modelled his fictional novelist on two most unlikely politicians, both, in 1971, as Atkins points out, conveniently dead.

literary world by Somerset Maughan's devastating portrayal of him as "Alroy Kear".* Greene's denial was *pro forma* too. His diaries reveal that he detested Priestley as a personality and despised him as a writer. He was to claim in his autobiography that he had never met Priestley personally. That was strictly speaking true. But he knew enough about Priestley from Rupert Hart-Davis to loathe him. Rupert had married Peggy Ashcroft at the end of 1929; in 1931, only eighteen months into the young couple's marriage, Priestley had had an affair with her that in effect destroyed it. Graham knew all this (though Peggy Ashcroft, then and later, did everything she could to hush it all up). He was, as always, passionately loyal to his friends. His friends' enemies were his enemies, and he never had any mercy on them. What better revenge for Rupert than to have Priestley savaged in a successful book? That is what he thought; and that, despite his later denials, is what he did.

The man most to be pitied in this literary/emotional imbroglio is Charles Evans, torn between two of his own authors, one ex-colleague, and a very reticent young actress. In the end a compromise was reached. Twenty-odd pages were rewritten, re-printed and rebound (at Graham's expense); all references to "the new Dickens", to pipe-smoking, to blunt fingers – Priestley's hallmarks – were taken out, and a ruinous libel action avoided. *Stamboul Train* appeared in the bookshops with only a week's delay – admirable Heinemann's! – and was received favourably by everyone except JB Priestley himself.

"The popular novelist," wrote *The Times Literary Supplement*, "though an admirable figure of satire is an unspeakable epitome of his kind". But nobody drew, at least in public or in print the overt comparison. "The Jew", the TLS review added, "illustrates all the characteristics of a Jew."

Myatt's father, with his white beard and old ringed fingers, Myatt himself with his fur coat, his two pairs of silk pyjamas, his spreading hands, "a trick of his race which he was consciously repressing", "his too familiar features, the small eyes, the large nose, the black oiled hair," are noticeably the Jews of popular fiction; and *The Times Literary Supplement* was right to fasten on the point. But right too to fasten on it hesitantly. For the Jew, if anyone, is the hero of *Stamboul Train*, Brutus to Dr. Czinner's Caesar, warm-hearted but inconsistent, an idealist and, in Myatt's case, a cynic only where money, Gentiles in business, and christianized Jews in social life are concerned. His portrait does not seem to have offended the reading public. What did offend them, however, were the open lesbianism and hints of homosexuality, the atmosphere of amoral fornication and sexual indulgence, in general the brilliantly and tenderly handled seduction of the chorus girl – a virgin

* In *Cakes and Ale*, published only two years earlier, which Walpole, as chairman of the Book Society Selection Committee, had been given to read. He read it and was horrified. But on Priestley's advice did nothing – a great mistake. For the portrait made him a figure of scorn for the rest of his life.

– by the Jew, and in particular the *obiter dictum*: "Novelists like Ruby M. Ayres might say that chastity was worth more than rubies, but the truth was it was priced at a fur coat or thereabouts." Book Society members returned their copies in shoals. "Are none of your members pure in heart?" wrote one. "This may be like life but if it is I don't want to read about it," wrote another.

★ ★ ★

It was a hard hard winter that winter. Charlie Sykes, the local madman, froze to death on his bed of straw in Broad Campden. On the bitterest night of the year a young woman walked out of one of the Council houses and drowned herself in the lake of Northwick Park. The old man who sold the *News of the World* in Chipping Campden was found hanging dead, aged 73. Nellie Greenall used to tell Graham about all these tragedies. She herself had chopped the top of her finger off in the garden of Little Orchard while chopping wood. Graham was indoors at the time and was more than thankful – for he was squeamish about blood – that she had not called to him for help. He remarked on the endurance of the lower classes, noting that in the pea-picking season Nellie had worked from four in the morning picking peas right through till eleven at night in the cottage. But his attitude was not consistent. When he discovered that she was taking time off for which he considered he was paying her, he was furious – to think of her doing that to an impoverished writer and his wife!

For at the beginning of 1933 money worries were as bad as the previous year even though *Stamboul Train* was selling 100 copies a day and had almost reached the 15,000 mark.* He dreamt he had murdered Priestley and was arrested at the Times Book Club and taken away in a Black Maria. This caused him, so to speak, to lose no sleep.

Slowly things took a turn for the better. First Peter Fleming, Derek Verschoyle's sidekick on *The Spectator*, asked him to take over the fiction reviewing for £5 a week. Next Derek Verschoyle accepted Graham's first non-critical piece "Death in the Cotswolds" – about the death, and strange life, of Charlie Sykes – and finally came an amazing offer of £150 for the serial rights of *Stamboul Train*.

Graham celebrated. First, on March 15th he celebrated, together with Annette, eighteen months' mutual acquaintance; then, two days later, with Vivienne, the eighth anniversary of their first meeting. He summoned her up to Town for the occasion. They stayed at the Kenilworth Hotel, had dinner at Schmidt's, went to see a René Clair at the movies (and also Raymond in "Kamet Conquered") – and, in their euphoria, forgot to take any 'precautions'.

The weather turned soft and springlike. On Palm Sunday Rupert Hart-Davis

* The royalties never reached Little Orchard. They were simply going towards paying back Graham's debt to Heinemann.

came over to lunch with Comfort Turner – and news that he had left the Book Society to become a Director, a very young one, of Jonathan Cape's. They celebrated again. Then the following Wednesday, came even more extraordinary good news. Twentieth Century Fox wanted the film rights of *Stamboul Train* and were offering $7500.

Everything seemed to be happening at once. Vivienne discovered she was pregnant and pretended to be horrified to please Graham. He was most disconcerted when he realized that she was only pretending. On April 25th news came that Muriel Dayrell-Browning had fallen and broken her leg. A worried Vivienne set out to visit her in the nursing home. By the same post came further news: that Vivienne's father, Sidney Dayrell-Browning, was dead.

And exactly a week later came the red-letter day when, as Graham triumphantly postcarded Hugh, a cheque for £1738.3.8d arrived from Twentieth Century Fox. Graham paid £100 into Vivienne's account at once and sent a cheque for £35 to Molly, his eldest sister, for a holiday. He and Vivienne went for a walk, hand in hand, blissful, dazed at their good fortune.

Who says that money does not bring happiness? After all the years of striving and anxiety Graham could at long last afford to relax. His good fortune was so sudden, so unexpected and so thoroughly and satisfactorily huge after so many disappointments and hopes falsely raised that it took him days to adjust himself to the fact that they were now well-off. Worries about the baby at once disappeared. Now Graham's first and foremost wish was to leave country life and country cottages behind him for ever. He and Vivienne caught a bus over to Oxford and went house-hunting. They settled on a flat at the far end of the Woodstock Road, not too far from Graham's old digs in Thorncliffe Road – modern, with both a refrigerator and a sunny bathroom, for £130 a year. Fred Hart, back from St. Kitts where Charles Wade had a plantation, was delighted at Graham's amazing good fortune but sad that Vivienne would be leaving Chipping Campden for ever.

Then it was up to London, Vivienne to stay overnight with her mother in the nursing home, Graham to walk with Aunt Nono in Battersea Park; down to Incents for a couple of days (Graham drew with his father at chess but only when Charles Greene had given him a knight); and across England for a springtime seaside holiday past the Mumbles in Swansea Bay.

Vivienne and Graham reached Sea Beach on May 21st, a Monday, to find two telegrams awaiting them. The first was to say that Muriel Dayrell-Browning was seriously ill. The second was to say that she was dead. For one ghastly moment Graham, who opened them, thought they referred to his own mother. When he broke the news to Vivienne, there came from her a shriek of despair.

Vivienne was terribly upset, and spent the next days in tears. She must have felt that what God gave with one hand – unexpected good fortune and an unexpected baby – He took back with the other in two equally unexpected deaths. Now her child would never know its grandparents; and her own mother and father would never see their first grandchild. Moreover her father had died – where? how? perhaps a lonely death in South America? – unreconciled to her; and she felt, Graham thought, unnecessarily guilty for having distanced herself from her mother too in recent years. She was so very upset that Graham was quite determined not to allow her to travel to London for the funeral especially now that she was bearing their child.

Muriel had died of a blood clot that suddenly passed from her broken leg to her brain. Her body was to be cremated at Golders Green. The Green-Armytages rallied round to Graham's appeals. Uncle Vivian, the Indian Army doctor, wrote to advise his niece not to come; and Uncle Bob telephoned. Vivienne finally gave way when Graham offered to go up to London in her place.

The funeral was held that Thursday. Graham had never been to a cremation before and he took it all in – the air of heartless sentimentality, the roar of the furnaces, the factory-like swiftness with which funerals followed each other, the coffin sliding in. There was a very pretty girl there, he noticed, who had been living in Muriel's Hampstead flat; and many years and many novels later he was to use his memories of the scene, still obviously perfectly vivid, pretty girl and all, in the last section of *The End of the Affair.*

★ ★ ★

Graham and Vivienne stayed on for another three weeks of almost perfect sunshine in Wales. By mid-June they were back in Chipping Campden. On June 22nd Graham went up to London to a literary tea-party given at the Carlton by Mrs Belloc Lowndes for Charles Morgan, who had just won the Hawthornden Prize. The guests sat in little groups at gold tables. Understandably Graham went on from this over-rarefied atmosphere to visit Annette. She was not, however, in despite his usual early-warning cable; and he spent a debauched evening instead, in the company of Archie Harding, Claud Cockburn's friend, touring the fleshpots.

Next day the Greenes moved. Mr and Mrs Graham Greene, announced their printed card, were now to be found at 9 Woodstock Close, Woodstock Road, Oxford, Telephone: Summertown 58173. Graham's stay in the country had lasted almost exactly two years; and had produced three books, plus, in embryo, one child.

★ ★ ★

Back in Oxford once again Graham bubbled over with literary energy. He read Robert Graves' marvellous autobiography *Goodbye to All That*; and was so impressed with the school jokes and the tale of Graves' expulsion that he decided to propose a symposium, via Rupert Hart-Davies to Jonathan Cape, to be entitled

The Old School; say ten young writers, ex-public schoolboys, each from a different school, each to write a chapter about their own ghastly experiences.

A week later he was reading Antonia White's convent-set novel *Frost in May*, and the project began to take shape. Betrayal, expulsion, secret police-like discipline – they were themes after Graham's own heart, and in his mind he broadened the scope of the book to include girls' schools as well as boys'. At Heinemann's Summer Garden Party he enrolled LP Hartley late of Harrow (and also of Balliol) and Theodora Benson late of Cheltenham Ladies' College. But it was at Oxford, at Headington, that he first met another novelist, also to be roped in as a future contributor, who was to become a lifelong friend. This was Elizabeth Bowen.

What most fascinated him about Elizabeth Bowen at this first meeting was her account of TS Eliot★ and his disastrous marriage.

Graham and Vivienne Greene's marriage was never to reach the tragic point of Tom and Vivienne Eliot's. Though it too was to end in separation, and though that separation, arguably, continued to worry, possibly indeed to torment, both of them throughout both their lives, there was never to be the appalling, if understandable, treachery and secrecy that accompanied the eventual committal of Eliot's Vivienne, against her will, to a lunatic asylum; where after eleven years of silence and restraint she was to die a miserable and lonely death. Graham and Vivienne were never to come to that; or indeed anything remotely like it.

Not that Graham and Vivienne's marriage can be described as happy, even in their new flat and even back at Oxford, the scene of their wooing. Graham for two reasons was restless. The first was the travel urge. Now that he had money in his account he wanted to get abroad, and make his name, as so many other adventurous young writers were doing†. Thus when on August 8th he received a letter from Nordahl Grieg suggesting an exotic and unusual voyage he was sorely tempted.

"I assure that you before now or later must come to Estonia," wrote the

★ Graham Greene was a great admirer of T.S. Eliot; and particularly of *The Waste Land*, which had appeared in Graham's first year at Oxford and which, certain critics say, influenced directly or indirectly all his later works. There were to be Plutarchian parallels between Eliot's life and Greene's life. Though they were to meet (via Herbert Read) only once or twice, and did not particularly get on, both shared many similar tastes – for practical jokes, for Victorian detective stories and for *erotica*. Both were in their time poets, playwrights, magazine editors and directors of publishing houses. Converts too, though to different churches. But the most extraordinary parallel of all is that both had married, after an Oxford romance, young women named Vivienne. Graham was superstitious about names, and this cannot have failed to strike him. It was indeed about this time that Vivienne dropped the two final letters of her Christian name – to become Vivien thereafter.

† Peter Fleming, for instance, had set out to Brazil on an expedition in search of the lost explorer Colonel Fawcett. Not only did he write a bestseller about it; but Geoffrey Dawson made him a Special Corespondent. He became Dawson's favourite young protegé as a result and was tipped as a future editor of *The Times*.

Norwegian – he had obviously taken to Graham immensely – "and please come now. It is a charming country, absolutely unspoilt, the cheapest in the world. I am a very poor author but here I can afford absolutely everything – a strange and marvellous feeling! If the weather is good do let us hire a sailing boat and go for a week among the islands. The population there has scarcely seen a white man before, and for a few pieces of chocolate we could certainly buy what native girls we want. Do come."

This was an almost irresistible letter; and one that showed a surprising intuitive understanding by Nordahl of Graham's tastes and desires – seeing that the two young men had known each other for a mere afternoon. Next day Graham bought an Everyman Atlas and noted in his diary an urge to set out for Tallinn. But it was not – or not yet – to be. For Graham had already arranged to set off – but with Hugh, and to Sweden.

Hugh had just come down from Oxford with a disappointing Second; and Graham wanted to offer him a consolatory holiday.

But the main reason for choosing Sweden as the destination was the next novel. Ivar Kreuger, the Swedish match king, had shot himself on March 12th, 1932, when the share value of his Swedish Match company had dropped from £180 million to £45 million. A year later a writer called George Soloveytchik has rushed out a quick biography, which Graham had reviewed for *The Spectator*. The book was not particularly well written but it was a good story, it stuck in Graham's mind and he told Hugh that one of the three main characters in his proposed new novel *Brothers and Sisters* would be modelled on Kreuger. He did not mention – perhaps he had not yet decided on it – that another of the main characters would be modelled, and extremely closely modelled, on their own elder brother Herbert.

Graham had rather niftily persuaded the Gotha Canal Company to give him a free return trip except for the food. The two brothers set out in mid-August, were away for three weeks, and most enjoyed themselves at Oslo where Graham met the translator of *The Man Within*, Nils Lie, and his very attractive girlfriend Ingeborg. This was the first but was not to be the only occasion on which he was immediately attracted to a Scandinavian beauty.

Back in England Graham celebrated his 29th birthday by writing his second general piece for *The Spectator*. Entitled "Two Capitals" – Oslo and Stockholm – it resulted, he told Hugh gleefully, in protests from both Legations.*

Hugh had decided to go out to Germany as a freelance for both *The Spectator* and the *Daily Mail*, and Graham was generously pleased that his brother thus

* Graham Greene's Oslo was full of pleasantly drunk professors, his Stockholm of aggressively and arrogantly drunk publishers. His main disappointment on the trip was that the character of Kreuger had failed to "come alive." It was to fail to "come alive" in the eventual novel too. But at least he had learnt the *Rumour At Nightfall* lesson; only write about countries when you have actually visited them in person.

avoided his own laborious beginnings in journalism. He obtained for Hugh introductions to leading lay Catholics in Munich from Father Bede Jarrett, of Blackfriars, an admired Dominican. Don't become a Buchmanite, he urged Hugh semi-jokingly; and, semi-seriously, do let me know if you become a Catholic in Germany. Graham's attitude towards his adopted religion was evolving; and this while he was writing, in Oxford, the *Brothers and Sisters* novel and awaiting the birth of his child – a much happier period.

But this was after the completion of *It's A Battlefield* and after, indeed, the disappearance from his life of Annette.

Chapter IX

Enter Moura, Boldly

There was trouble with Heinemann's over *It's A Battlefield*. Graham had not in fact finished writing it till August, just before leaving for Sweden. The typescript was, therefore, late in reaching his publishers and they could not publish that year. This annoyed both sides. But what Charles Evans particularly objected to was Graham Greene's perversity in once again including a satirical portrait of a well-known living literary figure only lightly disguised. Once bitten, Graham, he had thought, would be twice shy. But here after "Mr Savory" in *Stamboul Train* came "Mr Surrogate" in *It's A Battlefield*.

The satire is notably vicious. The portrait of Mr Surrogate, the bourgeois intellectual, the Bloomsbury Communist with his pink bedroom and his dead, malicious wife is a minor triumph. It is instantly recognizable as that of Middleton Murry, despite the too obvious divergences – Katherine Mansfield becomes a painter rather than a writer – just as the much more sympathetic portrait of "Lady Caroline Bury", with "her haggard sunken face" and her overwhelming desire to do good, is instantly recognizable as that of Lady Ottoline Morrell. All the literary world knew that Middleton Murry had confided the whole harried story of his married life to Lady Ottoline. "In her brain Mr Surrogate knew were stored all his wife's letters; but though he was embarrassed and embittered by the knowledge, he could not resist the compliment of her interest." All the literary world would have recognized the portrait, and chuckled at it. But all the literary world too – and that would include Charles Evans and AS Frere at Heinemanns – would have recognized in the very name of "Mr Surrogate" an open bow to Aldous Huxley*; and would have remembered Aldous Huxley's own, more ferocious, satires of both Middleton Murry and Lady Ottoline. In a sense, therefore, Graham Greene was repeating a trick already played. In another sense, it might even be said that, in Middleton Murry's case, he was hitting a man who was already down.

* *Brave New World* had come out in 1932; and Graham, a great fan of Huxley's, was writing *It's A Battlefield* in early 1933 – the obeisance, to the reading public of the day, was, therefore, transparent. The previous December Aldous Huxley (writing under the pen-name of Francis Iles) had given *Stamboul Train* a glowing review; which to Graham, coming from the greatest Balliol novelist of his generation, was both a surprise and an enormous delight – one that merited a response.

Greene did not attempt to deny, in his eventual Introduction to the book, that two of the major characters were based on Lady Ottoline and Middleton Murry. A third major character, the most rounded and human in the novel, is that of the Assistant Commissioner, an elderly policeman who has served in the East and now, back at Scotland Yard, finds himself to his considerable distaste involved not in mere detection but in the political implications of hanging a Communist murderer as well. Here too Graham Greene admits a real-life model. "My uncle Graham Greene," he writes, "lent a little of his stiff inhibited bachelor integrity to the character of Assistant Commissioner. My uncle though had had no experience of the Far East – that was to be mine nearly twenty years later, a curious foreshadowing."

This is no doubt true as far as it, cautiously, goes. But the real model of the Assistant Commissioner is Conrad's Assistant Commissioner in *The Secret Agent*. Not only do Greene's man and Conrad's man share exactly the same impersonal title, but both are confronted with obtuse and hostile assistants – in Conrad's book Chief Inspector Heat of the Special Crimes Department, in Greene's Superintendent Crosse of the Yard – and both too are involved in politics, to their disgust, by a smooth-talking Private Secretary to a Minister. Furthermore just as Greene's Assistant Commissioner is an old acquaintance of "Lady Caroline" – Lady Ottoline – who attempts to influence him, so Conrad's Assistant Commissioner has too "the great Lady" as his patroness, with, as in Lady Ottoline's case, her private salon. A final, conclusive, point: Conrad writes of his Assistant Commissioner: "His career had begun in a tropical colony." Both Assistant Commissioners, in the metropolis of the Empire, thus feel themselves uneasily out of their depth; chronology tells us which is modelled on the other.

Despite Greene's intense research – he had visited not only Wormwood Scrubs but also Wandsworth Prison, and Morlands' factory in Gloucester too, to get the authentic backgrounds – all the rest, the workers and the clerks, the Communists and the Soho waiters, their wives and women, all (except perhaps for the tiny indignant anti-Communist murdered policeman's widow, Mrs Coney) are somehow peculiarly lifeless and unconvincing. This is particularly so when compared to the vivid characters of the previous novel *Stamboul Train*. It is as if Greene, despite all his efforts to introduce vigour into the narrative, has temporarily lost that touch.

"The book," writes John Atkins,* "is heavy with individual misery. Greene's sense of insecurity, insufficiency and failure, with the possible addition of sexual maladjustment, came to a head here for the first time. There is no question of the

* John Atkins' excellent critical study, *Graham Greene*, first came out in 1957. It is perhaps the best book ever written on Graham Greene's works, intelligent, perceptive, fierce, enthusiastic, involved. A New and Revised Edition came out in 1966, together with a Preface by the author which laid into "the Greene claque" with great vigour.

mood being faked. It is also accompanied by a social conscience that later disappears."

This is strong stuff; and possibly over-emphatic. But certainly the contrast of moods between the vigorous writing in *Stamboul Train* with its generally affectionate treatment of the characters (even "Mr Savory", is, at moments, more sympathised with than mocked) and the stale displeasing atmosphere of *It's A Battlefield* is astounding. If, therefore, Graham Greene wrote *Stamboul Train* so well because he was happily in love with Annette, very possibly he wrote *It's A Battlefield* so badly because the love affair was, while he was writing it, going sour. Hence his 'individual misery' and his 'sexual maladjustment'.

The chronology here is all important. By mid-January 1933 Graham had finished the first section of *It's A Battlefield*, rather a good vigorous section, largely based on Conrad, featuring the Assistant Commissioner and the Private Secretary, and thus setting the scene. By early March he was reading Middleton Murry's *Reminiscences of Lawrence*, which he despised, and writing to Tooter – this was from Chipping Campden still – asking him to post on an enclosed note to Annette*. But there was a great disappointment in store when, after what seems to have been an unusually long period of abstinence, Graham finally revisited Annette in mid-March. She was ill in bed; and all they could do was to drink the bottle of Liebfraumilch which Graham had brought along, and to chat. This was not what he had had in mind.

From this point on the book progressed but the love-affair did not. Graham started the second section on April 4th; he certainly saw Annette for one hour on April 6th but a whole sentence is crossed out and totally illegible in the diary. So whether the visit was satisfactory is impossible to say. One rather doubts it. Annette may have been finding Graham too serious and too intense. For certainly after their next meeting five weeks later he went on to get drunk with his taxi-driver at a Gerrard Street club; and on this occasion the two words crossed out after the mention of visiting Annette appear to be: "for nothing". On May 24th, on his next trip to London, he did not even try to see Annette; instead he attempted to divert himself with another prostitute whom he had previously known, without much success. By this stage the book was almost two-thirds done; and very probably Graham was rewriting the second chapter, the factory scene. For this is, in the finished version, set in a match factory – which implies (the coincidence would, otherwise, be too great) that it was written after he had read the Swedish Match King's biography in March, and not before. In other words it seems probable that everything except what is now Chapter One (25-odd pages) was written, or re-written, in a period, early 1933, when Graham was on tenterhooks over his relationship with Annette.

Was she playing with him? The suspicion must have crossed his mind. Illnesses

* Presumably to avoid any risk of Vivienne spotting it en route to the Post Office.

and absences in the case of high-class prostitutes may of course be perfectly genuine; but then again they may be simply excuses for getting rid of importunate clients, perhaps in favour – there is just a hint of this – of a richer 'protector'. Certainly on June 22nd, though Graham sent Annette a telegram to say he would be there at seven, she was out when he arrived. And on his next visit to London, on July 12th, he went round twice without warning only to find no answer when he rang the doorbell. A woman living opposite gave him the depressing news, false or true, that Annette had gone to a nursing home.

On August 2nd he tried again, but found the flat still empty. An unsatisfactory fling elsewhere followed, and his diary entry reflects despair. Two days later he finished the novel; and a fortnight after that, without apparently any further attempt to see Annette, he was off with Hugh on the Scandinavian trip. And that appears to have been the end of that. By the time he came back in the early autumn, Vivienne was five months pregnant. Graham may have been both conscience-stricken and half way to recovering his moral balance (as the obviously growing influence of Father Bede Jarrett, of Blackfriars, indicates). In any case, he appears to have made no attempt to see Annette again. Instead, he set about exorcising her memory in the next novel, the Swedish novel, the one which he was now beginning, Opus VI.*

Meanwhile however he dedicated *It's A Battlefield* not to Vivien, his wife, but "For David and Anne (his agents) in London and for Nils and Ingeborg (his friends) in Oslo". This, in the particular circumstances of her pregnancy, must have offended her gravely; for Vivien was very sensitive to the outward signs of Graham's continuing affection and she cannot have helped noticing his distraction and restlessness in those first Oxford weeks. What must also have caught her attention was one of the late scenes in the novel: Jules Briton, a half-French Soho waiter (one of the least successful characters in the book) drives the flighty Kay out to Berkhamsted, attempts to seduce her against a tree trunk on Berkhamsted Common, and finally sleeps with her in a bed-and-breakfast cottage up in the nearby Chiltern Hills. Alone of the cast of *It's A Battlefield*, Jules is a Catholic. Not a very devout one, admittedly, and it is not particularly important – indeed nor is Jules himself – to the plot. But there is banter with Kay about marriage. "She was young and pretty and practised; he could not imagine a wife who would more ably stir his senses;" and at one stage he asks her "with comic hopefulness, 'You aren't a Catholic by any chance?'" Kay was not. "No, why? Why, do you want to marry me?" "I was just wondering that's all." "I'm not sure I wouldn't marry you," Kay says. "I'm fed up with gentlemen. They keep you waiting half an hour and then they don't turn up."

Kay is not a prostitute; but she does sleep around, and she has already slept with Mr Surrogate. If Kay is modelled on Annette, then the shy Coral Musker in

* Of which more in its place. See below, pp 93-94

Stamboul Train can hardly be. Neither of them may be, of course; or, alternatively, each of them may represent certain very different traits of Annette. It is infuriating to have no idea of Annette's looks or tastes or character. She may – it is a possible hypothesis, and an interesting one – have been French herself; and she, rather than the fictional Jules Briton, may have attended the French Church in Spanish Place off Leicester Square. Mass there is one of the few affectionately described scenes in the novel. But even Annette – if Kay is, at least partly, Annette – is portrayed without vigour or vividness; without bitterness too it must be said, but with a kind of frustrated sympathy understandable perhaps if Graham was wavering himself between hope and frustration in his own love affair.

* * *

Vivien gave birth. The happy event took place in Oxford on December 28th 1933. Under the sign of Capricorn appeared Lucy Caroline Greene. And it was a happy event. The proud father told the youngest uncle that though he was by no means philoprogenitive, Lucy did seem to him to be more intelligent than most babies.

The youngest uncle, who was by contrast to be the most philoprogenitive of the younger Greenes, heard such family news with particular interest. Hugh had met, in Munich where she too was staying for a period, Helga Guinness, the daughter of a banking Guinness, Samuel. They fell in love. Then in February 1934 Hugh was transferred to Berlin. His life at the time was the most fascinating of the lives of all the Greenes. He had done so well as a freelance in his two months at Munich that the *Daily Telegraph* agreed to take him on as their Assistant Correspondent for Germany, at a splendid nine guineas a week; this was to mark the real start of a distinguished and successful career. *The Daily Telegraph's* office on Unter der Linden was at the heart of Nazi Berlin; and of a country in the throes, or almost, of the 'second revolution' that Roehm and his Brownshirts were pressing on a reluctant Hitler. In neighbouring Austria Dr. Dolfuss was bloodily repressing his own socialist revolution (and Kim Philby was, with chivalrous concern, marrying in Vienna one of the potential refugees from this repression, the revolutionary Alice Friedmann). Far away in Central America General Anastasio Somoza's National Guardsmen were abducting the peasant leader, Sandino, whom they then shot, and, thus, martyred. The world was indeed a battlefield; and when *It's A Battlefield* came out, unexpectedly, on February 5th, it met with a very favourable critical reception. VS Pritchett gave it Graham Greene's most glowing review to date; and there was praise from both Ezra Pound and Ford Madox Ford. Middleton Murry did not sue for libel; nor of course did Lady Ottoline. But she did not, it seems, appreciate the portrait of herself – generally favourable but, here and there, barbed – and perhaps she particularly resented the implication that she was mortally ill. At any rate it appears that correspondence between Graham and Lady Ottoline ceased abruptly. She was in her sixties, her health did indeed start declining the following year, and she was to die four years later.

On March 12th Raymond Greene married for the second time. His wife was Eleanor Craven Gamble, an American, the daughter of Hamilton Rowan Gamble of St. Louis, Missouri; and they were (though not till after the outbreak of the Second World War) to have two children, Annabel and Oliver. It was a very successful wedding. The champagne flowed. Ghosts from Berkhamsted past – Barbara Porter, Jane Millicain, and Amanda – reappeared. Graham and Vivien were there; but Hugh was not. Instead, he sent Marion a letter that arrived on the very morning of the wedding, announcing his engagement to Helga Guinness – and thus almost succeeded in upstaging Raymond and Eleanor. Certainly a Guinness was a matrimonial catch that a Gamble or even a Dayrell-Browning was not – a feather in the Greene cap, an entry into the world of high society and wealth.

Hugh invited Graham out to Berlin. Graham was sorely tempted and thought indeed of looking up Count Bernstorff – Bernstorff had been dismissed by the new régime from the London Embassy (he was publicly anti-Nazi) and had retired to private life. But it was not Berlin, primarily, that attracted him. He wanted to go further afield. Nordahl Grieg was still in Russia, and Ingeborg had joined him there as his secretary. So Lapland, where he had hoped to go with Nils and Ingeborg was, infuriatingly, off. There was however another alternative. "I have just returned to Moscow from the country," wrote Nordahl. "What fun to meet you here! I am most likely to stay the whole of May; but there is a vague possibility of me going to Tiflis and Caucasus. In that case perhaps you will come with me?" It was an attractive possibility, particularly with Ingeborg there; yet expensive. And perhaps, too, Graham Greene had been put off Russia – in mid-March he was still wavering – by a new acquaintance, Malcolm Muggeridge.

The Manchester Guardian had sent Muggeridge out as their correspondent to Moscow, expecting him to be generally favourable to the régime. He hated it. He hated particularly the platitudes of the Fabian visitors, Bernard Shaw, HG Wells and the rest, who shut their eyes to trials, hunger and oppression. He left Moscow in the spring of 1933, quarrelled bitterly with *The Manchester Guardian* and wrote an anti-Stalin book, *Winter in Moscow* that, in the climate of the early Thirties, made him highly unpopular. But Graham Greene always liked, instinctively, people who refused to conform. Malcolm had left the USSR via the Baltic Republics; and Graham questioned him about them when the two met. For, as Graham told Hugh, it was not Russia he wanted to visit, but Estonia.

Nordahl Grieg had of course recommended idyllic Tallinn and its chocolate-bribable girls. But, more than Nordahl, much more than Malcolm, what decided Graham was someone else he met. She told him Estonia was marvellously cheap, with rooms in the top hotels for half a crown a night. There were two things he should visit, she added: a ruined monastery near the border and an age-old brothel in the capital.

Graham was fascinated by her. She was, he informed Hugh, an aristocrat who used to own an estate in Estonia, and Maxim Gorki's mistress.

This "aristocrat" was the indomitable Moura,[*] a person bound to appeal to a romantic like Graham: mistress not only of Gorki but also (which he did not yet know) of HG Wells; and, before that, as she perhaps assumed he must know – for the recent publication of *Memoirs of A Secret Agent* had made her notoriously famous for being so – of Robert Bruce Lockhart, the British Empire's 'Man in Moscow' during the Russian Revolution.

Moura had been slim and extraordinarily attractive as a young girl. In old age she was to become mountainous. When she met Graham, at a Jonathan Cape gathering, she was forty, ten years older than him, still in every way a woman of dazzling vitality. She sent him off to Estonia, and, most willingly, he went.

The plan was to see Hugh en route. So on May 4th Graham flew out to Berlin, still an adventure in those days.

He did not stay long among the Swastikas. The arrangement with Hugh was that if Hugh were not free – it was a Friday night, and he does not appear to have been – Graham would catch the midnight train on to the capital of Latvia, Riga. He travelled third-class, on hard wooden seats and without food, all day long through the plains of Eastern Germany and Lithuania till, in the evening sunlight, the grey spires of Riga appeared. A week later he caught a small plane on to Tallinn, the capital of Estonia, his ultimate destination.

Riga with its droshky drivers had reminded him of a decrepit aristocratic Brighton minus the Grand Dukes who had once frequented it. But Tallinn was a combination of Autun, Istanbul and Montmartre. What most impressed him was the cheapness: a meal in the best restaurant for 9d and a carafe of vodka for 1/6d.

He never found the famous brothel. When he asked a waiter in Tallinn's most elegant hotel for directions, the man was baffled: "But there is nothing of that kind we cannot arrange for you here!" He did find, however, a delightful British diplomat, who happened to be the only other passenger in the little plane from Riga. They were both reading Henry James' novels; and immediately struck up an acquaintance.

JF Leslie was His Majesty's Vice-Consul in Tallinn, a bachelor, and a former arms salesman. He and Graham, as Graham recounts, became firm friends during

[*] Not, strictly speaking, an aristocrat by birth; born a Zakrevsky, from a wealthy family of Poltava in the Ukraine; but twice married into the Baltic baronage. First to Baron Djon von Benckendorff, father of her two children, murdered by roving bandits during the turmoil of the Red Revolution on his Estonian estate while Moura was in St. Petersburg, sharing Gorki's apartment with his wife, other mistress, children, friends – and seducing HG Wells on his visit to discuss World Literature with Maxim. Next (after facing a Court of Honour of the Baltic nobility) to Baron Nikolai Budberg; whose person she soon abandoned but whose name she always kept.

Graham's stay in the Estonian capital thanks to their shared interest in Henry James. What Graham does not say, but what seems a reasonable assumption, is that the Vice-Consul was in fact a member of SIS; and that this, therefore, was Graham Greene's first contact with the Secret Intelligence Service.

For after its débâcle in late 1918 when Robert Bruce Lockhart had had to stand trial in Moscow as a British spymaster, the Secret Intelligence Service had closed its Moscow station. Instead, 'C', its Chief, ringed revolutionary Russia with listening posts where his men would be safe from arrest and trial. There were Heads of Station in Bucharest, Budapest, Prague, Vienna, Warsaw, Stockholm, Helsinki and, opposite Helsinki and Stockholm, just on the other side of the Baltic, in Riga and Tallinn.

Tallinn was near to Petrograd; the obvious stopping-off place for refugees and White Russian intriguers (to say nothing of the reactionary Baltic barons) and there was certainly a Head of Station in Tallinn. Officially the Foreign Office disapproved of Consular staff being associated with SIS – the Head of Stations invariably used the 'independent' cover of Passport Control Officers – but in fact a Foreign Office report of a senior official's visit to Riga the previous October reveals that the "hidden ramifications" of Passport Control certainly extended, whatever the official rules, into British Consulates; and indeed, in such a small place as Tallinn,* were bound to do so. JF Leslie may only have been a small cog in the Secret Service's wheel; but that he was, and that the very idea fascinated Graham, a future literary venture seems, pretty conclusively, to indicate. Before the end of the War Graham Greene was approached to write a film synopsis. He did so in a dozen pages. He made the Secret Service – about which he was himself then considerably better informed – the background; and he set the story – in pre-war Tallinn.

* * *

From Tallinn Graham decided to return by railway to Berlin. He arrived at Riga at midnight, had two hours to wait, changed trains and reached Berlin in the morning – to be met by Hugh full of eager questions at the railway station. But they were not exactly the eager questions that Graham had anticipated. What was going on, Hugh wanted to know, in Latvia? What was all this about a *coup d'état* last night?

Graham was in the embarrassing position of having to admit that he, by far the most experienced of the two brothers, had committed that mortal sin of *reportage*,

* Tallinn, rated, however, a full British Legation, at Olai Tanan 17; with a diplomatic staff of four and another outlying Vice-Consul, J.P.Dicks, at Pürno. The Minister was Hughe Knatchbull-Hugessen, later so famous not for being a spy but for being most successfully spied upon – in the Second World War when Ambassador to Turkey by his valet 'Cicero'.

that journalist's nightmare. He had been, fortuitously, the man on the spot at exactly the right moment but he had noticed nothing. On the late evening of the night when he had stopped off at Riga, dictatorial powers had been seized by Ulmanlis; just as (which might have put a more alert reporter on the *qui vive*) they had been seized by Pats in Estonia only a month earlier. Admittedly Graham was in the Baltic Republics purely for relaxation. But a journalist is never entirely on holiday and he was, undeniably, at this period of his life a freelance journalist, with an outlet available in *The Spectator* for articles of just this sort. Indeed it might have given him a very useful *entrée* back onto *The Times* – had he noticed, and seized, the opportunity. And that was an *entrée* which he still very much desired.

There were other things he desired more, though; or at least with more immediate urgency. One thing in particular: meeting Moura again.

Chapter X

Brothers and Sisters – and Cousin Barbara

No sooner was he back in England therefore, than Graham went to see Moura. In Berlin he had thought of telephoning to ask her to join him there. In London he told her so; and it turned out that she had had, unexpectedly, a holiday and would indeed have joined him if only he had telegraphed. Or so she said. She told the young man that if she won the Irish Sweep, she would take him to Berlin as her gigolo.

Moura Budberg was an extraordinary woman, and it is no wonder that Graham, whose social horizons now that he was free of country cottages and total impoverishment had been expanding so fast, should have been fascinated by the first glamorous and cosmopolitan sophisticate in his life.

"Those who would understand Moura," her daughter Tania von Benckendorff has written, "are confronted and challenged with a paradoxical character full of deep divisions; with a story where rival versions conflict and the truth is elusive.* Those who knew Moura testify at once to her courage, her charm and her self-confidence; even her sharpest detractors do not deny her good humour, her warmth and her affection. And yet at the same time they also acknowledge the lack of scruple, the disregard for truth, the insatiable need of admiration and attention. One way she achieved this, without doubt, was by exerting an emotional pull: she once told a friend of mine that she thought men would remain attached to her if she slept with them... Once attached, she never let go; and yet this seems to have been part of the attraction for those caught in this way."

Was Graham Greene "caught in this way"? So complicated was Moura's love-life already, in 1934,† that she would hardly have had time for a fling with

* A fine sentence; for 'Moura' substitute' Graham' and it would be almost equally true.

† What with the Congress of Writers that summer in Moscow and Moura's determination both to attend it and see Gorky, and to lie to HG Wells and pretend (when he joined her in Estonia) that she had not been back to Moscow at all. Where indeed she may also have added to her scalping list André Malraux, Graham's contemporary, the star of the Congress, whose masterful equivalent of *It's A Battlefield*, *La Condition Humaine*, had won him both the Prix Goncourt and an extraordinary reputation. HG Wells was angry, suspicious and very jealous about it all – and querulous about her mother to young Tania.

Graham. "Once attached," her daughter added, "she never let go"; so the conclusion must be that she was never properly attached to Graham. And yet a faint question mark must hover over this, as over so much of Moura's extraordinary life. If she did have an affair, however brief, with Graham, it is a tribute to her ability to recognize, and seduce, not only the reigning monarchs of literature but also their future successors, obscure princelings though they may have been at the time.

★ ★ ★

There was also the extraordinary affair of *The Old School* and Graham's own contribution to it. For this took the form, under the pretext of an essay on public school education, of a positively unpuritanical paeon to the pure delights of heterosexual sex.

The Old School came out towards the end of July, eight weeks after Graham was back from Estonia. As he had still been trying to find contributors at the end of February, it seems probable that it was only on his return that all the essays were in; and that he put the whole book together very hastily at Oxford adding a top and a tail – a Preface and a final summing-up essay.

Certainly the book gives every sign of hasty editing; or rather of no editing at all. Graham had justified his meagre editorial fee by assembling seventeen other writers and simply telling them to produce between ten and fifteen pages each on their own schooldays. He quite clearly made no attempt to impose a strong editorial line or to give a more coherent briefing.

The result was an awful mish-mash. Some contributors turned in fragments of autobiography about their childhood, to which their schools were merely incidental. Others seized the pretext to write generalized essays on education. Theodora Benson composed a light-hearted critique of her own character; Stephen Spender a more serious one of his father's. Anthony Powell was nostalgic about Eton, LP Hartley complacent on Harrow, and JN Richards positively grateful to Winchester. This was not at all the stuff that Graham had originally intended to give the troops.★ It was only Derek Verschoyle who came up to

★ Even Elizabeth Bowen described the extreme physical discomforts of her school as "salutary"; and the almost affectionate account of the horrors of Bedales by Grant-Watson – the cold baths the ice on which had to be broken, the excrement of the earth-privies which had to be wheeled out by the boys themselves and above all the incredibly dangerous level of bullying – makes Graham's own later descriptions of how he suffered for being teased at Berkhamsted seem, in retrospect, small beer indeed by the standard of the times.

The only two essays of lasting value and real feeling in *The Old School* are by Antonia White, a moving and beautifully written 17 pages entitled "A Child of the Five Wounds" on 'Lippington' and its code of manners and morals; and by Sean O'Faolain, on his wretchedly poor hedge-school, rat-invested, run by Christian Brothers near Cork – rough peasants themselves but, as he put it at the end, "truly brothers to us and I think we loved them".

scratch, launching an all-out attack against Malvern and, via Malvern, against the public-school system in general.

So when Graham Greene came to write his final essay, ostensibly on Berkhamsted and his time there, he could hardly insist on its horrors and awfulness: for, compared to the schools already described, Berkhamsted had been a haven of comfort, meek and mild; why, there had not even existed a minimal system of fagging and (as he remarked) the lavatories may not have had locks on their doors but compared to Malvern, where the lavatories had no doors at all, privacy was almost a privilege.

So, with a brief obeisance to his father's liberalism and to the good influence of several Berkhamsted masters, Graham proceeded to devote his remaining eight pages almost entirely to the subject of sex. Other contributors had referred *en passant* to sex (and, in general, the lack of it) at their schools; and Derek Verschoyle had referred to homosexuality as a "natural and transitory condition of adolescence", a view which Graham was quick to rebut, by implication, as regards Berkhamsted. It was unknown there. Everything, alas, was unknown there. He objected to the extraordinarily innocent atmosphere at his old school as regards "a normal sexual relationship". But he objected still more to the system of co-education at Bedales as described by Grant-Watson: "A 'comradely' no-nonsense-about-sex attitude between men and women is peculiarly repellent"; and he harked back to the old village school where children learnt about sex, naturally, in the farm-yard; or in cities, more naturally than from complacent masters' talks on the facts of life, from graffiti on lavatory walls. "They will have taught him (the child) at any rate that sexual enjoyment is neither solemn nor dull." It does sound rather like a lesson learnt from Moura here; certainly with her, even if only in imagination or in chatter, sex must have seemed frivolous, lively and highly enjoyable. Graham had, at least temporarily, shed his puritanism. It was not to last.

★ ★ ★

Amazingly, Graham never mentioned politics in his many letters of this period to Hugh. He did not refer to the shocking violence of Oswald Mosley's Blackshirt rally at Olympia; and he did not ask Hugh, three weeks later, about the far more appalling Night of the Long Knives in Germany. Hugh and *The Times* correspondent Norman Ebbutt had been playing tennis on June 30th when the news of the pre-emptive coup and Roehm's death came through from Munich, followed that evening by the return of the haggard Führer in person to the Templehof. Waves of summary executions and casual murders followed while next day, a Sunday, Hitler, smiling and relaxed, held a garden-party at the Chancellery. The easy general belief in Western Europe that Hitler's régime was basically fragile and certainly temporary, liable at any moment to be suppressed by the Prussian aristocracy or overthrown by the rallying forces of Weimar democracy, or even by revolution on the left, was shattered. To the country, and the world outside, Nazism revealed its ugly violence. Hugh covered these events; Graham appears to have, at least superficially, ignored them.

At the same time Hugh had other more personal matters on his mind. In mid-August he was back in London, staying at Barbara's elegant flat in Ormonde Gate. On October 24th he was back once more, for his wedding. He and Helga were married in great style at Chelsea Old Church, with Elizabeth again as a bridesmaid, but a grown-up one this time. The ceremony over, the wedding guests strolled down Chelsea Embankment to Cheyne Walk where the bride's parents, Mr and Mrs Samuel Guinness, were holding the reception. There, over a glass or two of champagne, Graham accosted Barbara with an extraordinary proposition which she eagerly accepted. Later, more sober, he was (she says) to repent of the idea. She did not. It was all a month or two ahead, in any case. Meanwhile he had his *Brothers and Sisters* novel to finish. And, before the end of the year, he finished it.

* * *

Graham always had trouble with titles. *Brothers and Sisters* made way for *The Shipwrecked*,* only to end, finally, as *England Made Me*. Graham would have done better to keep his other tentative title choice: *The Expatriates*. It may have seemed too pedestrian. But it was in fact most entirely accurate.

For Krogh/Kreuger, the putative leading figure, soon faded – or rather, to borrow Greene's own phrase, never "came alive" at all; and the other Swedish characters, from Pihlström the journalist to Professor Hammersten, the Shakespeare scholar, are mere extras, thrown in to add – as indeed are the street-names and scenes and buildings of Stockholm itself – a little local colour. It is the English expatriates and their lives that are important to the author. These range from a visiting family from Coventry via the (caricatured) staff of the British Embassy to a pair of leading and subtly drawn characters: Hall, Krogh's loyal bodyguard, his left-hand-man; and Minty, the spidery little journalist, the Old Harrovian remittance man who has known better times and places but now – ageing, alone, yet curiously at ease in his debased obscurity – has no real hopes or ambitions left. Minty, like Mabel Warren, is a memorable creation.

But the two main actors in the drama, the two whose interaction electrifies thoughts, memories, dialogue and plot, are indeed a brother and a sister. Kate

* Taken from a quotation from Ortega y Gasset found in the *Adelphi*, which Graham had, long previously, noted in his diary. *England Made Me* was first published in France as *Mère Angleterre*; Graham liked neither the title nor the translation, and after the War it reappeared as, indeed, *Les Naufragés*. In the USA too a post-war edition entitled *The Shipwrecked* sold far better than the original *England Made Me* had done.

Farrant is Krogh's secretary and mistress. Anthony Farrant is her ne'er-do-well roving twin. Their relationship lies at the heart of the story. "Anthony," Graham Greene was to write years later, "was someone I knew very well and whom I had lived many years on intimate terms with… I had shared some of his adventures."

Anthony Farrant is a feckless, charming, well-dressed cad, almost but not quite a confidence trickster, full of hopeless schemes for making money, utterly unreliable, yet with a curiously old-fashioned sense of loyalty and indeed – hence the title – patriotism. Wherever he is – and in Chapter Two he looks back on the long odyssey that has led him from India to Bangkok to Aden, expelled from the clubs, sacked from his jobs, despised by his fellow-countrymen – he remains obstinately convinced that he is still the salt of the earth, an English gentleman.

It comes therefore as little surprise to read, almost ten years later,* this gloss by Graham Greene on his previous remarks:

"I was quite satisfied with my portrait of Anthony. Hadn't I lived with him closely over many years? He was an idealized portrait of my eldest brother, Herbert."

But what of Kate, Anthony's sister – as efficient and matter-of-fact as Anthony is shifty and hopeless? "The subject", Graham Greene continued, "was simple… a brother and sister in the confusion of incestuous love… They were continually on the edge of self-discovery, but some self-protective instinct warded off, with false or incomplete memories and irrelevancies, the moment of discovery. Kate was nearer to knowledge than Anthony and both used their superficial sexual loves, Kate with Krogh, Anthony with Loo, to ward off the real thing."

Kate is, unlike most of Graham Greene's fictional women, a strong character, concisely drawn, whose only weakness is her yearning and protective love for her brother: "She might have been waiting for her lover" – the story begins, in a bar in Stockholm with Kate wondering whether she will recognize Anthony. "But she knew him at once by the small scar under his left eye, the round face which looked as if only that day it had lost its freshness, like a worn child's, the bonhomie which even a stranger would not trust." "I've resigned," he tells her. "But she had heard that tale too often; it had been the yearly fatal drumming in their father's ears which helped to kill him."†

Kate, as Graham Greene himself rightly says, is his most successful portrayal of a woman, "with the possible exception of Sarah in *The End of the Affair*". But the character of Sarah is undoubtedly, indisputably, modelled on that of a real woman, a woman Graham loved. Whom is Kate modelled on? Or, to put it another way, what was it that induced Graham Greene to write a novel based on the potentially

* After, therefore, Herbert's death. The change in the phraseology used is interesting. There is nothing now about having shared Anthony's adventures or having lived on intimate terms with him. Had those phrases been a placatory gesture of sorts, 35 years after the event, to a possibly still-offended brother? Could a book of this sort ever be forgotten? Forgiven?

† So the novelist reverses his wishes (Cp p 39) and kills off the honest, worrying narrow-minded *paterfamilias* again, as in *Anthony Sant*, his first novel (p 21) rather than the black sheep of a son.

incestuous love between a brother and a sister in the first place? It is not the most obvious of themes. One feels that there surely was, whether consciously or subconsciously, some strong compelling reason.

This is a potential minefield, and it behoves the biographer to tread warily. But what is certain is that when, a few months later, *England Made Me* came out, none of the Greene clan could have failed to recognize, in Anthony, Herbert.*

But who did they recognise in Kate Farrant?

There *was* a Kate in the family – Kate Greene, the youngest of Uncle Eppy's three daughters, just twenty at the time. Kate was very close to her brother Felix. What was *her* reaction to the book? Kate, Barbara, Ave, Elizabeth, Molly... Did love, or potential love, between first cousins seem to Graham almost incestuous? Had Herbert been particularly close to Molly, his elder by only fifteen months? Was Graham extrapolating his own feelings for one of his sisters or cousins onto Anthony Farrant in the novel? Was there another pair, in all those possible combinations of the twelve first cousins, who were too close, and known to be so, for their own and their family's comfort? Or was the novelist simply inventing a situation that evidently obsessed him and yet that had no basis at all in fact?

★ ★ ★

What is undeniable is that Graham Greene did foist onto Anthony Farrant his own, and not Herbert's, experience. The novel is pervaded by nostalgic memories of Soho, and of Annette. Annette is not described. But she is not disguised either. Graham uses her real name and his own memories – of meeting Annette and thinking "she's the goods", of Annette's torn photograph (but this may be a fictional touch) inscribed "With love from Annette", of Annette "intent and quiet and affectionate behind the drawn blinds in the half light".

But he had begun writing the novel in the autumn and winter of 1933, and his main, his most vivid memories, are of the emptiness in Soho, of the disappearance of his beloved, as if, by writing, he might exorcise the loss.

"When I pushed the button no bell rang and the light on the landing had been disconnected. The wall was covered with pencil notes: 'See you later', 'Off to the baker's', 'Leave the beer outside the door', 'Off for the weekend', 'No milk this morning'. There was hardly one patch of whitewash unwritten upon and the messages were all of them scratched out. Only one remained uncancelled, it

* An "idealized portrait"? Possibly, in the sense that, though Anthony/Herbert is murdered in the novel, his death is due, indirectly, to a noble action, the defence of an oppressed young Swedish worker against the viciousness of his capitalist employers. That said, no elder brother can have enjoyed seeing himself portrayed in print as a feckless cad by a more gifted younger brother. Nor can Audrey have been pleased. Nor, surely, Mr and Mrs Greene – though Vivienne has said that Mrs Greene detested her eldest son. The family dynamics were already, obviously, most complex. The additional complications caused by the publication of such a *roman à clef* are impossible, now, to calculate.

looked months old, but it might have been new, for it said: 'Gone out. Be back at 12.30, dear', and I had written her a post-card saying that I would be coming at half-past twelve. So I waited, sitting there on the stone stairs for two hours, in front of the top flat and nobody came up."

Three times at least in the novel Graham comes back to this memory, this scene. It is tenderly done. Indeed the whole book is tenderly done and suffused by a general affection of the novelist for all his characters. Even Sir Ronald, the fussy effeminate British Ambassador and Captain Gullie*, the poker-playing military attaché are sympathetically mocked. Compared to *It's A Battlefield*, and despite the theme of incest, this is a marvellously sunny book, marred only by the lifeless frigidity of Krogh. Even the killer Hall is, as Graham Greene's next and most central killer was to be, a man admirable in his way; and particularly for his loyalty. There is no "virtue of disloyalty" paraded in this novel. Hall is loyal to Krogh, Krogh to Kate, Kate despite everything to Anthony, and Anthony to his own code. It is a fascinating exercise to re-read the book as if one were sitting in Herbert's armchair at Oak Cottage, Plumpton. Through the ironies and the occasional spitefulness a haze almost of admiration for the brother who had once been a boyhood hero and then a failed bohemian adventurer still fitfully glows.

* * *

It was at Hugh's wedding that Tooter had said to Graham "I can't come myself. But why" – nodding at his sister – "don't you ask Barbara? She's at a loose end at the moment" – or words to that effect. So Graham had done so.

"'Why don't you come to Liberia with me?' I was asked by my cousin Graham, and, having had a glass or two of champagne, it seemed a remarkably easy thing to do. I agreed at once.'"

Those are Barbara's words. Later, according to Graham , when he had sobered up, he tried to dissuade her from coming; and in order to put her off, sent her the League of Nations report stressing the fearful conditions in the interior, and the ghastly diseases ranging from elephantiasis via yaws and hookworm to malaria and leprosy. She found it "far from comforting". Barbara had not exactly been brought up hard. As she put it herself:

"All my life I had been used to well-cooked food and beautiful clothes, a lovely house filled with people who smoothed out for me as far as possible the rough patches on my road through life. I was taken care of and spoilt both by my family and my friends, and the little, dull, tiresome everyday household things were automatically done for me. I had liked to find my evening clothes spread out for me ready pressed on my bed, my bath ready for me, and then to come down to a dinner lit by candle-light. Beauty, comfort and a good deal of luxury had been part of my life."

* Hughe Knatchbull-Hugessen? And Major Giffey, Head of Station, SIS, Tallinn?

Yet Barbara, despite appearances, was not just another Bright Young Thing. She was, in her own words, which do not do her justice, "tall and hefty". Tall, certainly – like almost all the younger Greenes six foot or more – and vigorous too; but "hefty" gives the wrong impression. She was an extremely attractive young woman. At twenty-seven, however, and unmarried – an unusual thing for upper middle-class girls at that period – she was at a turning point in her life and needed, even more than Graham, a change of scene, an adventure. So far from putting her off, reports of danger, diseases, even cannibals, attracted her. After all, she came from an adventurous and unusual family. She was rather pleased that all her friends thought her mad and were sure that, if she went, she would never return. "So I wept a little, and boasted a lot, and went to a great many farewell parties, and tried very hard to look like an explorer as I left London in a thick mackintosh and a 'sensible' hat. And gradually that sinking feeling left me, and I was left full of a glorious excitement."

What is far more extraordinary than her excitement is that Uncle Eppy and Aunt Eva appear to have raised no objections to the project. Barbara was of course grown-up and mistress of her own destiny; but in those days an unmarried daughter (unless she was an obvious rebel, which Barbara was not) would tend to obey her parents, particularly if she entirely depended on them for her money, her allowance, as it seems likely that Barbara did. The proposed trip was, after all, an extremely hazardous one, and not the sort of thing that young ladies, as opposed to young men, were meant to undertake. Uncle Eppy could have vetoed it on these grounds. He did not. No doubt he knew his daughter well enough to trust in her sturdy common-sense; and, after all, he himself as a young man had ventured into the wilds of Brazil, far from any British colony or influence, which was distinctly not the case with Liberia. "At last," he said to Barbara when she tentatively told him the news, "a daughter of mine is showing a little initiative."

But there was, obviously, another side to the whole business that all parties concerned, including the older generation of Greenes on both sides, must have considered with alarm, if not consternation. To put it bluntly, here were a young man of thirty and his first cousin, a young woman of twenty-seven, intending to go off for a long voyage together and a trek through the jungle, and God knows what other adventures, that would inevitably throw them into continuous close proximity. Furthermore they were both members of a family where first cousin romances had occurred, and had continued to occur, with or without consummation. It must have looked like a recipe for trouble.

It is impossible not to wonder what Vivien herself thought of the whole situation. There was her husband leaving her literally holding the baby while he disappeared for three months on a long trip with an attractive and unattached cousin, considerably younger than herself – a cousin furthermore whose elder sister her husband had once been in love with. It was not, to say the least, a reassuring turn of events.

In the event however, Vivien need not have worried. When Graham's book, *Journey Without Maps*, eventually appeared, it was dedicated "To My Wife" with the most touching quotation underneath that he had taken from a poem by one of his *Old School* contributors, William Plomer:

"I carry you like a passport everywhere."

And it was true. Graham missed Vivien immensely during his time in Liberia; and longed again and again to get back to her; and indeed, somewhat to his own surprise, to his baby daughter Lucy too. As for Barbara, she got out pen and paper at a fairly early stage of the trip and wrote down what she thought of Graham. It is rather perceptive. But it is certainly not in the least romantic.

"His brain frightened me. It was sharp and cruel and clear. I admired him for being unsentimental, but 'always remember to rely on yourself', I noted. 'If you are in a sticky place he will be so interested in noting your reactions that he will probably forget to rescue you.'" There were no illusions about a *preux chevalier* there.

"Apart from three or four people he was really fond of," she continued (one wonders who Barbara was thinking of: Hugh, his mother, Tooter, and Vivien perhaps), "I felt that the rest of humanity was to him like a heap of insects that he liked to examine as a scientist might examine his specimens, coldly and clearly."

Barbara came to admire her cousin greatly, to find him, even, "the best kind of companion one could have for a trip of this kind". But it is perfectly clear that, despite the obvious temptations of propinquity, there was no romance of any kind whatsoever between them.

The shifting relationships between members of the Greene clan, and particularly between the twelve cousins, are fascinating still; full of odd surprises and surmises. What is peculiarly extraordinary about Graham's eventual account of the Liberian trip, his *Journey Without Maps*, is this: that in the original edition he does not even hint at the fact that he travelled to, from and through Liberia with a female cousin. On his side there was not only a complete absence of romance, there was not even the slightest literary bow to Barbara.* Ungallant certainly, discreet to the point of obsession, a touch dishonest, insulting even – but Greeneian to the core.

* "There are intriguing references," wrote John Atkins in his 1966 edition, "to a cousin who accompanied Greene on this journey. Both person and relationship are undefined and the personal pronoun is never used, except on one occasion when it is slipped in casually and yet, one feels, meaningfully. It appears that the cousin was a female."

Very probably influenced by these remarks – it is evident, particularly from the Introduction to his Collected Works, that he had read John Atkins' criticism most attentively – Graham Greene made *amende honorable* in 1978 when *Journey Without Maps* was re-issued in the Collected Works edition; re-dedicating the book to, this time, "My cousin, Barbara Strachwitz"; and paying her a very handsome tribute in the Introduction – though producing, as an explanation for her previous weird elimination, a small smokescreen of implausible verbiage.

Chapter XI

Explorer!

"In joy and gladness with our hearts united
We'll shout the freedom of a land benighted
Long live Liberia, happy land
A home of glorious liberty, by God's command."
Liberian National Anthem: The Chorus

Liberia was a very bizarre little country indeed, a tiny offshoot of the United States on the wrong side of the Atlantic Ocean, complete with its own President, Senate, Executive Mansion and indeed even a State Department. There was this difference: that it was entirely inhabited by negroes, and therefore in theory at least happily free from racial conflict.

Things however had not entirely worked out as planned. The freed negroes from America, settled by the anti-slavery societies, exploited "the natives" as ruthlessly as any white colonisers. From time to time the United States Government had to intervene. When Graham was twelve, the Frontier Force, under US Army Officers, struck at and subdued the Krus of the Coast, much as the US Cavalry had in an earlier epoch struck at and subdued the Sioux back in the motherland.

By 1930 the command of the Frontier Force, 3000 strong, had passed into the hands of an American negro, Colonel Elwood Davis, a ruthless and cruel adventurer, ex-US Army, a veteran of the Mexican Wars. There were rumours of horrid massacres in the interior. The British Empire despatched an emissary to the Kru Coast to investigate.

His report* was presented to Parliament in the early summer of 1934. It was this that had caught Graham's attention and had made him determined to get out to Liberia by hook or by crook. It was damning. The Krus of Old Sasstown had rebelled. Colonel Elwood Davis and the Frontier Force had swept down.

* "*Affairs in Liberia: December 1930 – May 1934.*" (Blue Book, Command 4614, 90 pp). The author, Mr DG Rydings, Vice-Consul, had made no secret of where his sympathies lay. The Sasstown Krus he described as "a virile, courageous and industrious race".

Seventeen villages had been destroyed, the whole of Old Sasstown burnt to the ground, 72 women and children brutally massacred. In Parliament the Foreign Secretary referred nastily to the "corrupt and inefficient oligarchy of Monrovia" and declared that "His Majesty's Government felt that it would be a dereliction of duty if the misgovernment of the native tribes by Liberia were allowed to continue".

So much for the villains of the piece: the government in Monrovia, and in particular the Frontier Force and its brutal black American Commander. But what of the heroes? Their protagonist was the splendid Paramount Chief Nimley of the Sasstown Krus who, with 12,000 of his followers, had taken to the bush and had made a ringing declaration appealing to the British Consul in Monrovia to intervene and save his people.

Graham's grandiose plan, therefore, was to enter Liberia from British territory, in the remote north-east of the country, cut across the interior with carriers – he was thrilled to find it was blank and unexplored on all maps available in London – and descend, surreptitiously and diagonally, to the Kru Coast where he would contact Paramount Chief Nimley in the bush. He would, like Peter Fleming or indeed like Allan Quatermain in *King Solomon's Mines*, have a purpose; and, if his quest succeeded, a highly newsworthy one. In any case it would be a real adventure, in *terra incognita*, a boy's dream come true.

His first move, therefore, was to contact Sir John Harris of the Anti-Slavery Society in London and obtain letters of introduction to Chief Nimley. Next he approached *The Times*.

This was the crux of the matter: to be appointed, as Waugh and Fleming had been, a Special Correspondent. But *The Times* were only moderately interested in Liberia and the woes of the Krus. They would give him, to his annoyance, no money, no official title, and no guarantee that any dispatches he might send would be published. But by all means let him contact Chief Nimley; and if indeed there was a story there... They provided him with a letter of accreditation "*To Whom It May Concern*" explaining that the bearer, Mr Graham Greene, might be doing a series of articles. It was not, from Graham's point of view, very satisfactory. But it was *The Times*, and it was, at long last a chance to find, or create, a scoop; to establish himself, and thereby to win, if things went well, fame and fortune. After all, his dispatches might, if the Foreign Office was seriously considering declaring a Protectorate and incorporating Liberia into the British Empire, just possibly swing the balance; indeed alter for the better the whole course of West African history. Who could say? It had happened before. For no newspaper was then as influential in forming policy as *The Times*.

The only essential prerequisite was that he should actually succeed in getting to the Kru country and meet Chief Nimley in person– he would be the first correspondent to do so. If that failed, all failed, and the trip would lose its point.

Graham therefore asked Heinemann for a special advance. *It's A Battlefield* had not sold well. But the manuscript currently in hand, *England Made Me*, was more promising in that respect and clearly owed a great deal to Graham's own initiative in travelling to Sweden. Charles Evans knew his author well enough by now to realise that Northern Europe was unlikely ever to be for Graham a source of startling inspiration. But what might come out of Liberia? Heinemann decided, with moderate enthusiasm, to back the trip; but only to the extent of £350. Graham had to write to Hugh to ask him if he knew of anyone in England who could lend him a revolver. For he certainly could not, he explained, afford to buy one.

★ ★ ★

In the circumstances the fact that Graham asked Barbara to come with him seems very odd. It was clearly not a trip to do without a companion; and none of Rider Haggard's heroes had ever set out into the bush alone. But with a girl? Hardly!

Nevertheless there was no question of Barbara crying off at this stage. Graham and Barbara Greene set out by train from Euston for their port of embarkation, Liverpool, stayed the night together at the Adelphi Hotel (where one of the awkwardnesses of a young man and a young woman travelling together and sharing the same surname must surely have become apparent*), set sail on an Elder Dempster packet, the *David Livingstone*, called in first at Tenerife, where to Graham's excitement, the film of *Stamboul Train* was showing (cleaned up by Twentieth Century Fox, unrecognisable, re-entitled *Orient Express*, a disappointment, but still for Graham his first filmed book ever); and on January 14th touched Africa, French West Africa, at Dakar.

Graham loved Dakar, his first sight of Africa, the men holding hands, the Syrian children going willingly to school in white topees, the lovely looking women in the market-place. "It was René Clair in its happy lyrical absurdity."

Then came the Coast proper. "There was no other Coast but the West Coast and this was it." There was an outbreak of yellow fever on the Coast, and port after port, from Bathurst south, was closed to the *David Livingstone*. On January 19th they finally docked at Freetown and put up at the Grand Hotel. "On the roofs the vultures sat nuzzling under their wings with horrible tiny undeveloped heads; they squatted in the garden like turkeys; I could count seven out of my bedroom window." Charles Evans had been right, Graham Greene had discovered the world on which his imagination was so delightedly to fasten.

★ ★ ★

* Neither of them ever mentioned this problem in their published accounts; but it must have continually cropped up throughout their trip. Perhaps they pretended to be brother and sister. It would certainly have made life much simpler, and they looked enough alike for the white lie easily to have passed muster.

Barbara had only had to worry about her clothes. Everything else was left to Graham. "He was somewhat vague and impractical," she had thought. But, "later I was continually astonished at his efficiency and the care he devoted to every little detail".

They had bought trunkloads of stores from England: a hammock, beds, hurricane lamps, mosquito nets, mosquito screens, a hypodermic syringe, a steel money-box, their tin basin bath and, the real life-saver, a case of whisky. To this were added in Freetown six cases of tinned food, more equipment, quinine (5 grams a day was the dose) iodine, boracic tablets and – even more of a life-saver than the whisky – a large supply of Epsom salts. All this was to require a team of over 20 native porters to transport (each carrying a load of 50lb) plus a headman; four of the porters were on rotating hammock -carrying duty for Barbara.*

As regards more important matters, the whole purpose of the expedition, Graham made rather a hash of things. The trouble lay in his mania for letters of introduction and for preparing the ground well in advance by asking friends or acquaintances to write out. The result was that the trip, which ought to have been comparatively clandestine, became semi-official. The British Chargé d'Affaires in Monrovia wrote to say that he had announced the Greenes' projected visit to the Secretary of the Interior of the Liberian Government and the Secretary of the Interior had circulated all the District Commissioners in the Western Province asking them to show courtesy to Mr Greene's safari. In one sense, of course, this was extremely reassuring; and inside Sierra Leone too Barbara and Graham were treated almost as official visitors, invited to a garden-party at Government House and accommodated at government rest-houses when, eventually, they went up the line. But the real snag was, obviously, this; if the Greene safari was announced, and expected, and known about at all levels of the Liberian administration, how were its members to slip unnoticed down to the Kru Coast and made surreptitious contact with Chief Nimley in the interior? In fact Graham's two objectives were contradictory: for what would make a travel book successful – the actual trekking – would be likely to make the journalistic aim, the contact with Paramount Chief Nimley and the Krus, much more difficult to achieve.†

Another letter of introduction, or rather warning letter, to a young man – "Jimmie Daker" – had resulted in a charming reply from him to London: he was

* "I could only use it occasionally," Barbara was to find, "just for five or ten minutes every hour or so. I liked walking but it was wonderful to be able to rest my legs now and then."

† When Barbara and Graham arrived at Freetown, they were contacted at the quayside on the instructions of a mysterious Aronstein who had cabled from London. (All this section of the original edition of *Journey Without Maps*, sub-headed *Signed Aronstein*, was eliminated from later post-war editions, probably for much the same reasons as the description of "the great buck form" of a Customs Inspector was also cut out). Their contact was "a very black gentleman," (*per* Barbara) whom Graham describes only as "Mr. D.", the Liberian rebels' representative in Sierra Leone. He suggested that they should *sail*, not trek, from Freetown to Monrovia and then from Monrovia catch the coasting steamer to Cape Palmas, the most southerly promontory in Monrovia. It would

ready to help the Greenes in every possible way and would certainly have servants lined up for them on arrival. They arrived. Jimmie had arranged nothing. But he invited them to golf, and a cocktail party, and bathing; and at the cocktail party they met a delightful old drunkard "Pa Oakley" who promised to find them servants, and, to their amazement, remembered. Next morning three of them paraded outside the hotel: Amadu, the head boy, a dignified grey-faced little man known as the best head boy all up and down the line; Souri, the old and toothless cook; Laminah, the second boy, young and in shorts, wearing a hat with a scarlet bobble, who was to look after Barbara.

"There they stood," she wrote, "in their flowing white robes, their heads bent, their caps held in both hands and pressed against their chests, their eyes lowered. Their dignity overpowered us. Would we ever be able to live up to them? They were completely silent. A little nervously and in rather literary English my cousin addressed them. By no sign could one see whether they understood or not. They bowed and disappeared."

As Graham put it, "I couldn't have imagined then the affection I would come to feel for them".

Freetown itself Graham loathed – not so much the decaying shabby little city itself as its inhabitants, and he was to mock them mercilessly in his book. "One cannot continue long to find the Creole's painful attempt at playing the white man funny; it is rather like the Chimpanzees' tea-party, the joke is all on one side." He hated the commercial English too, the men who were out there for eighteen months, drinking in the long bar of the City Hotel and talking about the "bloody blacks" and how little one could trust them. He had in fact an extremely conventional public-school attitude towards the whole colonial system – as was only to be expected from somebody who had once considered going into the Colonial Service himself. Sierra Leone was divided into the Crown Colony – basically Freetown with its 40,000 inhabitants, mainly English-speaking Creoles, and the 120 Englishmen whom, in Graham's view, they so painfully aped – and the hinterland, the Protectorate, where, Graham immediately noticed, the British Empire was as he expected it to be: at its best.

"The Englishmen here didn't talk about the 'bloody blacks' nor did they patronise or laugh at them; they had to deal with the real native, not the Creole,

sail past the Kru Coast where no whites would be allowed to travel. But once on board they could suddenly, having booked their passage, change their minds and demand to be put down at Sinoe, a little port roughly half-way between Monrovia and Cape Palmas. There, proceeding along the beach to Nana Kru, they could contact Dr V., an American missionary, who would pass them into the interior up a line of contacts that would lead them to Chief Nimley's hidden camp.

It sounds an extraordinarily sensible plan, quite easy to implement and quite likely to succeed. But Graham rejected it. The trouble was that it was in a sense too easy. For, if it worked, Graham would have a dispatch or even a series of dispatches for *The Times*. But would he have a travel book for Heinemanns? No.

and the real native was someone to love and admire. The Englishmen here were of a finer subtler type than on the Coast." Graham was at heart an Imperialist of the Henty sort, with both the traditional upper-class Englishman's contempt for the babus and his admiration of the unspoilt natives, and for the lonely heroes who ruled them.

* * *

They had landed at Freetown on a Wednesday. Early the following Monday morning they caught the twice-weekly train for the interior. Vast piles of their luggage were assembled on the platform and crowds of natives came, it seemed, for the sole purpose of cheering and waving them goodbye.

Two days "up the line" a lorry met them at Pendembu, the end of the line, and took them 18 miles by road to Kailahun, the border post. There they drank warm cocktails with the District Commissioner. "I liked him at once," wrote Barbara, "and one of his greatest charms, I thought, was that he had all my cousin's books in a row on the bookshelf. We could not have had a better welcome." Next day they left British territory, and British protection, and crossed the border into Liberia.

They were now on the edge of the immense Liberian forest which covers virtually the whole of the Liberian hinterland.

"We were now going to plunge into the greenish half-light of the bush," wrote Barbara. "Monkeys chattered and swore, birds called, and there was a strange buzzing from a thousand insects while frogs croaked from every stream."

The expedition, very Rider Haggard-wise, was finally ready for the great departure. Graham fixed his very British khaki solar topee firmly on his head. The loin-clothed carriers lifted up their loads under the genial direction of Vande, his shirt tail flapping outside his trousers. Amadu, Laminah and Mark picked up the three Revelation suitcases that contained Master and Madam's personal belongings. Old Souri carried, as was usual, a stringy live chicken or two trussed ready for the pot. Barbara hitched up her too short shorts; and the long long line set off winding down the path into the great forest with light, early-morning hearts.

They began the long march on Thursday, February 3rd. It was almost exactly a month later, on March 2nd, that they all reached the Coast, and the adventure, properly speaking, was over.

Those who want to read the detailed recital of those four weeks can do so in both Barbara's and Graham's books; and those who feel inclined to follow their footsteps should proceed, from the Sierra Leone frontier through the villages of Kpangblamai, Duogobmai, Nicoboozo, Zigita (which however they might do better to avoid), Zorzor, and then cut straight across through French Guinea – as it then was – to end up, back across the Mani River by dug-out, in Ganta, where they might ask if Dr Harley, the expert on Liberia's Secret Societies, is still remembered. This will take them, if they follow Barbara and Graham's pace, nearly two weeks. And, like Barbara and Graham, they will probably soon find the Liberia forest – which lacks wild life – very monotonous and uninteresting; and the excitement of walking through it and of sleeping each night in rat-infested village huts, with jiggers having to be cut out from under toe-nails, will soon begin to pall.

Barbara bore up to the stresses and strains of the march rather better than Graham. "Physically he did not look strong," she had noted early in her diary. But she became more and more impressed with his will-power and his determination and indeed his powers of leadership. The carriers would lie around at his feet in the evenings, gossiping and chattering, while Graham sat in his green folding chair like a benevolent father smiling down kindly but uncomprehendingly at them. "Graham from the beginning treated them exactly as if they were white men from our country. He talked to them quite naturally and they liked him." He had been told in Freetown, that blacks would only respond to blows and shouts. But he was always patient and polite. Whenever there was a dispute, he would listen to it gravely as both sides stated their case, only Barbara knowing that he was quite incapable of following what it was all about. Then silence fell while he considered the matter gravely for a minute or two before bringing out what was to become a splendid stock phrase: "I agree with Amadu. Palaver finished."

Only once did he let himself go, not against the carriers but against a chief's son, who had failed, despite promises, to supply the men with their evening chop. He sent for the man. The carriers stood around in a ring. Graham remained sitting. "Slowly, with many biting expressions and in good round terms that no-one except myself understood, Graham delivered his lecture. The effect on our men was miraculous. They loved it. It was as good as a show. I loved it myself."

★ ★ ★

Quite out of the blue, on the very first day of the march, they had found the President with a small escort in a village on their route. It had been immediately assumed, rather to Graham's embarrassment, that he was specially presenting himself for a Presidential audience. Dusty and dirty, "a little taken aback", he was slightly reassured by the attentiveness of the neat young ADC; and even more so by the appearance of one of the President's "most intimate friends", a Miss Knight. She never spoke a word – nor did Graham. She had slanting eyes ("black dreamy eyes" per Barbara); and as for Graham's own eyes, he couldn't keep them off her. She was, he was to remember, "the loveliest thing I saw in Liberia". So if it hadn't been for the President's vitality and joviality, his appearance would have been almost an anti-climax. As it was, one phrase in particular that he used struck both Graham and Barbara. She had asked him whether his authority was the same as an American President's. More, he said, in his strong American accent, the words running away with him. "Once elected and in charge of the machine, why then, I'm boss of the whole show."

Quite obviously, from their accounts, neither Barbara nor Graham were able to take a black President – the only one in the whole world and in charge of a tinpot little country – at all seriously. Indeed Graham was to write, of his carriers, that there was not one of them "who would not have welcomed white intervention"; and of the country in general: "everywhere in the north I found myself welcomed because I was white, because they hoped all the time that a white nation would take the country over". Still, they had both liked President Barclay as a man; and it was undeniably a little awkward that Graham had felt obliged to tell him that they were going no further into the interior than the centre of the Western Province, where they were expected. It might have been very embarrassing indeed if, after an encounter with Chief Nimley, they had been picked up, and perhaps even confronted by the President in person with this lie direct. But from the fifth night of the march, when they had stayed at the evil village of Zigita, Graham was never really well again. Only continual doses of Epsom salts and whisky, and willpower, kept him going. The rainy season was looming, money was running short; and so at Ganta Graham took the bitter decision to cut almost straight down to the Coast towards Monrovia via the Grand Bassa. This meant in effect waving goodbye to any hopes of reaching the Kru coast and Sasstown and Chief Nimley. It meant, in short, that the expedition had aborted.

But fate did the next best thing. She suddenly presented them, at the town of Tappee-Ta, almost half-way along the trail to Grand Bassa, with the villain of the piece, Colonel Elwood Davis in person.

★ ★ ★

From the first day onwards Barbara and Graham never walked together. She followed him, like the rest of the long line of carriers, in Indian file. "To be alone with one companion for several weeks on end in uncomfortable and strange surroundings," she later wrote, "means that one either grows very fond of him or comes to dislike him intensely." Luckily she had discovered that she both liked and respected Graham. But however much she liked him, to watch his long socks slowly slipping down over his calves to lie, like a concertina, in a wrinkled pile around his ankles gave her the heebie-jeebies. She was too polite, however, much as she longed to, to ask him to pull them up – or even, indeed, to mention his socks at all.★

★ Graham was equally polite. Only at the very end, when she proposed packing them to take back to England, did he finally let fly and "with all the wealth of phrase at his command" inform her exactly what he thought of the rig of her shorts.

However, even *faute de* Barbara, Graham was conscious of them. When, having heard as they approached Tappee-Ta that the Frontier Force was there in strength, he saw a stockaded compound, each gate guarded by an armed sentry in red fez and pastel uniform, with the Lone Star Flag of Liberia fluttering above from a staff in the middle, he felt – as he followed the sentry in, towards a verandah crowded with blacks in smart tropical suits and military outfits, smoking cigars – very dirty indeed in his stained shorts and "rather absurd, with my stockings over my ankles". He was also sporting (which he does not mention, but Barbara does) a rather scrubby little beard.

He was a little uneasy too. They ought not to have been in the Central Province at all, and he feared the wrath of the Colonel, whom he visualized as a ferocious black tyrant.

A conference was on in the palaver house. Towards five o'clock a bugle blew; and the man whom his friends admiringly, his enemies derisively, described as the Dictator of Grand Bassa stepped out.

This was the first sight Graham had ever had of a type that he was to be fascinated by throughout his long life, the flamboyant military adventurer; and it was almost a case of love at first sight. Colonel Davis had a clean well-fitting uniform, a neat black pointed beard, and he carried himself with a swagger. He at once reminded Graham of that hero of Conrad's, Captain Blunt, whom he had used as a model in his own earliest novels, and whose motto was: "I live by my sword". To be fair to Graham, he impressed Barbara equally. To her he resembled a "handsome villain" in an old-fashioned play, tall, straight and good-looking. "No longer could I think of him as the cold-blooded murderer of women and children. His personality was too colourful, his gestures were too theatrical." She was fascinated. Graham sent a note across to ask him for an interview. The reply came back at once. Though Colonel Davis had had nine hard hours in the Council, he would see Mr Greene for just a few minutes.

Graham left Barbara to walk across to the compound. Night fell. The few minutes lengthened into over an hour. Barbara re-read Saki and Somerset Maugham. At last Graham reappeared.

"We want some whisky," he announced.

"I always have a glass of Ovaltine at the end of a day's trek," explained the Colonel, with a flash of his gold teeth. "But just tonight…"

By the end of that evening (and indeed of the following evening when he was in a sentimental mood and almost finished all the whisky that the whites had left) he had pretty nearly won Graham over entirely to his side. He was obviously a brave man and an efficient one – even Mr Rydings' hostile report had made that much clear. But he was also very proud of his achievements, perfectly prepared to talk about everything and answer any questions, and ended by convincing Graham (probably perfectly justifiably) that there had been no massacre of women and children at all, that it had all been a hotch-potch of lies and misunderstandings got up by his enemies to discredit him. Indeed Chief Nimley began to appear in a very different, rather brutal, and much less attractive, light.

He told them all his adventures. He told them, with great charm, about Liberia.

"Liberia is a beautiful country. A beautiful country. I ought to know. I guess I've seen most of the world. But when I hear the young men of Monrovia saying that they want to see Europe or America, I say to them – see Liberia first. And I think that's a beautiful thought. See Liberia first. That's what I say. See Liberia first."

He talked non-stop. There was one story that so pleased Graham and Barbara that they both recorded it.

"I've been glad to see you," he said. "Do you know what the captain of a liner once told me way out in mid-ocean? He pointed to the lights of a little ship passing by and: 'Davis', he said, 'I have three books in my library. The first is called *Ships That Pass in the Night*". The Colonel paused, and looked at the Greenes. "Can you guess what the others were?"

"No," said Graham.

"*The People We Meet* was the second. And then the captain looked at me for a long time and finally he said, 'The third book is called *The People We Love*.' I guess that's a beautiful thought."

Conticuere omnes... Graham and Barbara and Colonel Davis fell silent, reverently sipping their whiskies, as at the passing of a goddess. In those moments Liberia, and a certain kind of love too – something more in any case than mere maudlin sentimentality – held the two white adventurers and the legendary black, all three of them together, folded away in its thrall.

★ ★ ★

Even as they arrived in Tappee Ta, Barbara had noticed Graham looked very unwell. "My cousin had certainly caught some strange internal disease. He felt sick, and yet he was hungry all the time." But he would not rest. He was longing to get down to the Coast and, as he wrote in his diary that night, desperate to see Vivien again.

So next morning, despite the fact that "Graham looked ghastly and was shivering", off they set. He talked incessantly about the Coast and Grand Bassa, "as if it was going to turn out to be a heaven on earth". Barbara was more than worried. "As I saw him in the early morning light, his face grey and drawn, his hand shaking even more than it usually did as he poured the Epsom Salts into his tea, I became scared." She became even more scared on the long day's march. Graham "had a strange stupid expression on his face and sometimes he stumbled slightly as though he could not see very well". It was a nine-hour trek. "De cook plenty tired," Laminah told Barbara. They were all plenty tired. Graham was tottering when they reached their resting place, Zigi's Town.

That night he nearly died. His temperature went higher and higher. Barbara wrapped him up in blankets and gave him plenty of whisky and Epsom salts, hoping desperately that she was doing the right thing. The thunder roared, her head ached, the carriers quarrelled. She smoked an extra cigarette and thought, quite unemotionally, about what she would do if the worst happened – how she would have her cousin buried and go down to the Coast, with Amadu, and to whom in England she should send telegrams.

"I had supper by myself," she wrote. "The boys served me with grave faces. The same thought was in all our minds. Graham would die. I never doubted it for a minute. He looked like a dead man already."

* * *

So, had Graham Greene died there an early death, as he had always expected he would, before the age of 32, of some unknown fever in an obscure little African village, Amadu would have arranged for the grave to be dug and the body laid out and the carriers would have buried him, weeping. Mark, the Christian boy, might have carved a little wooden cross and Barbara, perhaps, have chosen an inscription: "Henry Graham Greene. Born 4th October 1904 at Berkhamsted in England. Died 25th February 1935 at Zigi's Town in Liberia, of an unknown disease, aged thirty. Poet, novelist and explorer."

He would have been remembered, then, only by his friends with regret but understanding; by some critics and fellow-writers too as a minor novelist of a certain promise; and of course by his family, his widow, and his tiny daughter.

But Barbara might have brought back his pencilled diary and given it to Vivien; and there she would have read in her husband's shaky hand as he lay dying his final heartfelt message of love to her, written at 8.32 p.m. precisely; and his last stoical sentences. Thus, courageously, without self-pity, with the traditional stiff upper lip, and with his last thoughts for Vivien, Graham Greene might have quitted in obscure virtue this vale of tears.

But it was not to be.

Chapter XII

Clapham Common

In early April, on a windy, rainy, bitterly cold morning, Graham and Barbara came home to England. It was four a.m. They sat, silent and depressed on their boxes in the dark customs house, waiting for an official to come and wave them through. Then they said farewell. Vivien was arriving later that morning in Dover to welcome Graham back. Barbara did not stay to meet her.

★ ★ ★

The trip, since Graham's near miraculous recovery at Zigi's Town, had been an anti-climax. They reached Grand Bassa, caught a small boat (full of Opposition politicians) leaving for Monrovia, spent a few days there, and then, via Freetown sailed home. Barbara had hated every moment of her time in Monrovia, with its thirty white inhabitants, endless boring parties and continual drinking. Farewells, as Byron had said and she was to quote, should be sudden.

But, instead, the trip had dragged drearily on; and by this time she and Graham had nothing more to say to one another. Indeed their last really happy evening together – Graham had noted it too, in his diary – had been at the pleasant village of Nicoboozo, way back on February 6th, only three days into their trekking – "one of the last times," as Barbara put it, "that we could talk completely naturally to one another". "We never really quarrelled," she specified, "not once." But Graham "would sometimes become rather obstinate, hanging on to some small unimportant point like a dog to a bone." So subject after subject, beginning with politics, had been set aside by mutual agreement "marked carefully 'Not wanted during voyage' till gradually practically nothing remained on the last day or two of our trip except the enthralling subject of food".

On the cargo boat coming back, Barbara, unutterably bored and tired of being both filthy and without decent clothes to wear, watched the burning sunshine plunge into storms and fogs and the days creep by till finally they docked at Dover. Graham meanwhile kept unsociably to his cabin, scribbling away at a piece of writing that was to become his most famous long short story, *The Basement Room*. This story alone would have justified Charles Evan's gamble. For though it was not directly inspired by the West African trip, though indeed with its luxurious setting in a Belgravia mansion, its butler and housekeeper, its references to Green Park and Belgrave Square, it was a pure piece of shipboard escapism, yet the whole atmosphere is impregnated with Graham's recent experiences. Philip's absent father has been a District Commissioner at Bo, up the line; and Baines the butler, whom the boy Philip loves and admires, is himself an "Old Coaster" and proud of it.

Down in the basement living room Baines entertains the boy with ginger-beer and stories of the Coast; and it is this particular sense of the great wide world beyond that enriches, so skilfully, the otherwise claustrophobic atmosphere of *The Basement Room*.

"'Why,' said Baines, bowing his thin grey hair with embarrassment over the ginger pop, 'I loved some of those damned niggers. I couldn't help loving them. There they'd be laughing, holding hands, they liked to touch each other… It wasn't love, it didn't mean anything we would understand.'"

So when Philip, not understanding, accepts the bribe of the Meccano set offered to him by Mrs Baines, and the Baines' world thereby crumbles, it is as if not the Land Benighted but the Happy Land itself is lost, to Philip/Graham, for ever.

"He never opened the Meccano set again, never created anything, died, the old dilettante, sixty years later with nothing to show rather than to preserve the memory of Mrs Baines' malicious voice saying goodnight, her soft determined footfalls on the stairs to the basement, going down, going down."

★ ★ ★

Paradoxically, it was not Heinemann's who published this small masterpiece. They had to content themselves with the eventual travel book, and with a future new novel, a "thriller", on both of which Graham set to work immediately. It was a minor publishing firm, The Cresset Press, that got hold of *The Basement Room* and they brought it out, with seven more of Graham's short stories – all much much shorter and slighter than the title story – in a small volume; which, as a gesture of gratitude which one hopes he appreciated, Graham dedicated to Charles Evans.

That was thanks to the ebullient John Hayward, literary adviser to The Cresset Press; and it was John Hayward too – he was literary adviser, formal or informal to all sorts of shy people, it might be said to have been his chosen role in life – who arranged for Graham to write and have published by another even tinier publisher, an extraordinary little work entitled *The Bear Fell Free*.

This is a book that Graham Greene was never to mention in any account of his life or writings. Yet it is an extremely handsome production, thin, large and flat in format, with twirling GGs on the end papers, surmounted by lightning and Maltese crosses entwined, the sort of book that any author might be proud to produce from the shelves where he keeps his collected works. It has moreover a great rarity value. Only 285 copies of the first edition were published of which

250, numbered and signed by the author, were put up for sale. And there has been no further edition.

It is only when one turns to the text of *The Bear Fell Free* that one gets an inkling of why Graham Greene preferred, basically, to suppress it. The story is very slight, only seventeen pages long, and barely deserves such an elaborate presentation. But it is the setting, and the style, that cause disarray. These are unrecognizable – particularly the latter. Here is the last paragraph and the last (title-giving) line describing the final air crash.

"Birth and death simultaneously tainted with each other – birth and suicide in the maternity ward, guilt and suicide in the trenches, in Jane's flat guilt and suicide. Patient serious Baron tasting from the first of the final soapsud, soapsuds in settlement, soapsuds in Parliament, soapsuds in Buckingham Palace. Money for nothing wrenched from Mrs Farrell's womb, sherry circulating through the broken neck, unbearable agony of the cracked skull in Jane's bed. Prayers no good for something already happened, memory no good with no past, hope no good with no future, love no good with no end and no beginning.

"The teddy bear fell free."

Graham Greene had long been fascinated by flying. This tale of a drunken bet at an "Atlantic Flight Party" and the subsequent tragic accident is obviously experimental; and, with its stream-of-consciousness technique and its rich upper middle-class characters, largely derivative. It was probably written *before* the trip to Liberia. The pilot's name, Tony Farrell, is remarkably similar to that of Anthony Farrant in *England Made Me*; and *England Made Me* too has stream-of-consciousness passages that, though in a very minor key compared to those of *The Bear Fell Free*, do indicate a certain fascination with this technique. It is just as well that Graham Greene did not pursue this line, for such techniques were in effect a form of sophisticated reversion to the introspection of his early novels. But it is understandable, indeed admirable, that he as a writer should have experimented with different methods. He was not a third-rater, incapable of taking a risk.

★ ★ ★

It is a pleasure indeed to contemplate Mr Graham Greene at this point in his life. For at long last he was firmly in charge of it. Up to his thirtieth year he had been buffeted along in a fairly chaotic manner. "*Factus de materia levis elementi*;" he might, with the Archpoet, have said, "*Similis sum folio de quo ludunt venti*." But he wasn't, in fact, made of light stuff. Adversity and uncertainty had strengthened him. Mr Graham Greene at the age of thirty was not the wind's plaything any longer. He could now be pretty sure that any book he might write would be published, any proposal he might submit would be seriously considered. If not yet a successful, he was certainly an established author; and, as he told Hugh happily, an incredibly busy one. He had two books to write – his travel book about the

Liberian trip and his new hopefully money-spinning thriller;* and, he promised his agents that autumn, he was devoting himself entirely to getting them both done by Christmas.

Graham and Vivien, with Lucy, moved from Oxford to London in the early summer of 1935, that is to say only weeks after his return from Liberia. With the lease of a house in London he set himself up, finally, as an established family man. His marriage appears to have been going well at this point. Another child was soon to be on the way, and this without any of the heart-searchings that the announcement of Vivien's first pregnancy had caused. There was a nursery, there was a German maid, Frieda, there was a cook. It was, in effect, an establishment.

Not in the smartest part of London. The Greenes' new home, 14 North Side, was well south of the river; but on the north side of Clapham Common – hence its name. The house however was a large Queen Anne house, in a terrace of large Queen Anne houses; its elegance compensated for its position. Five minutes' walk away was the Redemptorist Church of St Mary's; where Father Trollope had become a much-loved Rector; and it at first seemed a fair assumption that Graham and Vivien came to live on Clapham Common at Father Trollope's plea or suggestion. But that is wrong. Father Trollope had died in 1933, two years earlier.

So if it was not religion that induced the Greenes to set up house in Clapham Common, it must have been money. Even then, even though life and leases south of the river were comparatively cheap, Graham Greene could not possibly have afforded to set up an establishment in London on his earnings from authorship alone.

But he did not have to; for he now, at long last, had found what he had so long been looking for: a regular job in journalism. He had become film critic for *The Spectator*.

* * *

Graham Greene's first film review appeared on July 5th 1935, by which date he was already installed at 14 North Side. Thereafter week after week he would eagerly open the gilded invitation cards, spend his mornings at the press performances and write his column (of approximately 750 words, covering,

* *England Made Me* came out in June, it was dedicated to Vivien "With Ten Years' Love 1925-1935", which must have thrilled her, and was well reviewed by, among others, Peter Quennell in *The New Statesman*. But it sold only just over a thousand copies in England (and less in America). Since *Stamboul Train* three years previously, Graham Greene had been a financial disappointment to his publishers. They wanted another popular success. So did he. He had made up his mind therefore to write a fast-moving thriller that would, like *Stamboul Train*, be snapped up by a film company. But, being the man he was, he had, even in a popular thriller, to experiment. He decided to make its protagonist a peculiarly repulsive murderer; and gave him a black name, Raven, to match. It was a new challenge. Could he pull it off? Time would tell.

usually three films) once a week for *The Spectator*. His first stint lasted for almost exactly as long as his predecessor Charles Davey's had done – slightly under two years. He took a break after his column of May 7th 1937; and then came back to *The Spectator* just over a year later – rather a dramatic year for him – on June 10th 1938; continuing till March 15th 1940, after which Basil Wright took his place. Strictly speaking therefore it was for slightly under three and a half years, for two periods of almost equal length, rather than for four and a half years at a stretch that Graham Greene reviewed films for *The Spectator*. But it was the closest thing he ever came in his pre-war life to a regular job and one that imposed, because of its constraints, a regular pattern on his way of living; and in any case in those years he saw, and reviewed, an awful lot of films. He became part of the film world; and the world of films, which had always fascinated him, became, and was to remain, much more directly than before, a very important part, of his own life.

The position of film critic of *The Spectator* was not then, and is not now, a particularly influential one. But, as Anthony Powell was to remark, Graham Greene reviewed films differently, in marked contrast to the usually rather moderate tones of the balanced film or drama critic. "Greene fulminated like a John Knox of movie criticism, sometimes demanding maiden tribute, sometimes denouncing the sins of the flesh. Every phrase was forged in a white heat of passionate feeling, emotive images abounding, such as Von Stroheim, 'climbing a ladder in skin-tight Prussian breeches towards an innocent bed'. This calling of fire down from heaven – and up from hell – on the cinema and all its works, did not remain unanswered, but retribution was still several months ahead."

So very quickly Graham Greene carved a position out for himself as an unusual, highly forceful and very readable film critic. It should not be deduced that he was always on the attack. On the contrary, in his very first column of July 5th 1935 he described one of the four films reviewed, *Abyssinia*, as "the finest travel film I have ever seen... made by a Swiss expedition, with an admirably plain commentary."* He rather favoured documentary, particularly realistic documentary with poetic implications of the Anglo-Soviet school. What he loathed and despised were pretentious historical costume dramas, of which the screens were full, especially when they were made by foreigners masquerading as Englishmen. Against foreigners making foreign films – against Americans making gangster films, for instance, or light comedies or musicals – he had no prejudices at all. And about the French he was almost invariably ecstatic. He enjoyed too the

* Graham Greene's review shows that he shared none of Evelyn Waugh's pro-Fascist and anti-Abyssinian prejudices. "It (the film) leaves you with a vivid sense of something very old, very dusty and very cruel but something dignified in its dirt and popular in its tyranny and perhaps more worth preserving than the bright slick stream-lined civilization that threatens it." Three months later, on October 2nd 1935 – Graham's birthday – Mussolini invaded Abyssinia and the era of the Axis invasions began. (See the present author's *Haile Selassie's War*).

actresses, particularly foreign ones; but his critic's compliments are never mere fluff. Of Garbo he wrote, for instance, "no other film actress can so convey physical passion that you believe in its dignity and importance, and yet there is no actress who depends so little on her own sexual charm".

Yet he felt very keenly – it comes out in almost all his columns – that it was a British film critic's principal job to encourage all that was best in the British film industry and to savage all that was worst.

So it was natural enough, given his tastes and his background, that he should have been drawn, at first, into the rather intellectual, very serious Grierson/Rotha/Wright/Cavalcanti set.

⋆ ⋆ ⋆

Despite his new job, despite his long trip to Liberia, despite the new house and the two books on his hands, an almost irresistible letter came from Moscow, from Nordahl Grieg.

"I have borrowed the flat of Boris Pilnyak who has written 'Volga Falls Out in the Caspian Sea', (of course all Russian writers call their books after some river, they are even worse than you English who always find some very exclusive quotation as a title)... I am sure you will like to live in Moscow, there is such an enormous mass of people – a vast multitude of races, hopes and disappointments. And your hatred to nature can easily be satisfied here, there is no nature for many hundred miles, only something flat and stupid under an idiotical sky. So come for some months or more."

Almost fatally tempted – a few months' absence wouldn't have done much for his career or for his marriage, either – Graham Greene roughed out a synopsis for a short story: "Miss Mitton in Moscow". Would the *News Chronicle* commission it, he asked his agents.* Interestingly, for it was his first venture into that field, it was to be a spy story, and 10,000 words long. And would the *News Chronicle*, he wrote to Nancy Pearn on October 21st, please make up its mind as the boat he was planning to catch was leaving for Moscow in ten days? But the *News Chronicle* turned it down; and Graham Greene returned to his morning film press shows, problems with the house ("What *do* you mean about the roof?" asked Nancy Pearn) and the exciting prospects – fulfilled in this case – of ten days at Easter *en famille* in Dartmouth.

The Liberian travel book proved extremely difficult to write, or at least to

* Almost simultaneously with Graham's move to London there had been a flurry in the agency world. Spencer Curtis Brown, not a likeable man, had taken over his father's agency, and as a result both David Higham and Laurence Pollinger had left, taking Graham Greene with them. They joined forces with Nancy Pearn to form a new agency: Pearn Pollinger and Higham – offices at 6 Norfolk Street off the Strand.

make interesting. When it came down to it, very little had actually happened on the trip – certainly no excitements like the wars, arrests and escapes that Peter Fleming* had experienced in China and Manchuria; and a trek through a dank forest was even more tedious in itself, as indeed both travellers had found, than a walking tour through the Chilterns and the Cotswolds. Nevertheless he finished it as promised, before Christmas, and on January 4th 1936 the new 'shocker' too.

It was the latter he was counting on to make money with. Buoyed up by enthusiastic reactions both at Heinemann's and Doubledays, he wrote cock-a-hoop to Hugh, to congratulate him on Helga's pregnancy and to warn him that his own family was also on the increase. Despite this fraternal domestic bliss in both Berlin and London there were nostalgic yearnings; harking back to the brothers' trip to Scandinavia together, and to Nordahl's friends. For Ingeborg appeared in London in May with her new husband, utterly desirable in every way – that still tantalisingly elusive figure in both their lives.

Hugh's child was born first, on June 10th – his first child, a son, Graham Carleton Greene. Graham Greenes – old uncle, new uncle, nephew – now spanned three generations in a sort of cross-linked genealogical pattern. Tragically, Tooter's wife, Lola Bell, died five days later. Vivien was having a difficult pregnancy. But all went very well on the day itself. Francis Charles Bartley Greene was born on September 13th. Douglas Woodruff, *The Tablet's* new Editor, wrote to congratulate "you both" on the "accession." "May *The Tablet* grow faster than your family!" He would be printing, he added, Graham Greene's first chronicle the following week; and was enjoying his book.

Which book he did not specify. Both books had been out for several months. *Journey Without Maps*, the Liberian travel book, was the first book to appear – and to disappear.

Out in May, it was withdrawn in December. Graham had invented the name "Pa Oakley" for the drunkard who had been at the welcoming cocktail party for himself and Barbara in Freetown. Unfortunately a genuine Dr PD Oakley had emerged from the woodwork, the head of the Sierra Leone Medical Service and, utterly offended, was issuing writs. As all bar 200 copies had been sold, the prickly Doctor seemed to have won nothing but the book's suppression.

And that, it must be admitted, was no real loss to literature. *Journey Without Maps*, divided into three parts and twelve chapters with numerous sub-headings, illustrated by fourteen very dull box-brownie photos, was a far worse travel book than Barbara's own account, *Land Benighted*, which was to appear two years later. Partly because it was particularly pretentious. In the first few pages there were quotations from Henry James, Burton, Céline, Santayana, references to Conrad, Herr Hauser's *The Inner Journey*, and – welcome light relief – to *King Solomon's*

* Peter Fleming's second travel book, also a bestseller like his first, *Brazilian Adventure*, came out in 1934. It was entitled *One's Company: A Journey to China.*

Mines; sneers at Beverley Nichols and at Cecil Roberts. Get on with it, the reader wants to cry. But even when Graham Greene does get on with it, he pauses for long stretches – two pages here, three pages there – of retrospective flashbacks into his own past life: his childhood, Nottingham, trips to Paris and Estonia, horror stories of the Cotswolds, the Old Etonian with the interest in flagellation in Kensington Gardens, 'Major Grant' and the brothel off the Strand.

One can see why he did it. When *Journey Without Maps* reappeared in the Collected Edition of Graham Greene's works in 1978, he added a long *Introduction* with a very elaborate explanation of how he was "haunted by the awful tedium of A to Z" and needed to add a parallel, interior journey supporting the "uneventful record" with "memories, dreams, word-associations". But, though this makes it of interest to a biographer, it ruins *Journey Without Maps* (which in any case remains basically an A to Z record) as a travel book. The device is a failure.

In Barbara's book the real interest lies in the interplay of the two characters, her reaction to Graham and Graham's to her, and both of theirs to the different situations they face. This he in his book had oddly, disappointingly, deliberately ruled out. Nevertheless what is extremely striking about the two books by the two cousins is how closely they tie up on the actual details and events, and on the people met on the Liberian trek. There are virtually no contradictions. Indeed the only major difference of emphasis is Graham playing down his own near-death in true stiff-upper-lip fashion, while Barbara gives it its full due. But so unusual is it to have two accounts of any event that coincide almost exactly in different witnesses' eyes that this is most certainly a point worth stressing.

★ ★ ★

In another of his Collected Edition *Introductions* written so many years later Graham Greene turns on his commentators:

"Some critics," he writes, "have referred to a strange violent 'seedy' region of the mind (why did I ever popularize that last adjective?) which they call Greeneland, and I have sometimes wondered whether they go round the world blinkered. 'This is Indo-China,' I want to explain, 'this is Mexico, this is Sierra Leone carefully and accurately described. I have been a newspaper correspondent as well as a novelist. I assure you the dead child lay in the ditch in just that attitude. In the canal of Phat Diem the bodies stuck out of the water... But I know that argument is useless. They won't believe the world they haven't noticed is like that."

Greeneland had not yet been coined as a useful shorthand critical/descriptive expression.★ But, with the publication of *Journey Without Maps*, seediness

★ And Graham Greene was not always so averse to its use – in yet another *Introduction* talking of ennui in the tropics, and its remedies, he writes, less defensively and more percepiently than above, "Greeneland, perhaps: I can only say that it is the land in which I have passed much of my life."

certainly had. Mr Greene may have repented of it later on; but in his book on Liberia he positively wallowed in the seedy.

Right from the start "There seemed to be a seediness about the place you couldn't get to the same extent elsewhere, and seediness has a very deep appeal". Thus Liberia: only a mild contrast to the initial "seediness of civilization", and "the natural native seediness" of the Adelphi Hotel, Liverpool, from which, via the seedy Pole on the boat out, and the seedy British colonials in Freetown, one advances to (or, as the author prefers, one arrives back again at) a whole sub-section entitled THE SEEDY LEVEL; and to the conclusion, memories and past life summed up thus: "This may explain the deep appeal of the seedy. It *is* nearer the beginning; like Monrovia its building has begun wrong but at least it has only begun." So in some curious way, seediness – as opposed to "the smart, the new, the chic, the cerebral" – is innocence.

It can, therefore, reasonably be said that the only lasting contribution to the Greene *oeuvre* that sprang, fully-armed, from *Journey Without Maps* was the concept of seediness. But what a contribution, and how much Graham Greene enjoyed, at the time, making it. If ever after it was to cling to him and to his works like a cloak of Nessus, *fiat justitia*, one might say, rather than the Greenian *ruat coelum*.

Chapter XIII

Among the 'Dark Aliens'

"Murder didn't mean much to Raven." From its very opening line the 'shocker' grips and, gripping, moves on, in a way that the travel book utterly fails to do. Perhaps it was too much even for Graham Greene, for all his skill in keeping many literary projects in the air simultaneously, to try to juggle with two such very different books. One had to suffer. It was not *A Gun For Sale*.

In America, where it was published simultaneously by Doubleday Doran, they changed its title to the more meticulously correct *This Gun For Hire*.

"We loved the main literary problems posed," wrote the *New York Herald Tribune's* book reviewer. "Will Chumley kill Anne before Jimmy gets there? How many more will be shot? And will Anne be able to stop the European war? In our opinion the war petered out, but the running excitement, assisted by the author's nervous style, is well worth your money."*

It is easy enough to pick holes in the plot of *A Gun For Sale*, which depends on an extremely unlikely chain of coincidences. But the chilling opening sequence, the murder of a War Minister and his aged secretary in some (unnamed) Balkan country by a hired killer, only needs to be compared with similar political assassination scenes in contemporary thrillers to be recognized for what it is, a small masterpiece of skilful craftsmanship that owes nothing to portentously precise description of weapons and muzzle velocities; but everything to the deft little touch, to the eggs boiling on the stove and the old woman's macabre toughness.

There is a conventional hero to the story, Detective Sergeant Mather of the Yard – Jimmie – but he is almost entirely a cardboard figure, a plot convenience. On the other hand the heroine, Anne, has much more spunk than most of Graham Greene's heroines. She is not managed by but manages men and situations – hired killer and policeman fiancé alike, not to speak of the oily, lecherous Mr. Cholmondeley (did they use simplified spelling in the US edition, one wonders?) – and of course prevents a European war too.

On this last point it is worth noting that Graham Greene's extraordinary political prescience – so often to be more immediately obvious in his later

* $2.

novels.* For when *A Gun For Sale* was finished, that is to say in January 1936, Hitler had not yet invaded the Rhineland – that was to come in March – the Popular Front had not yet been elected in France – in April – Abyssinia had not yet been annexed by Mussolini – May; nor above all had the Spanish Civil War, the real precursor of war in Europe, broken out – not till July. So to set his thriller against the background of an imminent European war complete with air-raid practices, ultimatums, public fear and newspaper headlines was a rather risky, not at all an obvious gambit on the author's part; one that was to prove oddly accurate.

And whatever the American critic may have thought, the death count for a Graham Greene novel was not particularly high: only the Minister and his secretary at the beginning, and, at the end, the two villains, Mr Cholmondeley the middleman who has hired and double-crossed the killer, plus his boss, Sir Marcus, the armament manufacturer with the "old thin body" – who is "as painfully aware of his bones as a skeleton": a masterly character sketch, based on the notorious 'merchant of death' Sir Basil Zaharoff. Even the policeman, apparently mortally wounded, is announced to be recovering in the last scene; and hero and heroine – Detective Sergeant Jimmie and Anne – misunderstandings over, have marriage and a happy ending before them. " 'Oh', she said with a sigh of unshadowed happiness," – an unusual last line sentiment in a Graham Greene novel – " 'we're home' "

But Raven the killer of course dies too, shot in the back by a policeman; and, were it not a thriller that must by the rules of the genre have a happy ending, the story might with much greater logic have ended then, with Death coming to him in the form of "unbearable pain". For Raven is the real hero of *A Gun For Sale*. "It was as if he had to deliver this pain as a woman delivers a child, and he sobbed and moaned in the effort. At last it came out of him and he followed his only child into a vast desolation."

What a hero. Raven is the lumpenproletariat made flesh – undersized, ignorant, brutal, self-centred, self-pitying, vicious. His creator takes an almost perverse pleasure in loading the dice against his creature. Raven's father has been hanged. His mother has committed suicide, sawing at her throat and almost cutting her head off with a bread-knife. He has spent his childhood in a Home. He has no friends. Above all, worse of all, he is physically deformed. "He's very ugly through and through. That lip of his. It gives you the creeps." Again and again Graham Greene insists on Raven's hare-lip and the disgust it arouses, even in himself, perhaps in himself most of all. For Raven knows he is unlovable.

And yet by the end of the book so great is Graham Greene's skill that we have, like Anne, almost come to love Raven – Raven the indomitable, with his dogged determination to hunt down and kill the men who have double-crossed him, and his undoubted rat-like physical courage. It is a *tour de force* of the novelist's craft.

* As for instance of Russian missiles in Cuba (*Our Man in Havana*) or of ever-increasing American interference in Vietnam (*A Quiet American*).

No hero of any of Graham Greene's novels less resembles his author; and one might add too that no novel is less autobiographical if it were not that most of the action, after the opening scenes in Soho and King's Cross, takes place in a wintry Nottingham, lightly disguised as "Nottwich". But, though the décor of Graham Greene's Nottingham is all there in place – the two rival newspapers, the upmarket *Journal* and the downmarket *Guardian*, St Mark's RC Cathedral, the river, the railway station, the hotel, the theatre, the single tart in the town centre – it is only a bleak Midlands setting, less real now, one feels, to Graham Greene than "The Coast", than West Africa, than Liberia, than, indeed, what was to become Greeneland.

The isolated pair trapped in the railway sheds with death and the authorities roaming outside – consciously or unconsciously Graham Greene used the same setting, (though in England this time, not in far-away Subotica) as he had done in *Stamboul Train* for the long central *tête-à-tête* sequence where doomed man and baffled girl approach half way to love. Even more than in that previous successful thriller, less deliberately, more pervasively, the influence of the cinema, of the visual, dominates *A Gun For Sale*. Both literature and life may have provided a certain inspiration. But over the whole tale of the hare-lipped murderer, hunting and being hunted, looms the influence of such films as Fritz Lang's *M*, the influence – all to the good – of the movie masterpieces.

In the year 1936 Graham wrote no books, set out on no travels. Instead he went to the cinema. Films dominated his life. During its early months he was settling into his stride as a critic, lambasting in particular his preferred *bête noire*, Korda, and, wherever possible, Moura's elderly lover too. In February his target was *The Shape of Things to Come*, "the vast expensive Korda-Wells film of the future" given form by "the meaningless machinery of Mr Wells' riotous fancy." Three months later: "The dialogue of English films is notoriously bad, from Mr Wells downward." Then, in June, followed a particularly blistering attack.

"England," wrote *The Spectator's* film critic, "of course has always been the home of the exiled; but one may at least express a wish that *emigrés* would set up trades in which their ignorance of our language and culture was less of a handicap: it would not grieve me to see Mr. Alexander Korda seated before a cottage loom in an Eastern country, following an older and a better tradition. The Quota Act has played into foreign hands, and, as far as I know, there is nothing to prevent an English film unit being completely staffed by technicians of foreign blood. We have saved the English film industry from American competition only to surrender it to a far more alien control."

Alexander Korda did not exactly boast of the fact that he was born in Pusztaturpazto, in the County of Jasznagykunszolnok, but he certainly made no attempt to disguise his Hungarian origins. He was a phenomenon, soft-spoken, charming, part adventurer, part artist, part businessman, part *boulevardier*. He had written on films in Budapest, he had directed films in Vienna, in Hollywood, in

Berlin (with the Viennese Max Reinhardt, the uncrowned king of German theatre), in Paris. In November 1931 he first landed in England, and within three months of landing he had founded his own film production company, London Films, choosing, defiantly, Big Ben as his trademark.

By 1936 Korda, and London Films, were triumphing. Korda was no aristocrat – he was the son of a bailiff and looked like one, small, rather plumpish and bespectacled. But admiration for England, and for the British Empire, were second nature to him now, and he cannot have appreciated the suggestion, brusquely enough put, that he should get back to his weaving in Eastern Europe and quit these Anglo-Saxon shores.

Graham Greene rose to his astringent peroration:

> "Watching the dark alien executive tipping his cigar ash behind the glass partition in Wardour Street, the Hungarian producer adopting Mr. Wells' ideas tactfully at Denham, the German director letting himself down into his canvas chair at Elstree, and the London film critics (I speak with humility: I am one of them) exchanging smutty stories over the hock and the iced pudding and the brandy at the Carlton, I cannot help wondering whether from this great moneyed industry anything of value to the human spirit can ever emerge."

The Spectator's film critic was making himself no friends at all in the film industry with reviews like these. On the other hand he was speaking for the little group of basically public school and university-educated documentary film-makers whom he so admired. Alberto Cavalcanti, with seventeen years film-making in Paris behind him inspired this little world – a highly civilized man; and for him (formally for the GPO Film Unit) Graham produced a very short short called *Calendar of the Year.* It was his only venture into documentary film production; a world a little too austere in fact for his taste. But it was, as it were, the first lick of the cat's tongue; and with any luck, he told Hugh, he might be able to concentrate on films and give up writing for good.

In May that year Paramount purchased the film rights to *A Gun For Sale* for $12,000 even before its publication. With that sale Graham Greene's money worries were, at last, virtually over. His social life boomed.* But his feet itched.

* Parties with Lotte Reiniger, dinners with Mrs Belloc Lowndes, drinks with Basil Wright and John Grierson, pub-crawling with Dennis Kincaid, press lunches at the Carlton, literary gossip with Charles Evans (on Francis Brett Young's most thrilling sexual experiences) with Herbert Read (on Richard Aldington's two Patmore mistresses) and with Denyse Clairouin, Graham's Paris literary agent and translator, whom he very much liked, (on James Joyce's mad daughter). He met Tom Harrison, author of *Savage Civilizations*, at the first public showing of television ever. Next day Harrison invited Greene to join him on an expedition to Papua New Guinea; Graham was very grumpy about the family responsibilities that, obviously, ruled out four-year expeditions.

In June he was writing to Hugh, proposing that they both learn Spanish and go to Spain together. Perhaps for a holiday in October? It would, Graham added quite correctly, be an excitement.

On July 7th *A Gun For Sale* was published on both sides of the Atlantic; and, with excellent sales reported, even more money was on the way. Exactly a week later the Spanish Civil War broke out. There was to be no holiday for Hugh and Graham in Spain that bitter autumn.

Not that it was impossible to get out there. Hemingway went out, Malraux went out, George Orwell went out. As early as September 16th when the first Battle for Madrid was at its height, the *Daily Worker* proudly reported on its front-page that its man-on-the-spot 'Frank Pitcairn' had joined the Steel Battalion of the 5th Regiment of the Republic's Army under his real name: Claud Cockburn. In the autumn Claud published one of the first first-hand accounts of the Civil War in book form, *Reporter in Spain*; and subsequently spent his time trying to override the Foreign Office ban on his return. Meanwhile Graham was at Midhurst in Sussex, watching cricket and suffering from boils.[★]

In September Graham launched a second broadside against a second Wells/Korda film, *The Man Who Could Work Miracles*. But it was noticeably less vitriolic than his onslaught in June. And by November he was being almost respectful to a film actually directed by Korda, of the "historical waxwork" variety he might have been expected to hate: *Rembrandt*. The change in emphasis, on the surface astounding, is less so when one knows the background. By mid-November Graham was himself on Korda's payroll, writing him an original film script of 12,000 words for £175 down, whether it was used or not; with a further salary of £125 a week for four weeks to come for work on the film should it be accepted. And it was accepted. The *bête noire* was a 'dark alien' no longer.

In his autobiography Graham Greene enters feature-films in a single dismissive sentence: "From film-reviewing it was only a small step to script-writing." I doubt it has ever been quite as easy as that for any film critic to switch *métiers*. The contact may have been John Sutro, up at Oxford with Graham, whose father Leopold Sutro the banker had been Korda's original backer and was still very much on the board of London Films.[†] But John Sutro does not yet seem to have been as great a friend of Graham Greene's as he was later to become. Possibly Korda simply used his notorious charm to entice Graham to join his stable – as he had used it on so many upper middle class or upper class Englishmen before him;

★ That, though true, is a little unfair. He still had those family responsibilities, and, of course, his job.

† Indeed on the November day that Graham gave Korda his first favourable mention, Evelyn Waugh went down to Denham Studios where, by Korda in person, he "was told of a vulgar plot about cabaret girls which he wants me to write. John Sutro motored me back to London." Unlike Graham, Evelyn proved impervious to Hungarian charm; and *Lovelies from America* was never made.

though never before on one so acidulous in his hostility.* Their first meeting must have been edgy, at least on Graham's side. His own account of it has the faint air of legend.

"When we were alone, he asked me if I had any story in mind. I had none, so I began to improvise a thriller – early morning on Platform 1 at Paddington, the platform empty, except for one man who is waiting for the last train from Wales. From below his raincoat a trickle of blood forms a pool on the platform."

The outcome in any case was positive; Graham Greene, hitherto hostile film critic, was commissioned by Alexander Korda, much-criticised film producer, to write a film story entitled *Four Dark Hours*. Thus began a great and rather astonishing friendship that was to continue, for both of them, till Korda's death. It was, in its own way, another great victory for the Hungarian and one that was to bring him profit too in the long run – though none immediately.

Film histories describe *Four Dark Hours*, justifiably, as a "sleazy little Soho thriller". Graham Greene is credited with the story alone; the script as such was written, or rewritten, by two experienced hacks, Edward O Berkman and Arthur Wimperis. There is some doubt as to who actually directed it: William Cameron Menzies or William K Howard.† In one sense it hardly mattered. *Four Dark Hours* made no-one's fame or fortune. Shot in January 1937 at Denham, just 65 minutes long, it was not released till three years later, in 1940, under the title of *The Green Cockatoo*. In 1943 it was re-issued with yet another title, *Race Gang*. In the opening scene 'Dave Connor' (played by Robert Newton) is indeed dripping blood on No. 1 Platform at Paddington, stabbed to death by racecourse gangsters whom he has double-crossed. The last title was therefore the most apposite. That was what the film story was about, gangsters, and that was what the title should also have been, *Race Gang*.

William K's previous film *Fire Over England* was released in February and reviewed in *The Spectator* a month later. Graham Greene began his review biliously enough:

* Waugh apart, Korda's stable of writers included one Prime Minister's son, Anthony Asquith, one notable peer, Lord Castlerosse, and two well-born members of the House of Commons, Oliver Stanley M.P., Lord Derby's son – and Winston Churchill M.P., the Duke of Marlborough's grandson. Winston did better than either Evelyn or Graham: he made £10,000 out of Korda for a script that was never shot.

† Probably in the chaotic but creative confusion of Denham Studios where directors and writers were switched from one project to another with bewildering speed, William K Howard completed what William Cameron Menzies had begun. William K was a man after Graham's own heart, an American who used to start the day with a teapot of whisky, who had four Zane Grey novels to his credit, and who in 1933 had had an enormous success with *The Power and The Glory*. Graham was to remember, consciously or subconsciously, both that title and the Zane Greys. As for Graham himself, the story goes that he was replaced as the scriptwriter – sacked, that is – when he tried to slip in a scene too violent for Korda's taste.

"Herr Pommer, the German director, and Mr William K Howard, the American director, of Mr Korda's great national Coronation-year picture of Elizabethan England have done one remarkable thing; they have caught the very spirit of an English public schoolmistress's vision of history." As for the story, "the distinction is between Papists who burn their prisoners in the name of religion and the honest Protestants who sail round the world and singe Philip's beard, sportsmen all. No stench from Campion's quarters offend the nostrils here."

Having launched that barb at William K (presumably as an Irish immigrant's son, a Catholic, though one who might understandably never have heard of the martyred Jesuit) Greene continues in a very different tone:

"Nevertheless this is the best production to come from Denham yet." The sets were magnificent, the direction spirited, the acting far better than was usual in English films. And: "Mr Laurence Olivier can do the hysterical type of young romantic hero with ease."

There was a barb there too all right. At the time the review was written Graham was working on his second film, an adaptation of a Galsworthy short story. Mr Laurence Olivier and Korda's new young leading lady were to star in it. This was Vivien Leigh; and during the shooting of the Galsworthy she fell in love with the 'young romantic hero' and he with her. As the story, *The First and the Last*, was a creaky melodrama, as the director was the pompous Basil Dean ("I was nicknamed 'Sugar', he later wrote, "for what reasons I know not, but the sobriquet pleased them mightily for they burst into laughter whenever they used it"), as the result would obviously be no great shakes, the loving but adulterous pair behaved with complete insouciance. To cap it all, they took off before the end of the shooting for a week's jaunt to Denmark, to play in *Hamlet* at Elsinore. Korda knew all about it. As an understandably aggrieved Basil Dean wrote, "It was a public relations exercise to please as well as to publicise the young lovers. I was certainly 'the fall guy' in that merry plan!"

Graham Greene was on the surface tolerant enough of all these goings-on; after all, he was only a year or two older than Larry, and could hardly wear a glum and moralising face. But he had given up his job at *The Spectator* (his last review appeared on May 7th) to be full-time on the set; and basically he resented the not-so-young lovers' merry antics. Years later he could still blame them for "going off for a weekend of love" and returning in "the wrong spirit".★

★ ★ ★

★ Vivien Leigh was twenty-four at the time, Laurence Olivier thirty. This film too was canned; and was also eventually released in 1940 (under the title *Twenty One Days*) when Vivien Leigh, thanks to the enormous success of *Gone With The Wind*, had become an international star of far greater drawing-power, then, than Olivier. They both, the story goes, went to see the film unofficially when it opened in America, but were so bored by it that they walked out.

Film writing, begun with such high hopes six or seven months earlier, was turning out to be a dismal dead-end. It was a particularly humiliating experience for a film critic who knew exactly how films should be written and directed in theory, to be associated, in practice, with two minor, abject, and faded, projects that had ended up canned. In anything involving his own writing Graham hated to fail. He also hated to waste anything that he had written if he could possibly find a use for it. Thus in March 1937 he found a surprisingly fruitful use for the screenplay of *Four Dark Hours.*

This is how it came about. "Portrait of A Maiden Lady" was the title Graham had chosen for a vitriolic, vigorous review of Beverley Nichols' latest literary offering. Beverley Nichols – his critic's conceit was – must be, to judge by "her" writing, a middle-aged spinster of conformist views and delicate timidity. The review, naturally enough, was noticed and chuckled over far and wide.* Meanwhile Graham was doing his bit for what he considered real literature, sending off four of RK Narayan's short stories to his agents with an enthusiastic encomium attached. Nancy Pearn replied acknowledging the short stories, congratulating him rather archly on his "latest Domestic Event"; and adding that the Editor of Nash's, by far the best-paying of magazines, had seen and admired his Beverley Nichols article and wanted to meet him.

It was back in the autumn of 1936 that Graham had met Mr Mealand, the Editor of this long-vanished magazine. In February 1938 Nancy Pearn passed on to him Graham's screen dialogue for *Four Last Hours* (which had then just been shot). A month later, on March 8th, she brought Graham excellent news; Mealand had liked the dialogue, and he wanted Graham to go ahead and write up a long/short story of 45,000 words around it, eliminating the film technique. Nash's would use it as a "one-shot" and pay £250 for the use.

And that is how, from the secondhand dialogue of a "sleazy little Soho thriller", *Brighton Rock*, generally considered to be Graham Greene's first masterpiece, came to be born.

First had come real life; Herbert, the worldly elder brother sparking off Graham's interest in the Brighton race-gangs and their favourite Soho pubs.

Then had come *A Gun For Sale*, the thriller. Graham, when he first met Korda, had not improvised the beginning of a film story, whatever he may later have thought. He had taken a little scene from *A Gun For Sale* and it was that – Raven's first murder – that he had rehashed, as the opening sequence of *Four Dark Hours.* Thriller: screenplay; screenplay: short story; short story: thriller. That was the sequence that brought Graham Greene back to writing novels again; and without the screenplay in the middle and the film's failure, and the fortunate commission from Nash's, who can say whether *Brighton Rock* would ever have been written?

* Why exactly Graham had it in for the founder of the *Oxford Outlook* is not clear. Usually in his literary 'feuds', a personal dislike of the writer, as well as of the writings, was involved.

The dying man on the railway platform, dripping blood, murdered in a race-gang war... in *A Gun For Sale* that had been Kite, leader of a rival race-gang; killed by Raven, waiting for him on the platform with a razor when the train came in. In *Four Dark Hours* it had been Connor, dying of stab-wounds inflicted by race-course gangsters whom he had double-crossed; staggering towards a phone-booth, dripping blood, to mouth a mysterious dying message about "the Green Cockatoo". In *Brighton Rock* (as Graham and Nancy Pearn soon came to call the long/short story, for of course Korda retained the rights to *Four Dark Hours* and they could hardly use the title officially) Kite is dead, and Raven is dead. But it is Kite's mob, and its struggle to dominate Brighton race-course and the Brighton protection rackets against the much more sophisticated Colleoni outfit that is at the centre of the plot.

"Hale knew, before he had been in Brighton three hours, that they meant to murder him." That is the opening line, as gripping, from the other side, that of the hunted rather than the hunter, as "Murder didn't mean much to Raven".

And the double-crossing Hale is indeed murdered, not at the railway station this time, for he knew Kite's mob would be watching it; "and it was always easy to kill a lonely man at a railway station," as Kite himself had been killed. Terrified Hale, abandoned for a moment by the blowsy good-natured Ida Arnold as, unknown to her, Kite's mob close in on that sunny banal Bank Holiday afternoon, is killed among the crowds of holiday-makers there on the waterfront.

" 'I liked Kite,' the Boy said. He stared straight outwards France, an unknown land." The 17 year-old Boy, Kite's successor, is the leader of the vicious but pathetic remnants of Kite's mob. "It had been Kite's territory, it had been good enough for Kite, and when Kite had died in the waiting room at St Pancras, it had been as if a father had died."

Not so. Raven, the murderer of *A Gun For Sale*, begat – at least in a literary sense – the Boy, the murderer of *Brighton Rock*. They are two of a kind though intriguingly different: the elder man vicious, ruthless, vengeful, self-reliant; the youth vicious, ruthless, spiteful, hesitant. Just as Raven was hunted by the police, simply; so the Boy and his pathetic 'buer', Rose, both 'Romans', are hunted by a far more relentless pursuer, Ida Arnold, and in a far more complex quest.

Graham worked fast. Instructed in early March to produce 45,000 words, he sent in 30,000, 155 pages, on April 9th. But it was no longer, for its author, just another simple 'shocker'. As he warned Nancy Pearn, there was already a great deal more to it than that. Religion, ethics, their contradictory nature... She was not, however, to scare off Nash's with a word of this!

It may have scared them off. Certainly the planned 'one-shot' magazine thriller had very quickly turned into a much more complex undertaking, with overtones and undertones of moral theology that seem almost designed to baffle the characters involved, the reading public, the critics and indeed, very possibly in the end even their author. By the late summer of 1937 there were difficulties over publication; and finally, in September, Graham had to accept a cheque for only £60 and the return of his manuscript, unpublished. He had to set the story aside too – by then of course it was swelling way over the 45,000 word mark towards full novel length – and concentrate, for six months that might have become a lifetime, on a full-time job and a new career. But the potential novel was already *en route* to success. For, no sooner had the 'one-shot' been rejected by Nash's, than Graham Greene's agents sent the typescript off to Heinemann's.

Chapter XIV

Blood of the Martyrs

"*To the Writers and Poets of England, Scotland, Ireland and Wales*" read the questionnaire sent out in early 1937 by Nancy Cunard and signed by her and eleven intellectuals or writers, including Aragon, Auden and Spender.

> "This is the question we are asking you:
> Are you for, or against, the legal government and
> the People of Republican Spain?
> Are you for, or against, Franco and Fascism?
> For it is impossible any longer to take no sides.
> Writers and Poets, we wish to print your answers."

And, sure enough, the answers were printed, and published, before the end of the year.

Naturally almost all of the writers and poets were pro-the People and against Fascism; they included a great number of Graham Greene's friends and acquaintances, ranging from Herbert Read and Antonia White via Cyril Connolly to writers such as Ford Madox Ford and Aldous Huxley, whom he admired. As the preface to a recent book subtitled 'Writers on the Civil War' puts it, "the absence of Graham Greene from the survey has long intrigued". Indeed it has, even after more than fifty years. There is no suggestion that Graham Greene was not sent the questionnaire. He was one of the more prominent members of the younger London-based intelligentsia; and his books were decidedly left-wing, anti-Fascist, in tone and sympathy. Even his most recent thriller had had a suitably vicious and capitalistic arms manufacturer as its principal villain: and more serious previous novels such as *It's A Battlefield* had been sympathetic to the Party; and critical only of its ineffectiveness in England, which most certainly was not a fault with which it could be reproached in Spain. Graham Greene was an obvious name on the long and distinguished "For the Government" list.

But his name did not appear. He did not, like James Joyce say "No! I won't answer it because it is politics. Now politics are getting into everything." It would have been most unconvincing if he had, in view of his intense interest in politics. He did not, like a handful of famous authors, adopt a rigidly neutral stance – just as well, for if he had done so, he would have found himself in the uncomfortable company of HG Wells for whom the real enemy of mankind "is not the Fascist but the Ignorant Fool" – just the sort of block-headed Wellsian truism he had so taken against in his film criticism. And he did not, like Evelyn Waugh, point out that the questions were loaded: "As an Englishman I am not in the predicament of choosing between two evils… It is mischievous to suggest that such a choice is imminent". No, Graham Greene backed away from the issue by not answering the questionnaire at all. And, even more evasively, when he came to review the published results, the questions and answers, in a December issue of *The Spectator*, he made no comment whatsoever on the Spanish Civil War or on the opinions, right or wrong, of so many of his contemporaries and fellow-writers. He simply used "the publication of the little booklet *Authors Take Sides*" as a peg on which to hang a long piece of about 1200 words on "an earlier group of English writers who intervened in Spain a hundred years ago"; and thus to re-tell the tale of *The Episode*, General Torrijos, and Carlyle, Sterling and his doomed cousin Robert Boyd, throwing in the Cambridge Apostles,* Tennyson and Hallam, as the link. The article, totally irrelevant to the Spanish Civil War, and not even pretending to draw useful parallels, must have infuriated all those readers (and writers) who were expecting from Graham Greene at least some indication of his own political views and standpoint.

What needs to be understood, though, if any sense is to be made out of this rather queasy and, to be fair, untypically passive episode, is the acute embarrassment of Graham Greene's position. He was a left-wing intellectual, widely known as such, and therefore expected automatically to be anti-Franco and pro-the Spanish republic. But it was much less widely known that he was a Catholic. And, because of his intensely private nature, it can have been barely realized at all – except among the (very limited) readership of *The Tablet* – that he was in fact going through a Catholic phase that, ten years after he had actually joined the Church, amounted, almost, to a second conversion.†

There was however no question of Graham Greene taking an overtly pro-Fascist or pro-Franco stand, like Waugh and so many of the other Catholic writers

* Which must have appealed to the Cambridge Apostle Anthony Blunt who was also writing for *The Spectator* as Art Critic; and whose pro-Marxist sympathies were not concealed. Kim Philby on the other hand, Greene's future superior, was reporting for *The Times* on the Fascist side; and was indeed to be decorated by the Generalissimo in person.

† There are numerous indications of this in Graham Greene's private letters and diaries of the period; which unfortunately cannot, for the legal reasons explained in the Preface to this book, be quoted here. But see below, pp 132-133 for the arguments supporting this theory

of *The Tablet* group* when, precisely by Franco and his supporters, thousands of workers and intellectuals were being executed. It would have gone against the grain of his whole life, and all his writings, to date. It would have been intellectual high treason.

But equally there could be no question of him rejoining the Party, of fighting *à la Malraux* with the International Brigades or even supporting the Spanish republic that was guilty of permitting the massacre of thousands of still more defenceless bishops, priests and nuns. His was an impossible situation. Right-wing Catholic intellectuals fell automatically into line on one side, left-wing Protestant or agnostic intellectuals in far greater numbers on the other. But for left-wing Catholic intellectuals, faced with such a stark 'no quarter' conflict, the only real solution was to keep quiet, lie low and, no doubt, thank God that they were not born Spanish.

★ ★ ★

In fact Graham Greene did make one attempt to see for himself the fighting in Spain. It was certainly in 1937, almost certainly in the second half of May, and his aim, logically enough, was to join and report on the only Spaniards whose viewpoint more or less coincided with his own. Equipped by the Basque Delegation in London of President Aguirre's Catholic but Republican Government with a beautifully-sealed *laissez-passer* and the address of their contact in Toulouse, Graham caught a 5 a.m. train down from Paris – only to find at Toulouse that the Basque agent, *le patron* of a small bar, was unwilling to fly him across to Bilbao† because such flights had now become too dangerous. So our hero returned disconsolately to London, dreaming of Merle Oberon, Korda's leading lady, as he dozed fitfully on the wooden third-class seats on the long way back.

This seems a pretty half-hearted attempt; and it contrasts only too dramatically with Herbert Greene's. Herbert got out to Spain during the first nine months of 1937 not once but three times; and how Hugh and Graham metaphorically grind their teeth when they learn at the end of the year that Herbert is about to produce a book on his melodramatic on-the-spot experiences; when neither Hugh, the

* Is this unfair to Waugh? "I am not a Fascist nor shall I become one unless it were the only alternative to Marxism," he had added. However he had just published *Waugh in Abyssinia*. Its hymn of praise in the last chapter to Mussolini's noble road-builders bringing civilisation to the barbaric Abyssinians makes embarrassing reading even now. "A pro-Fascist tract," Rose Macaulay dubbed it.

† Despite the "Ring of Steel" Bilbao fell to Franco's troops on June 17th; so Graham Greene's attempted visit must obviously have been before that date. A Foreign Office file headed "Mr Graham Greene : Visit to Bilbao" was dated March. It has been "weeded". Probably however it refers to an approach by him asking for advice before his trip.

reporter, nor Graham, the writer, have as much as set foot in the arena where, it seemed at the time, all Europe's future, and England's too, was being decided.

"I am warning you, Greene," said a very high official seated in a small room in the British Admiralty overlooking Horse Guards Parade, "that if you are not more careful you will one day find yourself in the Thames." At first reading Herbert's book, *Secret Agent in Spain*, seems the most incredible mish-mash. He is working for a mysterious employer in London, known only as Y, with an office in Great Tower Street. One begins to wonder whether in fact Herbert, like the mythopoeic Anthony in *England Made Me*, had not simply made the whole thing up. But then the little details begin to become convincing; the meetings with Henry Buckley of *The Daily Telegraph* and Sefton Delmer of the *Express* in Madrid, the description of the Victoria Hotel in Valencia, the dedication to the Dean of Rochester, who had married Hugh and Helga, was a friend of cousin Charlie Fry, Curate at St. Luke's Maidenhead, and had been out in Republican Spain at the same time. It cannot all be invented. Even the very high official in the British Admiralty – after all, that was exactly what Uncle Graham had once been, and no doubt Uncle Graham had retained his contacts with Naval Intelligence.

Besides, there is an engaging modesty and self-deprecation about Herbert's writing that carries the ring of truth. On his third and final trip in June, he ships his Morris Eight via the AA across from Newhaven to Dieppe, and decides to take his wife and her sister down on a pleasure spin as far as the French frontier; from where he proceeds on with "Stanley Carr, an old Army friend". In Barcelona he runs out of money, and has to call on the Anglo-South American Bank to tide him over. It sounds typically Herbert. There are no hair-raising escapes, or near-captures by the insurgents, or even sights of the battlefield. As for what he actually did, who precisely he spied on, or even whom for, he is understandably discreet and modest. "I do not even know," he writes, "for whom my employers were working." And again, in an epilogue to Mrs Haden Guest who had written to him: "Since reading your book, I have learnt that you were a secret agent of Franco," he replies, very reasonably: "Mrs Guest may have more information thanI have myself. I have no direct contact *to my knowledge* with any agents of Franco. There are many countries today interested in Spain, apart from the two sides to the dispute." There is, admittedly, a mysterious X in Madrid, of whom Herbert has his suspicions. In London he reports – it seems that no more than Graham could he resist the chance of acting as a double agent to the Second Secretary of the Spanish Embassy "useful information" (not specified) "with regard to another party of espionage agents with whom I had been in contact." But he is always loyal to Y, to whom he transmits coded documents from Tarragona and Madrid. All we learn of the mysterious Y is that "he is neither a Spaniard nor a Jap". But those who have read the book do not doubt that Herbert did go to Spain, that Y did exist, and that the author was, if not exactly a Secret Agent, at least a courier.

Secret Agent In Spain was written by Herbert at his Sussex cottage in October/November 1937, published by Robert Hale early the next year and well-reviewed by the critics. "The story is amusing and exciting and told with great frankness," said the *TLS*. In *The Spectator* John Marks recommended it "as having the puzzling appeal of a detective slice of real life". And to the readers of *The Daily Telegraph* Malcolm Muggeridge explained that: "These journeys led Mr Greene into a variety of adventures which he describes with zest".

Twenty years later Hugh and Graham played Herbert, as if in delayed revenge, a rather mocking trick. They compiled, and published under their names, an anthology of spy stories entitled *The Spy's Bedside Book*. It included one entry from *Secret Agent in Spain*. They headed it "A Spy Advertises"; and they chose not any of the rather good stories or incidents that Herbert had described in the body of his book, but an unfortunate late-entry Foreword that he added somewhat hysterically just before publication.

"To anyone whom it might concern:" it read. "I think it advisable to state that I have no documents of any importance in my own possession in connection with any other country or work I have undertaken. I am making this statement as, on January 4th 1938, a friend and I left a certain Embassy in London. We were followed to Victoria Station, where I caught the 5.35 train. From there on, my memory is a blank until I found myself in hospital the following morning. Some papers of mine were missing. I will let the *Mid-Sussex Times* complete the story:

> **Accident in Mid-Sussex.**
>
> Mr W.H. Greene, of Oak Cottage, Plumpton, is in the Haywards Heath Hospital suffering from head injuries sustained in a motor-accident at Plumpton last week. He was found lying unconscious near his damaged car.
>
> *Herbert Greene*

To anyone reading this anthology (it was reissued in 1984) the inclusion of this apparently pointless little story must seem baffling. Herbert was understandably both furious and disappointed that this was what his two younger brothers had chosen to quote.

* * *

1935 had been for Graham a very good year: tremendous changes of scene – what with Liberia, then the move to London, then the new job and the films – and great bursts of creative writing combined. 1936 had been a very successful year financially, thanks mainly to Paramount and to the generalized success of

A Gun For Sale; and had not been a bad year for the paterfamilias either. But 1937 was proving most frustrating. Greenes were on the move everywhere, not just Herbert to Spain, but Barbara off to Estonia, driving out in her Austin Seven to Kallijärv, the Benckendorff summer lakeside house, with – how things tied up! – Tania, Moura's daughter.* But Graham was kicking his heels in London, or, at best, – in third-class trains to and from Toulouse, a frustrated film-maker, a bored film-critic, a novel-writer *malgré lui*, tied down by his household and his house and his responsibilities when he knew exactly where he wanted to be. He wanted to be in Mexico. And why did he want to be in Mexico? He knew exactly why he wanted to be in Mexico – because they were persecuting Catholics there, and he wanted to go out, see for himself and write a book about the persecution.

It had all begun, I think, with Evelyn Waugh's book on the martyred Elizabethan Jesuit Edmund Campion. Being Waugh's, it was a highly polemical account deliberately designed to infuriate the Protestants.† It came out in the autumn of 1935 – the chronology, the sequence, is rather important for the theory – and Graham reviewed it in *The Spectator* on November 1st. It was, he wrote, "a model of what a short biography should be. Sensitive and vivid, it catches the curious note of gaiety and gallantry,… of an adventure which, in spite of the end of Tyburn, was never sombre."

Waugh was delighted with this review. He took *Campion* very seriously indeed, more seriously than his novels or travel books, and such delicate praise was balm indeed. From this moment can be dated the real beginnings of Evelyn's warm feelings for Graham and his always affectionate, though sometimes pleading, friendship.

As for Graham Greene, there can be absolutely no doubt that the book affected

* And they were all writing books about their adventures too. Barbara's book on Liberia, *Land Benighted*, was in fact not to be published till 1938. In 1981, when it was republished (under a new and more tactful title *Too Late To Turn Back*), she explains, in a fascinating Introduction, that she had never had any intention of writing a book at all; but Uncle Eppy when ill had enjoyed her reading extracts out of her diary; and when, quite by chance, "the manuscript fell into the hands of a publisher", he had "insisted on bringing it out exactly as I had written it".

This explanation carries almost as little conviction as Graham's remark (in his later Introduction) that he had never noticed, on the trek, Barbara making notes at all. For Barbara was determined to make her name too and become a writer (as indeed, later on in her life, she did – *God of a Hundred Names* is her best-known book, an "instant bestseller"). She had had an article on Liberia printed in the *Daily Chronicle*. She never refers to this, or other, journalistic results of her trip. But they certainly impressed Mr Yapp, Our Man in Monrovia, who in his November 1935 "Summary of the Last Eighteen Months" to the FO peevishly complained of her "stupid and unnecessary reference to the President's clothes being aired on the balcony of the Mansion House." "We are all obliged to do this here," he added.

† The Protestant Truth Society attacked it in a letter to *The Listener*, and Rose Macaulay was to condemn it for "its excessive hostility to the Anglican church". Waugh must have chortled with glee.

him immensely. His future writings were to show, again and again, how great an impression upon him the tale of Campion, and his martyrdom, had made. It was as if Evelyn Waugh had introduced him to a certain side of English Catholicism, the blood and the suffering, that he had never, with his traditional, rather patriotic, liberal and therefore anti-Catholic upbringing, known about, and certainly not visualized before. His wife would have been too squeamish to instruct him in the horrors suffered by the English Martyrs. From the Blood of the Martyrs springs the Faith of the Church. The notion cast its appeal.

That February Graham Greene had been at death's door, always a shaking experience, often with a delayed effect. At Zigi's Town, Heaven, Hell, Death and Judgement – the 'Four Last Things' of the penny catechism – had loomed. In November came Greene's realization of the heroic nature of the English Catholic past, and of the bloody persecution, the rack, the trials, the hangings, the cutting-down and disembowellings while still conscious, the castrations and the quarterings that Elizabethan Catholics like Edmund Campion or Robert Southwell or John Gerard or scores of other priests infiltrated across the Channel had to face; and of how, voluntarily, almost gaily, these young men had crossed the Channel to meet an almost certain death.

And now, three hundred and fifty years later, the same thing was happening in Mexico. Greene was to fasten particularly on the story of Father Miguel Pro, like Campion a young man and a Jesuit. "He came back to his own country from a foreign seminary," Greene was to write, "much as Campion returned to England. We know how he was dressed when a year and a half later he came out into the prison yard to be shot, and he may have worn the same disguise when he landed (the equivalent of Campion's doublet and hose): a dark lounge suit, soft collar and tie, a bright cardigan. Most priests wear their mufti with a kind of uneasiness, but Pro was a good actor. He needed to be. Within two months of Pro's landing President Calles had begun the fiercest persecution of religion anywhere since the reign of Elizabeth."

Never mind the last wildly untenable generalization. Greene is writing as an apologist, not as a world historian. And what is clear is that his frame of mind by the end of 1935 – that is to say *before* the Spanish Civil War, with all its killings of priests, bishops and nuns had begun – was already so exalted, almost, that Frank Sheed, the Catholic publisher, obviously saw in young Greene the man to go out to Mexico and write a book about the persecution of the Church there.

It had however been ten years since Father Pro had landed at Vera Cruz; and it was only in the southern State of Tabasco, ruled by Garrido Canabal and his Red Shirts, that the persecution was still in full swing, with masses forbidden, churches raised, priests, when caught, put up against the wall and shot. It was to dangerous Tabasco, therefore, that Graham planned to go. It would, Graham warned Hugh without trepidation, be far, far worse in every way than Liberia.

Money was the difficulty. Sheed and Ward were a small firm, and Graham wanted £500 in advance to cover his travelling and writing expenses. Negotiations had begun in early 1936; half-way, that is, between the appearance of the Campion review and the outbreak of the Spanish Civil War. They dragged on inconclusively through 1936 and well into 1937. The trouble was that, by 1937, Graham was torn two ways. He wanted to go to Mexico, but his new American publishers, Viking, wouldn't back him, wouldn't put up the £250 necessary. And meanwhile, much more concretely, he was in the running for a new job; the literary editorship, as he told Hugh, exaggerating somewhat, of a new and potentially immensely successful magazine.

He plumped for the magazine. Who could blame him?

* * *

*Night and Day** was incorporated on April 1st, launched with a party at the Dorchester on June 30th, and appeared in print for the first time on July 1st. "Looking back on it," noted 'Slingsby', the chatty editorialist, in the second issue a week later, "the publication of the first number was a pretty hectic business... Our colleagues, haggard and unshaved, were for ever slumping forward on their desks with a groan, and we didn't feel too good ourself... Somebody kept on ringing us solely in order, when the telephone girl said 'Night and Day,' to reply 'You are the one'."

'Slingsby' was Peter Fleming; and among his haggard colleagues were John Marks, the editor, who had been the *New Statesman's* film critic, and Graham Greene, in effect the assistant editor, who had of course been *The Spectator's* film critic. They got on extremely well; and at first *Night and Day* seemed set for a brilliant, flippant future. The list of contributors who were roped in reads like a roll-call of contemporary English literature: Anthony Powell, Cyril Connolly, Antonia White, John Hayward, Malcolm Muggeridge and Hugh Kingsmill of course, Herbert Read, AJA Symons, VS Pritchett, John Betjeman, Christopher Sykes and even (thanks to Graham: his was the only short story ever to be published) RK Narayan. But the best of the writing appeared in three regular full page columns: Elizabeth Bowen on the theatre, Evelyn Waugh on books,† and Graham Greene on the cinema.

Graham returned to film criticism with all his usual vigour, praising (in the first issue) the "absurd heroics" of *We From Kronstadt*; and even awarding London

* The original idea for a "critically humorous" *New Yorker*-style magazine in London had come from Malcolm Muggeridge and his great friend, the ebullient Hugh Kingsmill. They had taken out an ad on the front page of *The Times*, proposing as its title *The Porcupine*.

† Graham had at first hoped that Evelyn Waugh would do the theatre. But on April 17th Waugh had married Laura Herbert, catholically; (John Sutro and Douglas Woodruff were invited to the wedding, but not, apparently, the Greenes), and, as Lady de Vesci had given the couple as a wedding present Piers

Films a splendid mixture of praise and blame for producing, instead of "the traditional Denham mouse", "a first-class thriller, beautifully directed, with... a nearly watertight scenario (only marred by a bath and bathe in the Naughty Wimperis* vein)". But the American studios were getting distinctly uptight with the impassioned Mr Greene. MGM cannot have liked his memorable description of their star, Jean Harlow, of the "restless shoulders and the protuberant breasts; her technique was the gangster's technique – she toted a breast like a man totes a gun". That appeared at the end of August, and as Miss Harlow had died before the film (*Saratoga*) was finished, it was not in the best of taste.

Worse, much worse from MGM's point of view, was to follow. In September *Film Lunch* appeared; and it began as wickedly as it was to continue:

"If ever there was a Christ-like man in human form it was Marcus Lowe.

"Under the huge Union Jack, the Stars and Stripes, the massed chandeliers of the Savoy, the little level Jewish voice softly intones. It is Mr Louis B Mayer, head of Metro-Goldwyn-Mayer, and the lunch is being held to celebrate the American company's decision to produce films in this country. Money, one can't help seeing it written on the literary faces, money for jam: but Mr Mayer's words fall on the mercenary gathering with apostolic seriousness."

There are swipes at all the bigwigs there: Hugh Walpole, Maureen O'Sullivan, Robert Taylor, Frank Swinnerton, an old target, Ivor Novello, even Korda. Graham Greene was no longer in the business of making any friends. Then, in his final paragraph, the bitterness of almost six wasted months rings out.

"He has spoken for forty minutes: for forty minutes we have listened to the voice of American capital itself... money for no thought, for the banal situation and the inhuman romance: money for forgetting how other people live: money for 'Siddown, won't yer' and 'I love, I love, I love' endlessly repeated. Inside the voice goes on – 'God... I Pray...' and the writers, a little stuffed and a little boozed, lean back and dream of the hundred pounds a week – and all that's asked in return, the dried imagination and the dead pen."

A savage, flailing Old Testament attack.

But in their turn the indignant followers of Baal were girding up their loins, poised to smite down this upstart scribbler.

The Moguls were on the war path.

★ ★ ★

Court in Gloucestershire, Waugh was stuck in the country and could not "do" the London theatres. In fact he turned out to be such an excellent book reviewer, so surprisingly sympathetic even to the authors most antipathetic to him, that his reviews alone would make *Night and Day* worth re-reading.

* Graham had taken a strong personal dislike to Arthur Wimperis, the namby-pamby script writer of *Four Dark Hours*; and could never resist having a crack at him now that aliens and Hungarians were, almost, off the target list.

October was a month of evil presage for Graham. It was the month in which an exasperated Frank Sheed warned the agency that unless Graham Greene got out to Mexico very soon, the religious persecution might well be over; in which case the proposed book would lose its value, and the whole project become pointless. Frustrated, at the end of his tether, Graham launched his blistering October 14th broadside on Louis B Mayer, MGM and the corrupting effect of the cinema in general; and then, two weeks later, played into his enemies' hands with his notorious October 28th review of *Wee Willie Winkie*. Pritt KC, *Night and Day*'s legal adviser, had stated "unequivocally" that it could be published without risk. He could not have been more wrong.

November began badly, and went from bad to worse. On November 1st a Board meeting was held. *Night and Day* was not attracting enough advertising; and the Managing Director, Ian Parsons, announced bad news: that unless £8000 of new capital could be raised, the magazine would have to fold. Next, the transatlantic potentates struck, not in fact in the shape of MGM, but in that of Twentieth Century Fox. They had, their lawyers claimed, been grossly insulted, accused of "procuring" their child star, the Nation's darling, Miss Shirley Temple, for "immoral purposes". Her "swaggering stride" indeed; "her neat and well-developed rump," "her dimpled depravity," forsooth; her "antique audience" of "middle-aged men and clergymen" responding to her "well-shaped and desirable little body", outrageous; "a complete totsy": the summing-up! Writs for libel went flying out against the printers, the publishers, the magazine itself; and the author of the article in question, Mr. Graham Greene.

"I suppose," wrote Anthony Powell in his memoirs, "a case might exist for considering Greene's notice 'bad box-office', but, even at that distant period, the notion that children neither had nor could express sexual instincts was, to say the least, an uninstructed one." This relaxed view certainly did not appeal to legal circles (Pritt KC excepted) and most certainly not to Lord Hewart, the Lord Chief Justice, who – it is the Lord Chief Justice's privilege – decided to reserve the case for his own court and his own judgement.

Hewart had been Lord Chief Justice, appointed by his crony Lloyd-George, since Graham Greene went up to Oxford. He was caustic, ironic, bullying, snappy, ill-tempered, and by 1937 getting noticeably worse. "Counsel for the appellant has raised six points in support of this appeal," he adjudged on one occasion. "In the first point there is nothing, and the same applies to the others. Five times nothing are nothing. The appeal is dismissed." Even without having read Graham Greene's comment on him in his private diary*, Hewart was obviously out for

* By one of those extraordinary foreboding coincidences that seem to punctuate Graham Greene's life, he had, a decade earlier when he was first in London, been taken by Eric Guest, a pupil barrister at the time, on a tour of the law courts; and had listened with utter repulsion to Hewart in the Court of Appeal. His description of Hewart's voice, manners and physical appearance is

blood, remembering how Oscar Wilde, an equally immoral young writer, had been demolished, for all his wit and bumptiousness, in the law-courts.

He must therefore have been bitterly disappointed when the libel action was settled by agreement. The terms were stiff: Shirley Temple was to receive £2,000 and Twentieth Century Fox £1,500 (£500 to be paid by Mr Graham Greene personally) for what the plaintiffs' counsel, Sir Patrick Hastings,† stated in the High Court, without contradiction, was "one of the most horrible libels one could well imagine" printed in "this beastly publication". He could not possibly read "this beastly libel" out in open court.

The defendants had hired not the misguided Pritt but Mr Valentine Holmes and, for the printers, Mr Theobald Mathew. Tendering his deepest apologies "on behalf of" (*inter alios*) "Mr Graham Greene", Mr. Holmes told His Lordship that there was no justification for the criticism of the film, which, his clients instructed him, was one to which anybody could take their children. (True enough: a subtly Greenian defence, perhaps. The point at issue was whether it was one to which any children could take their fathers.)

> "His Lordship – (Continued *The Times* Law Report) –
> Who is the author of this article?
> Mr Holmes – Mr Graham Greene
> His Lordship – Is he within the jurisdiction?
> Mr Holmes – I am afraid I do not know, my Lord."

Hewart tried again with the printers' barrister.

> "His Lordship – Can you tell me where Mr Greene is?
> Mr. Mathew – I have no information on the subject."

This sort of bland evasion is not calculated to soothe even the mildest judge's breast. Breathing flames, Hewart declared "This libel is simply a gross outrage" before assenting, as he was obliged to – High Court declarations of settlement of libels are a mere formality – to the settlement on the terms announced. But he went on to promise, savagely, that he would "take care" to have "suitable attention" brought to the matter. This was nothing less than a barely veiled threat to have Graham Greene personally prosecuted, and jailed, for criminal libel.

vivid and nauseating; but cannot, alas, for legal reasons be printed here. One feels almost that Hewart must have read it; but that of course is impossible. If he had done, that would explain, indeed almost justify, his venom. Clairvoyance?

† "Less sanctimonious at his own table," writes Anthony Powell of Sir Patrick, "where I had dined as a young man."

But where *was* Graham Greene, meanwhile? Lurking in disguise somewhere in The Strand, shielding his well-known features with hat-brim and scarf, like Raven his hare-lip? No, the missing man of mystery, whose whereabouts none of his own lawyers seemed to know, was at that particular moment way out of the jurisdiction; deep, at last and very wisely, in the wilds of Mexico.

Chapter XV

Alone in Hateful Mexico

Lawyers' conferences, serving of writs, statements of claim, pleas, rejoinders, backstairs negotiations: lawsuits do not occur overnight nor do legal settlements. So it was not till March 22nd 1938, that is to say almost five months after the Shirley Temple libel had been published, that the Lord Chief Justice assented to the terms of the settlement in the High Court.

And by then *Night and Day* had in any case ceased publication, its twenty-sixth and final issue having appeared on December 23rd. The magazine had lasted precisely six months. Graham was out of a job, that bleak Christmas; and, worse still, the Mexico project was off. Garrido Canabal had been driven out of Tabasco to exile in Costa Rica; the Red Shirts disappeared; and the persecution ceased. As Frank Sheed wrote to Graham's agents, "I am afraid therefore we shall have to drop it. It seems particularly unfortunate that the editorship of *Night and Day* should have prevented him going when we had arranged, and then proved impermanent." Sentiments that Graham could only miserably echo.

A ray of hope appeared in January: a splendid idea (or so it seemed to Graham) for a joint book on the Palestine Civil War with Malcolm Muggeridge, Graham to cover the Arabs, Malcolm to cover the Jews, both to meet up at the Holy Sepulchre. Muggeridge was delighted with the idea; at Heinemann's Graham tried to interest AS Frere, Charles Evans' joint managing editor and eventual successor. Frere was more Graham's type of person, a man of the world, a clubman, with a rather disreputable love life; and from this time on he was to become the man Graham Greene mainly dealt with at Heinemann's and one of his greatest friends and supporters. But on this particular occasion he was adamant – publishers were fighting shy of Muggeridge. Heinemann's would put no money up, either for Palestine or indeed for Mexico. What Heinemann's wanted was *Brighton Rock* completed and delivered; not its author disappearing into the blue.

Disconsolately, hating it all, finding the last 5,000 words more hellish to write than he had ever found any novel's ending to be before, his nerves in shreds, his future bleak,* Graham Greene gritted his teeth, and immersed himself in the joyless woes of Pinkie ("the Boy") and the dreadful joyful sins of Rosie, his girl; the morality of suicide, loveless sex, death-bed repentance, belief in Satan, despair and marriage *extra Ecclesiam*; the Jansenist theology of *Corruptio Optimi Pessima*; and the key *dictum* of the old priest in the final confessional (the first of Greene's fictional priests to be portrayed with any sympathy and the last till *Monsignor Quixote*, that work of his old age, to be in his professional role both understanding and effective): "You can't conceive, my child, nor can I or anyone the... appalling... strangeness of the mercy of God."

* * *

Then, just as he finished *Brighton Rock*, as if by miracle the clouds vanished and a golden lining appeared. David Mathew, a friend, a Balliol man, a priest and an historian,† was sure the Mexico book was still worth doing. Tom Burns, also a contemporary and a Catholic, had left Sheed and Ward to join Longmans; and had just published *Waugh in Abyssinia*. He was prepared, on Longman's behalf, to back Graham's Mexican project to the tune of £200. And suddenly, across the Atlantic, Mary Pritchett (who had now become his American agent) did her stuff, Viking ante'ed up, and Graham was off to New York at a week's notice, en route to Texas and Mexico; back, he hoped, in the middle of May.

He sailed out on the *Normandie* in early February; and he took Vivien with him. She needed a break from the two young children at 14 North Side, though obviously there could be no question of her taking weeks or months off to travel through Mexico with her husband. Besides, even if she had not had her family responsibilities, it would not have been in her character to do so. The plan was that she would make her own way home from New Orleans. To visit America in those days was still an expedition, and still a thrill. Vivien obviously adored every moment of it, and most particularly, perhaps, adored the fact that she had been invited to go with him by her husband.

"Dearest darling love," she wrote to Graham at the end of February from the

* Twentieth-Century Fox, he was persuaded, was trying to ruin him as a film-critic, have him blacklisted and broken. As for the horrid little Shirley Temple, she would cost him, he told Hugh, £250 at least (in fact it was to be twice as much). But all the same Hugh should go and see her in *Captain January*, her best film.

† David Mathew, the elder of two brothers, both at Balliol and both priests, was just about to become in 1938 Titular Bishop of Aetia and Auxiliary Bishop of Westminster. After the War, as Apostolic Visitor to Abyssinia, he wrote a book, *Ethiopia*, that was a much-needed Catholic counterblast to Waugh's slurs, which are still resented by Ethiopians to this day. But it was his younger brother Gervase, a freshman in Greene's final year at Balliol, by 1934 a Dominican priest and by 1939 Dean of Blackfriars at Oxford, who was Graham's real friend. It was to Gervase that he dedicated his eventual Mexican book.

airport at New Orleans – he had just left the day before for Texas and San Antonio – "I did love it so. I wanted to tell you at once how dear you are and how happy I've been with you for years and years and years and especially on this trip and the bits in New York you wrote of. It's funny that with me the strangeness of it all, and loveliness of being with you are almost concentrated in the Yama tea-room and seeing Rockefeller Centre in the dark with the skaters."

On and on her letter goes – one of the few from her to Graham that has survived – chatty, observant, written with a painter's eye for the colours of the scene outside her hotel window, illustrated with little sketches, naturally affectionate.

"After I saw you go away, dear heart, yesterday, I got two newspapers and a taxi to Canal Street (long dêtour because of crowds) and got a *most* curious silver or nickel brooch for Aunt Nono, representing one of the seven wonders of the world (Temple of Ephesus). The thing in front is a statue and there are two temples with columns in relief, but the funny thing is it has no back – between the columns you see the dress like this" (there are two drawings here in the margin).

"An old lady said briskly 'Ha! You an artist?' I said 'No, I'm just writing a letter.' 'Uh-oh. Wish I was as capable. Would you give me some notepaper?' So I gave her some. 'And an envelope, dear.' And away she went. (I expect her to return shortly for a p.c.)."

Vivien was never a negligible quantity. And her letters to Graham are, as letters, more readable, more varied, more full of incident, more naturally loving and, if no less long, a lot less heavy going than his to her. Also she evidently had a sense of fun which Graham did not. Graham paid tribute to her memories in his eventual book when he lay in southern Mexico in a hammock surrounded by snuffling pigs thinking "with longing of New York" – of Rockefeller Plaza "rising in icicles of steel towards the sky", the ice-skaters under the stars, and not the Yama tearooms indeed but, more upmarketly, "tea at the Waldorf, the little saucers of cinnamon sticks and cherries". Of course he did not mention that his companion had been his wife, any more than Barbara had been mentioned in the Liberia book. He liked to give the impression that he travelled alone.

And this time he was indeed going to travel alone; and in fact he hated it. He had tried to persuade Hugh to come with him, but the *Daily Telegraph* would not give Hugh leave. And Weston of the *Daily Telegraph* when approached by Graham's agents about a possible series of articles was "not very interested", especially as events in Central Europe were now beginning to dominate the news.

So he left Vivien in New Orleans; and on Saturday February 26th 1938 caught a train to Texas, to the city of San Antonio. His journey, properly speaking, had begun.

★ ★ ★

In one way the whole three months' trip can be plotted on a religious basis, from church to church, from Mass to Mass; almost from priest to priest. Even in New York Catholicism had been so much on his mind that when he called on Paul Rotha at the Museum of Modern Art's new Film Library he mistook Grand Central Station (which Rotha's office overlooked) for St. Patrick's Cathedral. Tom Burns had wanted his book to be, in style, "unofficial and quite personal". But its subject-matter was clearly defined: to present conditions in Mexico "with a special eye to the religious situation"; and Graham Greene, with his usual highly professional approach, took this brief extremely seriously.

So he was passed from hand to hand all down the line, beginning with the "old fiery half-blind Archbishop" and Catholic Action in San Antonio. He went to Mass in the tiny Cathedral there where the bones of the heroes of the Alamo are buried. "Did you Bob etc. to the Archbishop," Vivien wondered. "Or yammer and forget?" He went to a meeting in the park Father Lopez was organizing on behalf of Catholic Action, a strike of the pecan workers against their miserable wages. But it was all a little staid. "Catholicism, one felt, had to rediscover the technique of revolution," he later wrote describing the scene; a sentiment which he was to echo all his life. The Communists were later to take over the strike, and Father Lopez, outmanoeuvred, retired: "There was something a little pathetic about Catholic Action in San Antonio."

But the Alamo itself, the great heroic monument of San Antonio, monastery/fort preserved in the heart of the city, he did not visit. He ought to have done. By rights Mexico should have been one of the three vast North American Nations rather than very much the undersized poor relation of the demi-continent, half pitied and half despised. Graham Greene never really got the hang of this. Like all serious visitors to Mexico, he was to be bewildered by the nationalistic inferiority complex that turns so easily to xenophobia, and repelled by the incessant, almost pathological, propaganda in favour of the Mexican Revolution.

So Graham Greene hated Mexico, without really understanding why. He loathed the country and he loathed the climate and he loathed the food, and generally speaking he loathed the people. He got on fairly well with the priests and bishops he met, though always with an undercurrent of unease. "I have never been in a country where you are more aware all the time of hate," he was to write. Cruelty, treachery, fake emotions, false bonhomie – he was hardly to have words too harsh for the Mexicans.

It was not so to start with. From San Antonio he took a lift to the border, to Laredo; crossed the Rio Grande Bridge by taxi, and spent the night on the Mexican side, in Nuevo Laredo. From there he caught a train to the great northern city of Monterrey; in Monterrey he went to Mass at the cathedral. It was Ash Wednesday, the beginning of Lent. Hundreds were queueing up to receive the ashes, old peasant women were following the Stations of the Cross; and there and then, "on the strength of a happy mood, I was ready to think of Mexico in terms of quiet and gentleness and devotion".

★ ★ ★

San Luis Potosi was also " a lovely town"; it still is. It lies pretty nearly half-way between Monterrey and Mexico City on the direct train route. But then as now few foreigners stop off at it; then as now the hotels were – are – dirty and cheap. Then, as now, at the Cathedral peasants in from the country "kneel in their blue dungarees and hold out their arms, minute after minute, in the attitude of crucifixion". Then as now there is Benediction in the chirrurgeresque Templo del Carmen "bubbling crossly up towards the sky" where the Virgin "sits on an extraordinary silver cloud like a cabbage with the Infant in her arms above the altar", and all along the walls "statues with musty purple robes stand in glass coffins".

But the politicians – "plump men with blue chins wearing soft hats and guns on their hips" – have disappeared, at least in that form, from the balcony of the Presidencia in the Plaza Central. And outside the city there is no longer "complete irresponsibility – waves of it breaking over a countryside – lawless roads". The *pistoleros* have gone, the ranch at Las Palomas is a shelled deserted ruin where only an ornate but empty tomb in a half-tended cemetery bears witness to the existence of the General. And though there is still a Cedillo at Ciudad del Mais who bears a striking resemblance with his bull-like body his suspicious courtesy and his heavy mahogany face to the photographs and descriptions of his father, the whole atmosphere of tension and looming rebellion that so appealed to Graham Greene has vanished. This Cedillo breeds horses.

But the father was in his day a great man. Of the four sons of Don Amado Cedillo who rose against President Madero in the Civil Wars of 1912 General Saturnino Cedillo alone survived and grew powerful, to become under President Calles Governor of the State of San Luis Potosi.

They told Graham Greene that Saturnino – in San Luis Potosi they call him Saturnino to this day – had not enforced the anti-religious laws. He had explained to an American reporter, "perhaps I do not believe in all this religion myself, but the poor people want it, and I am going to see that they get what they want". They told Graham Greene a great deal about the General: a rebellion was being plotted, the rumour was, and at Saturnino's back were German advisers and a well-trained army of 15,000 men.*

* This was said not only in San Luis Potosi; but in an article published in the *New Statesman* on February 19, 1938: "From a Correspondent recently in Mexico" that concentrated on Cedillo waiting in the background "as the Mussolini-to-be of Mexico." Very possibly Graham Greene read this article in New York just after his arrival, made up his mind then and there to go to San Luis Potosi; and then tried (but failed) to get a commission from the *Daily Telegraph* to cover the story. The dates fit. Rightly, though, he never believed the rumours of the 15,000 men.

For the General was no longer Governor or even Minister or even military commander of the local Federal troops. In 1934, as Calles and Garrido Canabal had launched a fresh wake of religious persecution, San Luis Potosi had become, under Saturnino's rule, for a time the only safe haven in Mexico for priests and bishops. But the wily new President, Cardenas, who succeeded Calles wanted no Indian generals with power-bases in the provinces. So Saturnino was back at his ranch of Las Palomas, three or four hours' drive from San Luis Potosi, technically just a private citizen again.

Graham Greene had already missed one General at the Border – General Rodrigues, who was said to be massing 40,000 (mythical) Gold Shirts for an attack on Cardenas. He was quite determined not to miss this second one. But it was not so easy. As a previous British journalist, obviously rebuffed, had put it: "Today to the curious and unsympathetic he is not at home. He has nothing to say to them and does not wish to be bothered by their questions." It was only after days of waiting and long negotiations by telephone, and after assurances of secrecy, that because he was a Catholic Greene was finally granted an interview.

It was a whole day and night's expedition out and back over the whitened tracks to the great bowl of a plain in which, surrounded by the sierra, guarded by gunmen, Las Palomas stood. But it was most certainly worthwhile. For of all the characters who were to appear on the pages of Graham Greene's eventual travel book *The Lawless Roads*, only two come vividly to life – and one of these is a German romantic in the Epilogue, on the boat back to England. The other – the only other one of whom the reader retains a clear and vivid impression – is General Saturnino Cedillo.

The General stands out in *The Lawless Roads* much as the Colonel – Colonel Elwood Davis – stood out in *Journey Without Maps*. But this was the first Spanish-speaking General, outside the pages of literature and Carlyle, whom Graham Greene was to meet in the flesh; and he did not immediately take to him as he had to the whisky-drinking black Colonel with the sentimental memories. There was the barrier of language, of course. But there was also the fact that whereas Colonel Davis had looked every inch the military man, beautifully turned out in a trim uniform, alone among the politicians at Las Palomas waiting on the ranch's verandah with guns on their hips and elaborately worked cartridge belts, General Cedillo appeared unarmed, in "mufti, an old soft hat, a coarse shirt, and no tie".

He looked like a farmer, Graham thought. And when after long hours waiting and various meals and whisky served by impertinent maids, he at last agreed to answer questions, "there was something genuine", Greene felt, "in the bull-frog rage, the hopeless bewilderment of the man when I asked him about the German officers. He spluttered… I think he was inclined to hate the man who came bothering him with questions about Fascism and Communism. He swelled and sweated and said, 'Democracy'…"

Before dusk, before question time, he had insisted on driving his visitor and his interpreter round the farm, and they had bumped back in the dark as peasants drifted in towards the cookhouse, maids carried out smoking tin dishes, and from time to time cars would arrive with more armed men who guffawed around the verandah. The scene appealed to Graham Greene. "It was all rather movingly simple and, in spite of the guns, idyllic. The peasants sat silently against the cookhouse wall, with their rugs drawn up around their mouths. The general gave them no pay, but food and clothes and shelter and half of everything the farm produced, and ready cash too if they asked for it and he had it. They even took the fifty chairs he bought for his little private cinema. It was not a progressive relationship, it was feudal; you may say it was one-sided..."

But, *contre-coeur* perhaps, Graham Greene approved of it.

★ ★ ★

English writers need not often hope to have a particularly enjoyable time in Mexico; though by a sort of perverse masochistic justice the more ghastly their Mexican experiences are, the more stimulating they appear to find them, and the more success their eventual books attain. DH Lawrence's trip, in the early Twenties, finished disastrously with malaria and near-tuberculosis in Oaxaca and Frieda had a terrible time getting what appeared to be a dying man back to the United States. *The Plumed Serpent*, featuring Lawrence himself (from Chapter 11 onwards) as Quetzalcoatl, was the result. A decade and a half later, and more famously, Malcolm Lowry was, like the Consul, his *alter ego*, drinking himself nearly to death on mescal in Cuernavaca and writing, in snatches, his delayed *chef d'oeuvre* of the alcoholic life, *Under the Volcano*.★ By comparison Graham Greene's discomforts were mild. But, for all that, from the night he sailed from Vera Cruz in the *Ruiz Cano*, a rolling, half-rotting flat barge, across the Gulf till the night he arrived, after fourteen hours on mule-back at the Hotel España with its flowery patio, bed, sheets and bottle of beer in San Cristobal de Las Casas, exactly three weeks later, he was undeniably travelling rough and enjoying almost no minute of it at all.

The trouble was that Frank Sheed had been right. Greene had come to Mexico

★ "I had written," wrote Malcolm Lowry to his publishers Jonathan Cape, "a 40,000 word version by 1937 that Arthur Calder-Marshall liked; but it was not thorough or honest enough." He must have been in Cuernavaca when Graham Greene passed through.

As for Calder-Marshall, Graham had bumped into him only a couple of months earlier in Leicester Square. Calder-Marshall had just joined the Communist Party that morning. Everyone was joining the Communist Party at the time – Stephen Spender, for example, after much heart-searching, and John Langdon-Davies (also in the Leicester Square pub) who was to savage George Orwell's *Homage to Catalonia* as romantic deviationism in the *Daily Worker*. Graham thought them theoretical revolutionaries only, in fact soft at the centre; and was scathing about them all – though, interestingly, not about Calder-Marshall – in his private comments.

too late. The persecution in Tabasco had ended. Admittedly, all over this hot swampy little state, the churches were destroyed, and the priests had disappeared. All had been "hunted down and shot except one who existed for ten years in the forests and the swamps, venturing out only at night, his few letters, I was told, recorded an awful sense of impotence – to live in constant danger and yet be able to do so little, it hardly seemed worth the horror." He heard of this priest twice more. Once, in the capital of Tabasco, from the wife of a Catholic. "There had been one priest over the border in Chiapas but the people had told him to go – they couldn't protect him any longer."

"'And when you die?' I said.

"'Oh,' she said, 'we die like dogs.'"

That was all very interesting. But it was in the past. He met no priests in hiding, no latter-day Campions; and disused or destroyed churches have after the first impression only a marginal interest. There was one phrase that stuck in his mind, though. He asked an elderly Scots Catholic he met in Tabasco about the priest in Chiapas – Chiapas was the neighbouring state – who had fled.

"Oh," said Dr. Fitzpatrick, "he was just what we call a whisky priest."

* * *

It had taken the *Ruiz Cano* forty-one sweltering hours to cross the Gulf from Vera Cruz, the attractive port where (more or less) the Conquistadors had landed; and it is little wonder that, contemporaneously in London, the lawyers were unable to inform His Lordship of Mr.Greene's precise whereabouts. They docked at Frontera, the frontier town of the swampy roadless state. Sharks swam in the Grijalva River, vultures squatted on the roofs, and at nightfall the torment of the mosquito swarms began. Next day the *Ruiz Cano* sailed up the river through the banana plantations to the capital of Tabasco, Villahermosa, the "Beautiful City".

There in "the only possible hotel" Graham Greene took a large bare beetle-infested room with a high ceiling, a tiled floor, and a bed in its middle. He stayed there a week. He had learnt one lesson in Liberia. On that trip he had taken with him Burton's *Anatomy of Melancholy*; and it had made him melancholy. On this trip he took with him *Barchester Towers* and *Dr Thorne* and one reviewer was to remark that his main impression of Graham Greene's travels was of the author of *The Lawless Roads* lying in shuttered hotel rooms and reading Trollope. Truth to tell there was little else to see and little else to do in Villahermosa. The heat made the Gulf and Frontera seem, by contrast, cool and fresh. Every little detail of that long hot tedious week was to remain etched, willy-nilly, in Graham Greene's memory.

The capital of Chiapas, San Cristobal de Las Casas, had been described as "that very Catholic city" to Graham in Mexico City by its exiled Bishop, and he was determined to spend Holy Week there.

He tried mule-riding first – three excruciating days of discomfort with hammocks, storms, mosquitoes and the unvarying unending cry of *Mula Mula Echa Mula*. From dreary Salto fortunately a little plane took him on, as far as Yagalon, a village two thousand feet up where the climate was cool and he was marooned for a week, lodging with, among others, "a clerk I grew to loathe, a mestizo with curly sideburns and two yellow fangs at either end of his mouth". Wretched mestizo – that week in Yagalon was to lodge him in Graham Greene's memory, from there to be transplanted to the pages of fiction and to a certain unjustified immortality as the Judas betrayer of the whisky priest.

To get to San Cristobal de Las Casas Graham had to face another mule; but for the first time it seemed that he almost enjoyed the ride, the magnificent mountain scenery of northern Chiapas and the picturesqueness of the tiny machete-swinging Indians* who made his guide so uneasy. The first night they spent in a clearing that, with its round huts and courteous welcome, reminded Graham of Liberia. He "lay on the hard earth bed almost happy" – a typical qualification.

Next day, climbing higher, up to nine thousand feet Graham found his second wind. Like a scene from the past, on the high plateau men on mules cantered by, shepherding flocks of sheep and goats while an Indian herd in his pastoral tunic wound his horn and the pale golden light welled across the plain. It reminded Graham of the idyllic "England of the Conquest before the forests had been cut". That night, in bitter cold, they slept with two others in the empty mayor's office at the village of Cancuk. *Con amistad* said the mayor, entering late at night as the bearded men on the benches reached for their pistols; and then, at the word of friendship, relaxed. He "showed no surprise at finding four men sleeping in his office". Mexico was perhaps not so bad after all.

* * *

Las Casas is, like San Luis Potosi, a lovely place; but there was no *amistad* there for Graham Greene. He could not sit in the plaza for more than a few minutes without facing hostile stares from the students, and dangerous drunken gibes from

* As these pages are being corrected, in January 1994, the tiny machete-swinging Indians of Chiapas have risen in revolt against their Mexican masters, and the Bishop (no longer exiled) of "that very Catholic City", briefly captured by the rebels, is acting as peacemaker. It is a sort of irony that the Indian Catholic revolt, half expected by Graham then, should have broken out now, over half a century later, when least expected.

the *pistoleros* which he had to pretend to ignore, the traditional unpopular Englishman abroad.*

Nevertheless though the hostility thickened he stayed on at Las Casas for a week, tall gangly and out-of-place in a land where men like him might easily be knifed or shot in a bar-room brawl provoked by politics, the end Malcolm Lowry had given *his* hero, the Consul. Wisely therefore Graham kept out of the bars and in the churches.

It was Holy Week; and though the Cathedral was locked and bolted, most of the churches had been opened. So he went to Mass every day; and on Maundy Thursday thousands upon thousands of Indians poured down from the mountains and filled the streets with processions and laments on Good Friday. It was like an invasion. On Easter Monday he left; by road to unattractive Tuxtla, by plane to Oaxaca, by train to Puebla and by motor-coach to Mexico City. He showed a perfunctory interest in these places. Oaxaca was agreeable and Puebla had grace. But in Oaxaca dysentery struck and on an interminable train journey between the two he noted even more bitterly his growing hatred and contempt for the people of Mexico and for their repellent passivity.

Hatred dominated him, now. He was back in Mexico City (which he had hated before, whose "hatefulness" he had forgotten, and which he now hated again) to find awaiting him not the proofs of *Brighton Rock* which he had been expecting but a bundle of newspaper clippings. "JUDGE ASKS 'WHERE IS AUTHOR?'" had headlined the Daily Express. These did little to improve his already strained temper.

Eventually the proofs did turn up, after endless delay and repeated visits to various post offices that kept Graham in Mexico City for almost another week. By now he had one longing: to be home. The cheapest and quickest way back to Europe proved to be on a German liner sailing from Vera Cruz to Lisbon. He booked a third-class passage, caught the train down to Vera Cruz once more and went thankfully aboard for a ten-day voyage. His last gesture in Mexico was to slip the customs officer five pesos as a bribe not to open his bags – a final cause of resentment against the whole country and its whole corrupt ethos, no less piquant for being petty.

* President Cardenas had, for over a year, been moving, slowly, towards the expropriation of the foreign oil companies in Mexico. The oil interests were mainly British-owned, and expropriation, when it came, sparked off a political crisis, a run on the peso, fury in Britain and, eventually, the breaking off of diplomatic relations. To almost all Mexicans it was a much-admired assertion of Mexican independence and pride, but to Graham Greene, when he learnt of it on March 19th, as he was waiting in Mexico City for the train to take him down to the coast, it was simply this "sudden, crazy action" that reminded him of what DH Lawrence had written of Mexico: "Socialism here is a farce of farce, except very dangerous". By the time he had reached Las Casas, the British Government had sent a Protest Note to the Government of Mexico and the dispute was becoming envenomed. To be an Englishman in Mexico at the time was to be, therefore, an object of hatred.

Chapter XVI

Evelyn's Influence

Even in San Cristobal de Las Casas the Mexicans had been listening avidly (on the Spanish Service of the BBC) to the news from Spain. On the voyage back the German liner was full of Spaniards who, once Havana passed, revealed themselves as volunteers for the Generalissimo's forces. *Arriba España* and *Viva Franco* burst out exuberantly from that time onwards. Graham rather admired them all, noisy, carefree, going to the wars. He detested the Germans on board, though; with the exception of Kruger, a big pale man who hated Hitler and invited Graham to settle with him in the Amazon and find another wife there.

Kruger, and his complicated life story, fascinated Graham. As Kruger talked they leant over the rail looking at Havana. Havana fascinated Graham too. In Mexico City the Bishop of Tulancingo had described Havana as the despair of all good Catholic missionaries, the haunt of pimps, lounge-lizards and racketeers. But the third-class passengers were not allowed off at Havana; and Graham Greene was to wait many years till he could sample for himself the women, the cocktail lounges and Havana's other excitements.

They passed by another group of islands, the Azores, with which Graham Greene was, rather sooner, to be indirectly involved, seeing through the mist and rain the great white church at Flores – "At Flores in Azores Sir Richard Grenville lay" – a bad omen for Spain perhaps.

As they docked at Lisbon, the Spanish volunteers fell very silent. For them war was about to become a reality. Possibly for Graham Greene too? We do not know how he returned from Lisbon to England. The cheapest way would have been by rail to the Channel ports. There is some indication (the opening scene in his next thriller, set precisely on a cold cross-Channel steamer) that he did so; in which case he must have passed through Nationalist-held Northern Spain, very close to the war indeed. He keeps (if so) very quiet about this, and understandably. For there is something a little shaming about having been so close to the front and yet, apparently, to have made no effort to see for himself the fighting.

Once back, he was to put a new idea to Korda as the starting-point for an original film script: the Republican agent, sent to visit England on a desperate mission, coming face to face on the cross-Channel steamer, at the barrier between third-class and first-class, with the Nationalist agent, sent to England on a similar, rival mission; and the flash of recognition that passes suddenly between them. It was a good opening sequence, as good as the man dripping blood on Platform 1 of Paddington Station had been. But Korda turned it down, possibly (as he told Graham) because it was too sensitive a topic politically, possibly because London Films was, by mid-1938, in a bad way financially, possibly because Greene's previous attempts had not been too successful; and possibly, most intriguingly, because Korda himself was by this time becoming involved with SIS, the Secret Intelligence Service; and neither he, nor his new masters, would have cared to have agents and spies emphasised in contemporary guise in a Korda production.

But the idea stayed in Graham Greene's mind.

★ ★ ★

He came back to a Europe where tension was mounting, in the third week of May, over Czechoslovakia. There was near panic in London, Paris and Moscow as Europe found itself closer to war than at any time since July 1914.

But that interested Graham Greene much less than the news from Mexico. He was writing an article on General Cedillo that very weekend of the first Czechoslovakia crisis when a friend on the *Daily Herald* telephoned to tell him that the General had at last launched his long-expected rebellion.

Naturally enough Graham Greene was in a fever of frustrated excitement when the news of all this reached London. He had missed out in Mexico on the religious persecution by arriving too late; and now it seemed that he was about to miss out on the Mexican Civil War by having left too early. He was on to his agents immediately. Could they arrange for him to give a series of talks on the BBC? And to write articles in the *Evening Standard*? Above all, could they get him sent back to Mexico at once as a war correspondent?

They could not. Europe dominated editors' minds now; and it was just as well, in this last particular, that the agency failed. For Cedillo's rebellion was virtually over as soon as it had begun. The Federal columns reached and sacked Las Palomas, almost without resistance; and on May 26th Cedillo ordered his men to disband and to return to their homes. President Cardenas (despite having been bombed in person at San Luis Potosi by two of Cedillo's little planes) would probably have pardoned him even at this stage, or sent him into exile, but Cedillo was resolved, he wrote to one of his fellow generals, to "die on my feet like a man". With his son Heladio, his brother Colonel Cleophas, and twelve other close companions he took to the sierra. Had Graham Greene arrived as "war correspondent" in Mexico, he would have had either to take to the hills himself or to return, tail between his legs, to London.

At the very beginning of the next year, 1939, the final news was to come from Mexico. Captain Castrejon, commanding a column of *Federales*, had, early on the morning of January 11th, surrounded the hill of La Ventura where Cedillo and his small band of companions had spent the night. When the succeeding fusillade was over, Saturnino, his son Heladio, and the traitor Blas Ruiz, who had betrayed him, lay dead on the ground. Captain Castrejon identified the General's body by the magnificent pistol in his hand, with his initials carved upon it.

So ended the putative Mexican Civil War. A fortnight later Barcelona fell to the Nationalists, and the real Civil War, the Spanish Civil War, drew towards Franco's victory and its depressing, ill-boding end. On February 6th Graham Greene's Mexican travel book, *The Lawless Roads*, was published by Longmans, at 10/6d. It was 256 pages long, divided into eleven (titled) chapters and ninety sections, also titled. One of the three epigraphs, taken from a poem by Edwin Muir, explained the title.

> "And Without Fear the Lawless Roads
> Ran Wrong Through all the Land."

The worst might have been feared from the first part of the Prologue: "I was, I suppose, thirteen years old," it began ominously. "Otherwise why should I have been there – in secret – on the dark croquet lawn?" Six pages of childhood memories, of "horror and fascination", follow. But fortunately thereafter Graham Greene avoided the flashback and the "spiritual journey" which had made his Liberian travel book so intolerably pretentious, and concentrated on the simple A to Z narrative which he had previously so intolerantly condemned. It made a far better book; but still not a good book. "An honest but neurotic traveller," VS Pritchett called him with "a special eye for the uprooted character". "Mr Greene's is a good picture," Pritchett went on, "given its bias, of the present; it lacks history, as also he lacked much knowledge of the language;" and it was curiously elusive on controversial points like the real influence of the Church – and on himself. These were, for Graham Greene, good points in a very balanced review. But VS Pritchett ended on a note that must have both encouraged and worried him: "There is a sort of gentleness running through his fascination with corruption – perhaps simple English sentiment and the nostalgia of an isolated, injured mind".

Evelyn Waugh was, almost inevitably, more analytic in *The Spectator*. "I find it impossible," he began, "to write of *The Lawless Roads* in any but personal terms, for I have been awaiting its publication with particular curiosity." He had been out to Mexico himself, almost on Graham Greene's heels, but with his wife Laura and in high style, commissioned by Lord Cowdray's son, Clive Pearson, to write an anti-President Cardenas, anti-expropriation book – the Pearsons had invested heavily in Mexico – and a very bad book (*Pickpocket Government* was its original title, changed wisely to *Robbery Under Law*) it was to prove to be. "He was travelling as a poor man, I was a rich," Waugh went on. "There is a great deal to be said for travelling poor;... I have done a certain amount of that kind of travel and enjoyed it thoroughly in retrospect. The chief disadvantage is that the physical exhaustion incurred in getting from place to place often makes one abnormally unresponsive to their interest. Mr Greene, particularly, suffered from this. He makes no disguise of the fact that Mexico disgusted him." But then, as Waugh pointed out "in fairness", England appeared to disgust him too. "Mr Greene is, I think, an Augustinian Christian," Waugh continued, "contemplation of the horrible ways in which men exercise their right of choice leads him into something very near a hatred of freewill." This comment, I think, stuck consciously or unconsciously in Greene's palate – as indeed Pritchett's "simple English sentiment" must have done. Both reviews were of the sort to irritate, and therefore to stimulate him.*

In America the book was published under the less pretentious title *Another Mexico*. " 'Young intellectual' say his publishers...," wrote a reviewer, referring to the blurb: " 'young emotional' would have been a better tag for him." The whole trip was "jaundiced by his own instinctive dislike of anything not British. The consequence is a book in which purely personal prejudice controls every reaction." This was the first book his new publishers, Viking, had published: and they cannot have been exactly thrilled by their new author, so aptly and so fiercely criticized.

Sean O'Faolain later put it concisely and cruelly: Graham Greene had written "an entirely dreary book about Mexico". The wonder was, and is, that out of this entirely dreary travel book, out of a jaundiced trip to a country instinctively disliked, a magnificent novel should spring.

There is a mystery of creativity here. Graham Greene went to Mexico. He hated it. He hated the country, he hated the people, he did not speak the language, he felt only momentary flashes of sympathy or interest, he was glad to leave it, and them, behind. He wrote, because he was under contract to write, a book about his journey that he must have known was a bad ill-tempered book. Yet this very same country, this very same people, this very same trip inspired him to write one of his finest novels† – one of the greatest novels, perhaps, of this century.

How did this happen, and why? Unfortunately the clues are few – no diaries or journals of the writing period are available, and even some of the dates are speculative. Certainly, though, we can say this: that Graham Greene, back from Mexico in the spring of 1938, set to work to write his travel book and had completed it by the autumn of 1938. Then, dissatisfied with his travel book, conscious that he ought to, and could, make more out of his Mexican experience

* The one review that pleased him very much was sent in by the agency. "There is little in the book of the joy of travel and adventures," it began. "Yet *The Lawless Roads* is worth reading more than a hundred other books of travel. Mr Graham Greene is a man of letters and his book is a work of art."

† To be entitled – though not yet – *The Power and The Glory*.

than he had so far done, he set to work to use the same background for a novel. But it progressed slowly and with difficulty; and for a couple of months he almost abandoned it to write, in conditions of great speed and stress, a money-making thriller. He also wrote a radio play. But he did not abandon the Mexican novel. Though it seems that he nearly did – for in many ways its opening chapters were too like the Mexican travel book; and this must have depressed him. He had decided to set the novel in Tabasco, the 'Godless State', where he had spent such a tedious week; and he peopled the first fifty pages of the novel, Part One, with his usual collection of seedy expatriates and natives, half based on people he had encountered* at Frontera, the port, and in Villahermosa, the capital, and half on his imagination. That first part, Part One, is extraordinarily vivid and impressive; but it is cinematic in style, cutting swiftly from scene to scene, person to person – and one gets the impression that the foreigners, Mr Tench in the town and Captain Fellowes and his wife and above all their daughter Coral out on the banana plantations, are going to be the main characters in the drama that will follow. There is at this stage a hint, a very strong hint, that the novel is going to turn into a thriller, centred on the hunt for James Calver, the American gangster, wanted for bank robberies and homicide, and now known to be south of the border, inside Mexico.

The Mexican novel might very well have turned into that sort of a book, with the whisky priest, also on the run like the gangster, a mere lead-in character, and the drama being (as in *England Made Me* and *Stamboul Train*) essentially one of Anglo-Saxon expatriates in a foreign, violent setting. That would have been a typical-enough Graham Greene novel, and very good entertainment – even more excellent than before in the sense that Mexico was more exotic and, in the opening chapters, more vividly and precisely described than Sweden or Central Europe had ever been. After all, Greene had had days of tedious waiting in which to note down every telling little detail.

Fortunately that was not how it turned out. Why not? There is a theory that explains why not. It is backed up by chronology. The theory is this: that Greene was stuck at Part One, uncertain how to proceed, till the travel book came out in March, followed by the comments (by Pritchett put kindly, in the American

* It is instructive to compare pages 105-130, the twenty-five relevant pages of *The Lawless Roads*, to pages 7-58, the first four chapters of *The Power and The Glory* (Penguin editions). The American dentist, Doc Winter, of the travel book becomes the English dentist, Mr Tench, who dominates the first chapter, indeed the first line, of the novel. Even more strikingly, from *The Lawless Roads* "the chief of police, a big, blond, cheery creature with curly hair, dressed too tightly in white drill, with a holster at his fat hip" hardly changes, to appear in *The Power and The Glory* as "The Chief of Police..., a stout man with a pink fat face, dressed in white flannels with a wide-awake hat and a cartridge belt and big pistol clapping his thigh". As for descriptions of the buildings, the sharks in the Grijalva or the vultures on the roof-top, they are sometimes literally transposed, word for word from the travel book to the novel.

review cruelly) that here was a writer incapable of handling or appreciating anything not British. These comments stung. There then followed Waugh's final summing-up remarks in his *Spectator* review: which did not sting but, instead, stimulated; and set Greene tacking out on a new, more adventurous and much more creative course.

"So far," Waugh had written, "as the author had any particular purpose in his observations, it was to investigate the strength of the anti-religious policy of the governing gang. From this point of view, may I offer him one reflection? The Mexicans are not only the people who killed the martyrs; they are the people for whom the martyrs died." The last sentence is the sentence to take hold of; and consciously or sub-consciously – the theory goes – it first piqued, then stimulated and finally guided its destinee. What a triumph for both men – and indeed for the cause of positive reviewing – if true!

The dates fit. If Graham Greene began writing Part Two, the central hundred pages of the Mexican novel, in early March, shortly after these reviews appeared, he would hardly have been half-way through the whole book (ie fifty pages into Part Two) by mid-May. Certainly there is an extraordinary change of tone and pace in those central hundred pages. The cinematic thriller-style drops away, the expatriates and the 'Englishness' disappear, and Graham Greene enters into a totally different world of the imagination, which he barely knew by hearsay and even more barely by experience; that of the heart, mind, body and soul of a timid dumpy little Mexican priest, and the life and habits of Mexican officialdom, Mexican jails and remote Mexican villages. It is a total triumph. We feel with the priest, we feel with the villagers, we feel with the lieutenant of police (who bears no resemblance, bar incorruptibility, to Greene's British policemen). The priest is to be a martyr, and these are the people, the Mexican people, including his hunter and his betrayer for whom the priest is to die. There is no "simple English sentiment" here; no "instinctive dislike of anything not British" – quite the contrary. Distanced from Mexico, having emptied out in *The Lawless Roads* his disgust and distaste for it, Greene made as a novelist his most imaginative and successful leap yet.

Without doubt he had already been attracted imaginatively when he wrote, in *The Lawless Roads*, of taking off from the airport beyond the cemetery in Villahermosa (where by the great gateway stood "the black letters 'SILENCIO' and the wall where the prisoners had been shot"); and of flying away towards Las Casas: "Far below Tabasco spread out, the godless state, the landscape of a hunted man's terror and captivity – wood and water, without words, and on the horizon the mountains of Chiapas like a prison wall." That indeed became the whole setting and the whole story of the central part of the Mexican novel – the whisky priest on the run for a hundred pages, with the lieutenant of police, a good man but a fanatic, close on his trail. But as for the "Augustinian Christian" and his "hatred of freewill," *that* totally disappears. Nothing could be less inevitable than that the priest should be finally caught. Like Christ himself, he exercises the prerogative of freewill in the face of his own personal Judas, the yellow-fanged mestizo; and willingly, consciously, accepts the trap that has been set for him. So much for you, Evelyn, and all your theological criticism, Graham appears almost openly to be saying: do not try to tie me down within imposed limitations. It was a dialogue between Greene and Waugh that was to last throughout their lives, throughout their literary relationship.

In the final sixty pages of the Mexican Novel (Parts Three and Four) the expatriates reappear on the scene. And the American gangster-on-the-run does indeed put in a tardy entrance – perhaps the only real false note in the book, a mere plot convenience drifting in from a very different novel. Then, brilliantly, the end comes, through the eyes of Mr Tench, who is treating the chief of police for toothache:

"With his hand on his stomach he protested, 'Not another revolution?'

The Jefe levered himself upright and spat out a gag. 'Of course not' he said. 'A man's being shot.'

'What for?'

'Treason.'

'I thought you generally did it,' Mr Tench said, 'up by the cemetery?' A horrid fascination kept him by the window: this was something he had never seen. He and the vultures looked together on the little whitewashed courtyard.

'It was better not to this time. There might have been a demonstration. People are so ignorant.'

A small man came out of a side door: he was being held up by two policemen, but you could feel that he was doing his best – it was only that his legs were not fully under his control. They paddled him across to the opposite wall; an officer tied a handkerchief round his eyes. Mr Tench thought: But I know him. Good God, one ought to do something. This was like seeing a neighbour shot."

The half-page that follows is possibly Graham Greene's most affecting, and most restrained, description of a death in any of his novels; and so vivid that it lives before our eyes as it lived before Mr Tench's: a triumph of pity, terror – and imaginative empathy. Insular Graham Greene may once have been, insular he was no longer.

Chapter XVII

Enter Dorothy, Devotedly

Brighton Rock had come out in the United States the previous June, just after Graham's return to England; and the American reviewers had not cared for it. "It is all slightly preposterous," wrote one dismissive critic, "the sort of book one reads for relaxation." But it was a very different story in England. There, in July, with orders already in for over 2000 copies, Heinemann scrapped their planned advertisement in the Sunday newspapers and substituted instead a review that had appeared in *The Bookseller*. After quoting with approval the opening words, "The whole of the novel is as arresting as that first sentence," it had continued. "I shall be greatly surprised," added the anonymous but extraordinarily accurate reviewer, "if this fascinating story of a young gangster is not acclaimed as an addition to the permanent literature of our time." Richard Church, a new friend as well as a reviewer, went so far as to dub Graham the "El Greco among English novelists".

There had been one less comfortable comment in the *Daily Express*. "If this brilliant novel has a technical fault," their over-acute critic had written, "it is that of bringing about the boy's death by the same device that Stevenson used in the *Ebb Tide*."* Such coincidences are embarrassing; and it was certainly tactless of Julian Maclaren-Ross to come round to 14 North Side on the morning the review appeared carrying a copy of *Brighton Rock* wrapped in the *Daily Express*; and then to drop a "dreadful clanger" by asking Graham Greene whether he had read the *Express* review.

But Greene did not seem to mind. In fact he treated the young man – Maclaren-Ross was about ten years his junior and just beginning to struggle up the greasy literary pole – with great good humour. They hit it off together from the moment when Maclaren-Ross first saw him appear "quite silently in the open doorway" at the first-floor drawing-room.

"Seeing me there also gave him a start, and he took a step back. He was wearing a brown suit and large horn-rimmed spectacles, which he at once

* By, in both cases, vitriol intended for a victim exploding in the face of the villain and causing his death. Had the scene written by his cousin lodged in Graham Greene's subconscious?

snatched off,* as if they had been his hat. He was not wearing a hat and this was the only time I saw him wearing spectacles. I had not expected him to be so tall.

'I hope you haven't been waiting long,' he said. He had a spontaneous pleasant smile. 'Nobody told me you were here. Would you like a cigarette? Something to drink?' "

Graham Greene was always an excellent host, whose first question to all interviewers traditionally was to ask them what they would like to drink. After lunch† Maclaren-Ross and he settled down over the coffee and brandy to discuss "ruthlessness in the thriller", Greene's favourite example being from the *Four Just Men* by Edgar Wallace.

"'D'you remember what they did to the Spanish priest who's been guilty of Rape? When they condemned him to death he begged them to let him see a priest before his execution, and they showed him – a mirror!'

"He had given full value to the capital 'R' in Rape and his eyes swivelled, glinting towards me as when he'd told me about Sylvia and the Boy.‡ They had always an alert watchful quality, the eyeballs were slightly bloodshot and one had a sense of tremendous energy and fun triumphing over inner fatigue."

One separate scene is worth quoting in full, for it gives a very vivid idea of what Graham Greene was like as a father. Indeed it appears to be the only description in print of that side of his character; and indications are that the attitude implied is the attitude that remained constant throughout his parental life. He was not the ideal family man.

* Decades later in Cuba a *Granma* journalist deputed to entertain him noticed, and reported, exactly the same gesture. Certainly Greene did not care to be photographed wearing spectacles, and few, or no, such photographs exist.

† During which Mrs Greene "handsome with black hair, placid and sedate like a young Spanish matriarch" only opened her mouth twice; once when Graham tried to draw her into a conversation about books, and once to remind him that it was late. She does not sound a comfortable hostess.

‡ Earlier they had been discussing the reviews of *Brighton Rock* and the fact that the critics were bound to miss the theological aspect – especially the Catholic critics, whom Greene said 'with every evidence of delight' would probably be the worst of the lot. Maclaren-Ross admitted he was a Catholic.

"'In that case,' said Greene recovering, 'you must have enjoyed the bit in *Brighton Rock* with Sylvia in the Lancia.'

'I haven't got to anyone called Sylvia yet.'

'Oh well, you've that to come. Spicer's girl you see gets a sudden lech on the Boy, and she wants him to have a fuck in the back of a car.'

He shot me a piercing gunmetal glance to see my reaction to the use of the word, which itself was shot out like a bullet from the barrel of Raven's automatic: presumably as a Catholic I should have been shocked but my face remained impassive:

'And does he fuck her?' I asked.

'No. You see when the girl asks him if he's got a French let…' but at that moment his wife entered the room to announce that lunch was ready."

"When we rose from the table Greene said to me apologetically:

'It's an awful nuisance but They are asking to see you, I'm afraid. I wonder if you'd mind.'

'Why of course not,' I said mystified. 'I'd like to see Them very much.'

'I'm sorry but we'll get no peace otherwise,' he said, leading the way up another darker flight of stairs; I could hear a strange twittering sound coming from behind the door in front of which he halted.

'By the way,' I asked slightly nervous, 'What are They?'...

'They are in here,' Greene said, opening the door for me to precede him, and I found myself facing a large railed cot raised off the floor to about the level of my chest. From behind the bars of this cage two small, extremely pretty blonde children peered out at me unblinking. They were perhaps aged four or five.*

'Well, come on,' Greene said from behind me, 'Say hullo politely.'

He was addressing the children actually, but I managed a ghastly smile and a subdued Hullo. The children did not reply. Without speaking they continued to stare intently through their bars. Then to my surprise, and perhaps that of their father, they started slowly to grin, and the youngest gave a sort of gurgle.

'He looks nice, Daddy,' the elder one called out encouragingly...

'That'll do,' their father said. He explained to me: 'They insist on seeing everyone who comes to the house before They'll settle down,' and to the children: 'Shut up now and have your sleep' "

Maclaren-Ross and Greene went back to the drawing-room.

" 'Lovely children,' I said, 'charming' in the hearty voice used by my father when he'd survived a social ordeal and I was further relieved to see Greene had a brandy bottle in his hand.

He said: 'Who was it complained that not enough children get murdered in detective stories?' pouring me a large measure.

'A reviewer called Cyril Connolly,' I said. 'Thanks.'

'I expect you need it,' Greene said. 'There's that book of Philip Macdonald's of course *Murder Gone Mad*, d'you know that one?'

'Plenty of kids get it there,' I agreed. 'A massacre of the innocents!' "

It would be going too far to deduce from this that Graham Greene was thoroughly bored with his children. A few weeks earlier he had written to Hugh, whose baby son Graham had been taken ill, to say how fearfully upset and worried he had been when Lucy had had an infected ear. And indeed this was a period of intense concentration on the family and its future for all the Greenes. Uncle Eppy died that July, only just into his sixties. The Hall had gone, long before his death, and the connection with Berkhamsted was almost broken. But the question of what would happen to Harston House was looming; for Uncle Graham was 81,

* In fact Lucy was 4 1/2; but Francis just under 2. Maclaren-Ross was not a family man by nature, either.

and he and the aunts were childless. A great deal of correspondence went to and fro. Harston cost £500 a year to run, gardening, rates and housekeeping included, and Graham reckoned he was already spending about that on 14 North Side. Should he and Hugh perhaps take Harston over together? Or would it not be better for one of them to take it all? And thus avoid the complicated question of who exactly might be the squire? However the elder generation of Greenes was to turn out to be long-lived indeed; and Graham was never to succeed, willy-nilly, to Sir Graham as squire of Harston House.*

A pity: for the description Maclaren-Ross gives of him in London could well be the physical description of a youngish Cambridgeshire squire, almost at any period, period details apart, from the days of Cromwell onwards.

"He must have been thirty-four at the time, his lean face was unlined then, but the skin rough and a little worn: though his cheeks were carefully shaven there was still a suggestion of stubble. He smiled a lot and the set of his mouth was amiable rather than severe as in the photographs. His lightish brown hair was parted at the side and brushed in a slight curl over a broad bumpy forehead. He sat forward in the low armchair with broad shoulders hunched up, high and large knuckly hands hanging down with a cigarette fuming between the long fingers."

Cromwellian squire is wrong, though. Graham Greene was about, like many Englishmen, to enter an intensely patriotic phase, and his patriotism extended to embrace even the monarchy which previously he had so despised. The trip on which, he had told Maclaren-Ross, he was going abroad "tomorrow" was in fact a short assignment for *The Spectator* to cover King George VI's visit to Paris. The date was July 1938, the period was right in between the two Czechoslovak crises, and the purpose was to cement the *Entente Cordiale*.

Graham found it all extremely moving on the day, with the Spahi sabres flashing and the French crowds cheering; and he concluded that it was inconceivable that friendship between France and England should ever be threatened, and that the King was indeed among friends. An article thus written without the slightest cynicism or sneer at fine sentiments, including even a reference to the King as "a simple and kindly gentleman" came as a most extraordinary change from the unpleasant and carping references, so obviously the author's own feelings, to the monarchy and its futile pomp to be found in *It's A Battlefield*. It was as if, after the horrors of Mexico, Graham Greene was almost for

* Of the three "Harston aunts" only one, Florence, was to die just before the war on her 84th birthday. Aunt Polly and Aunt Helen both lived on into their nineties, as indeed did Sir Graham Greene himself, who survived, pretty hale and hearty, despite falling off an apple tree and breaking his leg, till 1950, when he finally expired aged 93. It is noticeable in the family correspondence about Harston that Herbert is nowhere even mentioned as having any possible claims upon Harston at all. Had the junior Graham Greenes moved into Harston, then they would have become the neighbours of the Walstons of Newton pre-war: a curious thought that must often have struck Graham post-war. But that fatal Lancelot and Guinevere encounter was not yet to be.

the first time in his life, appreciating the insular delights of England. Back from Paris he immediately set out on a walking tour; and meanwhile, as he told Maclaren-Ross, "I've just been asked to do a radio play". What was significant was the subject – "It's to be about Benjamin Jowett, the Master of Balliol, you know"; and, even more so, Graham Greene's approach, affectionate and almost – if it is ever possible to use such a word of Graham Greene – reverential.* Oxford, history and learning, the English countryside, his family, Harston House, the King – it was as if a great and unexpected surge of feeling, the love of country if a single phrase is needed, was sweeping over Graham Greene at a time when the country, *his* country, was in evident deadly peril.

The children had been sent out of London during the Munich crisis; but were back, that autumn, at North Side. Graham found it impossible to work from home. He had finished, bad-temperedly, the manuscript of the Mexican travel book, was starting on the Mexican novel (the writing of which he found to be a struggle – this was the early 'expatriate' section); and so, to make money, he determined at the same time to write another thriller, taking as his starting point the scene that Korda had rejected; the meeting of the two rival agents on the Cross-Channel steamer. To write two novels at once in a house full of children, disturbed by visitors and now telephone-calls, was, he found, impossible. So in order to write in peace he took a studio in Mecklenburgh Square, in the heart of Bloomsbury.

It was, in effect, the first time he had moved out of house and home to write on his own. Before that, whether in their first Hampstead flat, or in the Cotswold cottage, or at Oxford after Lucy's birth, he had always written his novels at home, in whatever room or part of a room had been reserved as his study. The move was understandable. But to Vivien it inevitably looked very much as if Graham was both abandoning her and beginning to distance himself from his children. And indeed so it came to pass. At Mecklenburgh Square Graham was not only free from family distractions, he was closer to others that he had probably given up for some time, in the effort, which he now tacitly recognized as failed, to establish himself in the role of paterfamilias. From this time on it seems fair to say that he never really lived together with his wife and children again, except episodically.

* *The Great Jowett* was eventually broadcast on May 6th 1939 – a very fine play, forty minutes long; indeed perhaps the most successful – because the most unpretentious – of all Graham Greene's plays. The scenes are all set at Oxford, in Balliol, to the background of Big Tom's chimes; and the play itself is a delicate, dramatic, well-deserved paeon in praise of Balliol's greatest Master, a man who had died eleven years before Graham Greene was born. "You couldn't have called a man like that a leader," says the commentator, "and yet somehow, between the dinner parties to the great and the translations from the Greek, he created an atmosphere in which leaders were born... not the greatest men, perhaps, who emerge from worlds stormier than Balliol... but men with a sense of philosophy and commonsense, who didn't, any more than Jowett, expect too much of the world." This from Graham Greene, without irony, without any reference to sex, sin, despair, betrayal or wickedness. It is an extraordinary transformation.

He dashed the new thriller off in a matter of weeks, starting each day with a tablet of benzedrine, and taking a second tablet at midday. Benzedrine had, Graham worriedly found, disturbing side effects: temporary impotency in his case which led him to renew his efforts to prove his sexuality.

There is a splendid Muggeridge story, that perhaps dates from this epoch, of how Graham burst in excitedly to see Malcolm Muggeridge, waving a copy of a rag that offered the services of a whipping lady (they were difficult to get hold of in those days, not advertised by sticker in every central London telephone kiosk as now) and eager in a state of high excitement to try them out – only, crestfallen, to have to report on his next meeting with the Muggeridges that the lady in question had had mumps, and she and her client had therefore abandoned the proceedings and had enjoyed an interesting conversation instead. Certainly Graham was to some extent at least back on the Soho beat at the time; he and Ronald Matthews, his future Boswell, had met at a Westminster party and, after striking up a loose literary friendship – they had both been at Oxford, both wrote and were both Catholic converts – had finally combined at about this period to ghost-write a prostitute's book of memoirs that had to be withdrawn following newspaper attacks on it as pornography.*

So the last months of 1938 may, to sum up, reasonably be taken as the period when Graham – for whatever reason: benzedrine, children's cries, sexual frustration, revived opportunity, or sheer boredom – broke away from the conventional constraints of married life, which had suited him so little. Of course the break was not final – it was indeed never to be final and it was certainly, at that time, not open. Graham remained very considerate to Vivien and a good provider, and kind enough father in his detached and brusque way. But from this time on he began to drift apart from his family and to spend less and less time in the house on Clapham Common. His marriage had lasted, if this be taken as its first breaking point – concealed of course from the children and due to cause Graham many subsequent agonies of conscience – almost exactly eleven years.

Certainly by the following spring he was having a serious affair with another woman: with Dorothy, Dorothy Glover. Unfortunately she remains a shadowy figure. She appears to have made little impression even on those few of Graham's friends who met her. She was a designer by profession, working in the theatre, using the professional name of Dorothy Craigie. She had, probably, a basement

* It was however eventually published in Paris, by the *Nouvelle Revue Française*; and reprinted nearly a decade after the War in England under the title of *To Beg I Am Ashamed*. The publishers were an obscure little firm called The Richards Press, of which however Martin Secker was a director. The author, a clergyman's grandchild, "born a lady" writes under the pseudonym of "Sheila Cousins"; and there is no open indication whatsoever in the published book that Graham Greene or Ronald Matthews had a hand in it. She does not become a prostitute till Chapter Nine (out of fifteen chapters) after the birth of an illegitimate son to a film scenario-writer in Soho; then there is a typically Greeneian passage on "short-time hotels in the terraces around Paddington Station."

flat in Bloomsbury.* Her mother certainly lived in Crowborough – at Alberta, West Bracken Road, not all that far from Incents, Beacon Road, where Graham's parents lived. It seems natural enough that they should have first met in Crowborough. Dorothy liked drinking beer and pub-crawling. She was easy-going, loyal and very obviously devoted to Graham. Vivien certainly knew nothing about her at this stage. But Dorothy was a spinster, unmarried; and the fiendish complexities of the situation that, by April, led Graham to believe that only a World War could sort them out were perhaps simply that she wanted Graham to divorce his wife and to marry her.

A curious passage occurs at the end of the Mexican novel: Mr Tench has received a letter from his wife. "'Hadn't so much as heard from her for – oh, twenty years. Then out of the blue she…' he leant closer and levered furiously with his pick: the jefe beat the air and grunted. 'Wash out your mouth', Mr Tench said, and began grimly to fix his drill. He said, 'What was I talking about? Oh, the wife, wasn't it? Seems she had got religion of some kind. Some sort of a group – Oxford. What would she be doing in Oxford?† Wrote to say that she had forgiven me and wanted to make things legal. Divorce, I mean. Forgiven *me*.'" What is curious about this passage is that it is the first of a whole series of passages, in later novels and plays,‡ where divorce, making things legal, is almost wistfully brought up as a possible solution to or by husbands in difficulties. But it never happened. Vivien never gave Graham his 'freedom'; nor is it probable, really, that he would have accepted it if it had been offered. After all the whisky priest fathers an illegitimate child in a moment of despair; but he does not commit the greater sin of marrying the mother; and the priest who in the Mexican novel does marry and thereby betray his Faith, old fat cowardly Padre José, is a figure of ridicule to all.

* * *

* It is described, without affection, in *The Confidential Agent*. "The place was stuffy with the smell of *pot-pourri* from a decorated pot on the mantelpiece; a divan covered with an art needlework counterpane: blue and orange cushions: a gas fire. He took it quickly in, to the home-made water-colours on the walls and the radio set by the dressing table. It spoke to him of an unmarried ageing woman with few interests." This is indeed so lacking in affection that there must be some doubt. Yet outside the hero, the hunted man, had found that "there was a little brass plate behind the bell: Glover." It is just the sort of half-clue Graham Greene enjoys dropping, particularly as he had put off would-be trackers by dedicating the book to "Dorothy Craigie" – her working surname – and giving this fictional Glover the Christian name of Emily.

† But it is Miss Glover who was involved with the Oxford Group (and a Crowborough connection) in *The Confidential Agent*. "It's religion," explains one of the characters, "but it's practical. It helps you to get on because you feel *right* towards people. We've had an enormous success in Norway." Was Graham mocking his new mistress perhaps?

‡ Most noticeably and fervently in *The Quiet American*; but also before that, in both *The Heart of the Matter* and *The Living Room*.

The Confidential Agent was published in September 1939, three weeks after the declaration of war. To later critics the benzedrine book seemed "a strangely phantasmagoric thriller" where "at first sight the foreign agents seem to have the stature of spirit visitors from another world."* Almost at the same time the manuscript of the Mexican novel, finished at last, was delivered to AS Frere. Graham asked that £150 of the advance should be sent to his mother at Crowborough; and therefore to Vivien and the children too, who had been sent down there in the first flurry of fear and excitement when bombing raids were expected at the very outbreak of war. £75 he wanted for himself. He was still using the Clapham Common house, almost empty now, as his official home, for it was from there that he sent a postcard to Laurence Pollinger informing him that he was proposing *The Power and The Glory* to Heinemann's as a title. "*The Power and The Glory* is good," Pollinger replied on November 28th, "and I only hope Heinemann doesn't discover it's been used recently."† Apparently they did not, for a couple of days later Frere wrote to the agency that, "I am glad Graham Greene has found a title for his novel. None of us has been able to think of a better one, so we shall go ahead."

Thus, without enthusiasm, the most famous title, and generally speaking the best-remembered of all the titles of all Graham Greene's novels, was reluctantly fastened upon.

★ ★ ★

The Power and The Glory duly appeared, on both sides of the Atlantic, the following March. In America Viking, less cavalier – or perhaps simply more conscientious and better-informed than Heinemanns – were not prepared to use

* At first the phantasmagoric repels. When D, the hero, encounters L, the anti-hero, on the Cross-Channel ferry – both "confidential agents" for rival sides in a civil war – the Kafkaesque use of initials rather than names seems both pretentious and unnecessary. Greene had a running battle with agents and publishers alike over this. But when one considers that this was Graham Greene's first spy novel as such and that Graham Greene himself was soon enough to be working for 'C', it rather falls into place; and the novel becomes as successful as it is interesting. Politically the novel is of the left; and it places the author at long last firmly on the side of the Spanish republic and against the lower-class Fascist thugs in Britain and their uneasy capitalist manipulators. The plot may be thin, the necessary coincidences for once far too transparent, but the middle-aged hero, the ruthless upper-class heroine, the sad Jew, the incidental scenes and backgrounds are all beautifully handled – particularly the whole sequence set in coal-mining country; and, in total contrast, the marvellous Entrenationo Language Centre south of Oxford Street with that nice little bow to Korda – "heart" in *Entrenationo*.

† This was not what Pollinger was referring to; but in fact Nordahl Greig had, in 1935, put on a play in Göteborg entitled *Our Power and Our Glory*. That was a couple of years after Graham and Hugh's trip to Scandinavia; but of course Nordahl may have been writing it when they met him there.

the title under which Phyllis Bentley had recently published *her The Power and The Glory*: a romance of Roundheads and their enemies. They entitled their book rather cumbrously *The Labyrinthine Ways*. It was, all the same, extremely well reviewed on both sides of the Atlantic, so much so that Nancy Pearn forecast to Graham – quite rightly as it was to turn out – "his biggest success yet".

By far the most interesting review was to come in May, in Issue No. 5 of *Horizon*. Arthur Calder-Marshall used the publication of *The Power and The Glory* as a peg on which to hang a complete assessment of "The Works of Graham Greene". Seven novels, two travel books and a recent collection of short stories* were listed at the end. Graham Greene must have read this, the longest, most studied and most important assessment of his writing to date with eager interest – and mixed feelings. For Calder-Marshall, who had obviously put an enormous amount of application and re-reading into his article, had here at its outset first coined the catchword that was to haunt Graham Greene, to his annoyance, all his life. He was analysing the novelist's "uniform vision".

"The setting may be London or Liberia, Stockholm Brighton or Tabasco," he wrote. "But they are all in Greeneland. The main character may be a drunken, adulterous priest, as in *The Power and The Glory*, a boy murderer as in *Brighton Rock*, a hare-lipped gunman, as in *A Gun For Sale*, or the pseudo-Harrovian cad of *England Made Me*. They are accurately observed. They speak their own language, usually. They have their own convincing histories, yet they are the same breed, Greenelanders."

And where was Greeneland? "'The seedy level!' That is the location of Greeneland." Calder-Marshall wound up his long, critical, intelligent review with advice that Graham was, eventually, to take. "If he is to continue along this course" – that is, choosing, as in *The Power and The Glory*, imaginative themes too ambitious for the thriller technique – "he will have to enlarge the territory of Greeneland and get it to a more variable climate."

But that was the last thing on Graham Greene's mind at the time. Even before *The Power and the Glory* had been completed, he was conscious that, as a novel-writer, he was fast running out of steam. He had difficulty bringing *Brighton Rock* to an end, *The Confidential Agent* had needed drugs, and *The Power and The Glory* had ground to a perplexed halt at the beginning. So now, instead of novels, a whole spate of proposals for non-fiction books flowed from his fertile brain: for a Restoration Anthology; for a Catholic Anthology; more elaborately, complete with synopsis, for a book on popular – and patriotic – adventure story writers,

* The Cresset Press published, just after the outbreak of war, a collection of 24 short stories, eight by James Laver, eight by Sylvia Townsend Warner (of Spanish Civil War fame) and eight by Graham Greene. For this, his first-ever collection of short stories, he chose three early ones – "The End of the Party", "I Spy", "Proof Positive"; three written in '35 and '36 – "A Day Saved", "Jubilee", "Brother"; plus the Liberian story, "A Chance for Mr Lever", and, as *pièce de resistance*, "The Basement Room".

The Heroic Age; for *The Refugee Ships*, a sort of pre-war Exodus; for a biography of Father Damien; and, stimulated by a bad American film, *Stanley and Livingstone* (which he reviewed for *The Spectator* a few weeks before the outbreak of war) for *The Rear Column, an African Mystery* "a fascinating study of the effect of hate, fever, fear and loneliness on a group of inexperienced adventurers". Though, like all the rest, abandoned, decades later heat, fever, fear and loneliness were to shape, against the same background, the last of Greene's great fictional heroes; though even then, in that work of almost theological despair, he could never quite bring himself to abandon, *pace* Calder-Marshall, "the thriller technique".

Chapter XVIII

Royal Marine Manqué

Madrid fell to the forces of Franco on March 28th 1939. Graham had already been accepted as a member of the Officers' Emergency Reserve before the vast and threatening military parade in Berlin which celebrated Hitler's 50th birthday four weeks later. The Wehrmacht invaded Poland; and, in retaliation, on September 3rd, almost exactly a month before Graham's 35th birthday, Britain and France declared war on the Führer, the Germans and the Third Reich.

All the indications are that Graham Greene desperately wanted to become involved. David Higham, an older man, was almost immediately called up from the agency. But Higham had had military experience and Greene had had none. For the rest of the year Graham marked time, writing patriotically, furiously, in *The Spectator* till at last he was summoned by the authorities.

"How do you *visualize* yourself?" asked the obviously perplexed general. They were, Graham decided dreading the thought that once again they would have the answer, "Intelligence".

"I suppose..." he replied, "the infantry".

There was an almost audible sigh of relief. But there is no reason at all to doubt that Graham meant it. He wanted to get into the Army, and he wanted to be an officer, and he wanted to fight his country's enemy. Herbert had been commissioned, just, into the Suffolk Regiment at the end of the First World War; and that was the obvious Regiment of the Line for Greene to join. His contemporaries were now getting placed rather rapidly. By the beginning of 1940 Evelyn Waugh had joined the Royal Marines; and Malcolm Muggeridge the Military Police (Field Security Wing) and was at Mytchett Barracks in Aldershot "greatly absorbed by his new experiences" as the agency informed Graham. "I heard a rumour," wrote John Hayward to Graham in March 1940 from Merton Hall, Cambridge (to which he had retired for the duration) "that you are in uniform. Is this true?"

It was not.★

★ Graham's War Office Board had been held on January 12th 1940; and at it he had been given six months Initial Leave of Absence. Rather oddly, he states in his memoirs that he requested this postponement of his call-up till June as he "needed a few more months to complete *The Power and*

"Almost every male I know," John Hayward had added, "seems to be involved somehow in some official job." Perhaps that piqued Graham and he decided then and there that he could not, like a poor, wheelchair-bound invalid, do nothing at all for the war effort. Within three weeks of receiving Hayward's letter, he had landed an official job, at a place that was tailor-made, theoretically, for all unemployed intellectuals, the Ministry of Information. It meant abandoning all hopes of the Infantry and a proper wartime career in uniform – that is, if he still had any hopes. But in any case there still appeared to be no fighting – except on the Russo-Finnish front where at last, on March 13th, the Finns admitted defeat of a sort and signed a ceasefire. Graham burst out into indignant verse again,* this time directed at the Russians alone, at their pretence of being "liberators" under the wilting portraits of Stalin, at: "The awful repetitions of the how-many-years-plan, the edited texts of Lenin", even loosing a satiric bolt in his general disgust at Russian films of the *Earth* and *Mother* ilk. Two days later he published his last-ever film review in *The Spectator* (in the issue in which Kate O'Brien reviewed, very favourably, *The Power and the Glory*); and by the beginning of April he was ensconced in the great rabbit-warren of the Ministry of Information building in Malet Street. Hardly was he there in place, in the Literary Section, ready to fight the propaganda battle for – among other things – the hearts and minds of Latin Americans,† than the real war broke out in Europe; and after eight months of nothing very much dramatic events began to tumble over one another in an ever-increasing spiral of excitement in the West.

But not at the Ministry of Information. The Ministry of Information was a place not so much of dullness as of enervating triviality. It was Chamberlain's riposte to Goebbels' Ministry of Propaganda; and it had been, from the beginning, about as much of an answer as Chamberlain himself had been to Hitler. "It would take hours to describe the perfection in which this piece of chaos has been organised," wrote an ex-chairman of the Conservative Party as early as October 1939. His complaint was that it was "directed exclusively by Communists, and like all intellectuals they are completely incompetent in the practice of human affairs". To remedy this he obtained a job there himself, as Controller of Production. Harold Nicolson saw it, almost simultaneously, from the other but equally unflattering angle. "The Ministry of Information... had

The Glory" This is totally misleading; for *The Power and The Glory* had been finished long before Christmas 1939. Nor did Graham have any other major work on the stocks. What, one wonders, was the real reason?

* On the collapse of Poland he had vented his feelings in a deeply felt but rather bad poem for *The Spectator* – in rhyming couplets recited alternatively by General Von Fritsch and Marshal Tukhachevsky – against Hitler and Stalin, the Nazi and the Communist, alike.

† "Coolly exploring the possibility of throwing stigmatic and other miraculous occurrences" into this particular battle, per Malcolm Muggeridge.

been stuffed by duds at the top and all the good people are in the most subordinate positions." To remedy this, he obtained a job there himself as Parliamentary Secretary to the Minister. Duff-Cooper took a balanced view of the inferno. "The presence of so many able undisciplined men in one Ministry was bound to lead to a great deal of internal friction." To remedy this, he became – shortly after Greene's appointment – Minister himself, replacing the first Minister, Lord Macmillan, a dud Scots (Communist) judge. In each of these cases the remedies turned out to be as bad as the disease. None of the three was a success at his job. None lasted long. But all lasted longer than Graham Greene.

This was not because he was bad at his job. On the contrary he seems to have been quite remarkably competent and orderly; arranging, for example, for Howard Spring to write a 7000-word pamphlet on "Life Under the Nazis" or for Dorothy Sayers to write a little detective story featuring Lord Peter's wife and mocking the absurdity of rumours.

Also, the company was stimulating. George Orwell was working on Far East Radio broadcasts. Richard Crossman was in the Enemy Propaganda Division, plus Elizabeth Bowen and a host of other friends. And from outside, in Bloomsbury, Graham Greene's admirers gazed at the skyscraper building in which the object of their admiration was working. "D'you see that?" said Bill Makins, *Horizon's* business manager to Julian Maclaren-Ross – they were both en route to an underground pub. "London University but it's now the Ministry of Information. Graham Greene works there!"

"Does he?" said Maclaren-Ross.

"He does," Makins said. Makins, a redoubtable figure, resembled Graham Greene, whom he had never met but whom he admired above all other novelists, in height, build and even in dress. "He may be in there working at this very moment."

"It was a solemn thought," recorded Maclaren-Ross. "We stood there looking towards the Ministry as if it was a shrine or a cenotaph."

Indeed a cenotaph was what Information most resembled – a tomb empty of meaning. The amazing thing is not that Graham Greene 'resigned': but that he stuck it out so long. There were moments of excitement, of course, but the excitement always seemed to occur outside the job and indeed almost exclusively to other people. Nordahl Grieg for instance suddenly reappeared, sailing o'er the foam from Norway, from Narvik to be precise, with, if not the King's daughter, at least the King's gold, Maria Theresa dollars included, saved from the clutches of the Germans by, among others, a spic and span naval officer who turned out to be Nils and successfully escorted by Nordahl to the Bank of England – to be followed a little later by King Haakon in person. This was high adventure, and Nordahl tracked Graham down immediately on arrival and summoned him to the Charing Cross Hotel where in Nordahl's room, on Nordahl's bed, surrounded by Nordahl's excited fellow countrymen, full of military plans and projects, the two discussed Marxism and Hemingway. That was at the end of April, Graham's first month at the Ministry. Then in May came the dramatic beginnings of the Ben Greene affair.

* * *

This was a bad, murky business that ruined Uncle Eppy's eldest son. Benjamin Greene was, at 6 foot seven, the tallest of all the immensely tall male Greenes, and by all accounts almost as handsome and attractive to women as his cousin Herbert. But unlike Herbert he was shy and could be gauche and abrupt. And unlike all the other male Greenes – bar, possibly, Herbert – who were, each in his own different way, utterly and ruthlessly resolved upon professional success, Ben was an idealist. That did not necessarily make him any the less ruthless. He had become a Quaker and a pacifist at Oxford, and had then, foremost among all the Greenes of his generation, hurled himself directly into politics; first as a Socialist parliamentary candidate, then as a prickly left-winger inside an increasingly divided and powerless Labour party; and finally, at the time of Munich, horrified at the thought of war with Germany, as a founder-member, with Lord Tavistock, the Duke of Bedford's heir, of the peace-seeking, reformist British People's Party.

Graham had never much cared for Ben who had been not only three years the older, but a junior prefect at Berkhamsted as well; and he had no time at all for pacifists. But he was a fascinated spectator of the Ben Greene affair, kept informed, blow by blow, by a worried Tooter. Imprisoned, totally unjustly, in Brixton Gaol under the notorious Regulation 18B on May 23rd 1940, Ben was not released till eighteen months later, in January 1942. The whole baroque episode deserves, almost, a chapter in itself: involving MI5, a homosexual German-Jewish refugee *agent provocateur* named Harold Kurtz, Labour Party infighting in high places, honey-traps, the Fraülein sister-in-law of the Head of Section II of SIS, Sir Oswald Mosley and the British Union of Fascists, the Anglo-German Information Bureau, Section B5G, a bisexual animal-loving former naval officer and agent-runner known only as "M" or "Captain King"; flats in Dolphin Square, Olga Gray and the Woolwich Arsenal, digs in Ebury Street, top solicitors, correspondence with Germans in Brazil, H St John Philby, Kim's father, detective agencies, 'Miss Coplestone', and, eventually, the House of Lords. In the saga of the Greene clan this business ranks very high; but perhaps not, regrettably, in this particular book.

* * *

In June, Graham's third month at the Ministry, came Dunkirk, the fall of France, fear of imminent invasion – and the publication, on that theme, of one of

Graham's most moving short stories, "The Lieutenant Died Last"*; and in July news that Denyse Clairouin had disappeared. This was doubly worrying, first of all because Graham had continually been popping over to Paris for the weekend or for a day or two, even a week, before the outbreak of war and had become very close to her, but secondly because Denyse had been acting as his agent not only in France but in Italy; and Graham was anxious about his Italian advance from Mondadori on their proposed version of *The Power and The Glory*. Had it come through, he wondered, before Italy had declared war; and, if so, where was the money now? War and turmoil might dominate; but literature, and literary business, went on.

Meanwhile it was back to the Ministry, and to its desks, memos, committee meetings and incessant internal wranglings. Graham saved his real opinion of its futility, stored it up, to give vent to it with real passion, in a short story, one of his best, that was published – not of course until after he had left the Ministry and even then, to his amused or infuriated ex-colleagues it must have seemed like an act of *risqué lèse-majesté* – one year later in John Lehmann's *Penguin New Writing*. He entitled his story, ironically, "Men at Work". Its background is the hour-long meeting of the Books Committee. It is a small masterpiece of sardonic irritation.

> "On Skate's agenda was written:
> (1) Arising from the Minutes
> (2) Pamphlet in Welsh on German labour conditions
> (3) Facilities for Wilkinson to visit the A.T.S.
> (4) Objections to proposed Bone pamphlet
> (5) Suggestion for a leaflet from Milk Marketing Board
> (6) The Problem of India."

And there an be no doubt at all about who 'Skate' is. "Richard Skate", the story begins, "had taken a couple of hours away from the Ministry to see whether his house was still standing after the previous night's raid," the house that was "cut off from him by the immeasurable distance of bombed London. He visited it hurriedly twice a week, and his whole world was now the Ministry, the high heatless building with complicated lifts and long passages like those of a liner and

* "The Lieutenant Died Last" is a highly patriotic story set in the Cotswold countryside, in the fictional equivalent of Chipping Campden, where a group of German paratroops have landed and, disguised as British soldiers, have seized a country village in collaboration with the local (Fascist) squire. The invaders are foiled, however, and destroyed one by one by an old poacher armed only with a shotgun. The 'twist' is that he takes them for Boers; and of the invading German force, the commander, the lieutenant, dies last. Appearing in June, with France collapsing, and the invasion of England threatening to become a frightening reality, it could hardly have been better timed. It was to have (for a short story) an unexpected sequel: as an Anglo-Brazilian director's first, and best, feature film.

lavatories where the water never ran hot and the nailbrushes were chained like bibles."

There Skate/Greene had watched as "the huge staff of the Ministry accumulated like a kind of fungoid life – old divisions sprouting daily new sections which then broke away and became divisions in turn" – the "five hundred rooms of the great university block" becoming as a consequence inadequate and his own "little dark room" constructed therefore out of plywood in a passage.

As for his work Greene obviously felt that it was a bad joke. Pleasant enough company yes, particularly at the various Committee meetings that would often end in general discussions of life and literature. But "Propaganda was a means of passing the time: work was not done for its usefulness but for its own sake – simply as an occupation. He wrote down wearily 'The Problem of India' on the agenda."

The sting of the story comes in the tail; and it resonates, even now, even at such a distance of time with Graham's ardent yearning for a real role in the war, for a return to the Mess rather than to the Ministry.

Lowndes comes in late, "smelling a little of wine", interrupting the staid deliberations of the Book Committee with news of daylight raids again. Hill cuts short his excited account of fifty Nazi planes shot down, fifteen of our own lost.

"'We really must get Bone's pamphlet out," said Hill.

Skate suddenly, to his own surprise, said savagely, 'That'll show them' and then sat down in humble collapse as though he had been caught out in treachery." He is soothed down. Then comes the last paragraph, Graham's own reminiscence of a splendour that he had once too briefly shared:*

"The Book Committee was over for another week, and since the room would be empty now until morning, Skate opened the windows against the night's blast. Far up in the pale enormous sky little white lines, like the phosphorescent spore of snails, showed where men were coming home after work."

* * *

At the end of September 1941, that is to say after one year of war and six months there, Graham left his job at the Ministry of Information. Whether he was sacked or whether he resigned hardly matters. Almost as soon as he got in, he had known he had made a mistake and had been longing to get out. "Went to Ministry of Information," noted Captain Waugh of the Royal Marines, up in London after a

* Just before the outbreak of war, Graham had, if only for a few hours, donned uniform and went up in the air as an observer on a RAF training exercise. It was 'Eastland' versus 'Westland', and he flew in an 'Eastland' bomber, a Wellington, out over the North Sea to then sweep inland, evading 'Westland's defences, and to machine-gun, in theory, "a whole quiet landscape". Low-flying was an experience that profoundly impressed him, "the most exciting sport in the world". "It had been a good day," he wrote. "Even if the war had been a real one, it would still have been a good day."

battalion field day, "where Graham Greene propounded a scheme for official writers to the Forces and himself wanted to become a Marine". That was at the end of May 1940; but Evelyn could not help. He had found it difficult enough to get into uniform, with the chance of active service, himself. In the year that was to come he saw active service off Dakar with the Free French, in Crete with the Commandos. But Graham Greene not only did not become a Marine, he did not become even a writer, official or unofficial, to the forces. From September 1940 to September 1941, with the world full of melodrama, thunder and excitement, with the war spreading into Russia, the Western Desert, the Middle East, the Pacific, and the Far East, for that whole dramatic second year of World War Two, he sat in London, writing literary reviews, doing for the war effort precisely nothing.

This is an accurate but unfair summary. Accurate in its gist but unfair in two respects: subjectively and objectively. Every man who has not been a soldier despises himself; and subjectively Graham Greene would undoubtedly have seized any opportunity that came up to be a soldier and to join in the fighting. But, through no fault of his own, no opportunity came. And objectively it is not quite true to say that he did nothing for the war effort. He became, like many intellectuals, a part-time air-raid warden; and this, because he stayed in London, because he made a point of staying in London, was, *pace* Doctor Johnson, the saving of him.

The London Blitz lasted for nine months, from early September 1940 till mid-May 1941. For all those nine months Graham Greene stayed in London, and he was proud to be a Londoner. He had rented a little mews flat, in Gower Mews, at Number 19, just across the road from his job at the Ministry of Information. Vivien and the children were safely* out of London, in the country, so there were no worries there. And as for the house in Clapham Common it was almost totally demolished during the Blitz. Nobody was in it at the time of course. Malcolm Muggeridge had come to London, and ran into Greene again shortly after this had happened. "I will never forget," he said, "the expression of utter glee that came across Graham's face when he told me that his family home had been destroyed."

Graham enjoyed it all: "the nightly routine of sirens, barrage, the probing raider, the unmistakable engine, the bomb bursts moving nearer, then moving away, hold one like a love charm". "Lying on one's stomach" in the basement

* Very safely – first at Crowborough; but Vivien did not find it easy to get on with her mother-in-law, Marion, whom she found rather cold. So they moved to Oxford, the safest city in England, the only one that Hitler (it later materialized) had ordered should never be raided; and stayed there throughout the War with old friends, for Reggie had become President of Trinity College in 1938; and so Vivien and the children were back as Stella's guests throughout the war, at the President's Lodgings, next door to Balliol. Oxford was indeed to be Vivien's home for the rest of her life.

"while a bomb whines across," he remembered with "almost a feeling of tenderness" Colonel Davis in Liberia and General Cedillo in Mexico. For "they started things in a small way while the world waited for the big event." "That is why," he concluded – he was writing an article just after having left the Ministry – "one feels at home in London... because life there is what it ought to be."

He left his job; but he did not leave his mews flat. For just under the School of Hygiene and Tropical Medicine in Gower Street was Number I ARP Post where, throughout the Blitz, he served as a warden. This was slap-bang in the centre of an area of about 600 yards square, divided into three "beats", that covered the best of Bloomsbury, bounded by Tottenham Court Road to the west and Russell Square to the east.

Within the three beats lay almost all his current life: the Post, of course, to which he would report every night he was on duty: when the air-raid sirens sounded at 10 p.m. But also Heinemanns, his publishers, at 99 Great Russell Street, the Ministry of Information in the great London University Tower, the British Museum and the Reading Room south of it. *The Spectator* too had its offices in Gower Street.* Dorothy was a shelter warden in Gower Mews, and he would go drinking with her in The Horseshoe in Tottenham Court Road, strolling at least once, sometimes twice, a week outside his "sector" to the theatres of Shaftesbury Avenue and the restaurants of Dean Street and Charlotte Street, occasionally going as far north as The Duke of Grafton, in Euston Road. It was in Woburn Square, on the 'North Beat', that he saw, with a sense of shock, his first bombed house, "neatly sliced in half" with its entrails exposed. But it was not till six months later, in April 1942 – on Wednesday the 16th to be precise – towards the end of the Blitz (though they were not to know it yet) that Bloomsbury suffered its first fearful pounding.

Graham had taken Dorothy to dinner at the Czarda in Dean Street when the sirens went off, alarmingly an hour earlier than usual. They walked back apprehensively to Gower Mews, wishing they had their steel helmets with them. Dorothy was on fire-watching duty that night, so they changed and went out on duty together, each to their nearby posts. It was after midnight that there was an enormous explosion in Malet Street, behind Alfred Place: and after that it was one damn thing after another: flares all round, casualties, stretchers, Graham cutting

* Derek Verschoyle had joined the RAF. Peter Fleming was with a sabotage outfit in the Middle East. As Literary Editor – always a somewhat nebulous title on *The Spectator* – Graham worked practically full-time at 99 Gower Street, in close contact with the editor, Wilson Harris; a man whom he disliked. The two got on each other's nerves, and Graham played some unpleasant practical jokes on his Editor. But the person he really had it in for was Noel Coward, whom he despised for so carefully being abroad during those dangerous times. On the other hand as regards Priestley, he recanted; he was full of praise for JP Priestley's BBC broadcasts, which in those dark months did so much to raise morale throughout the country.

his hand on broken glass, not quite certain how best to help, dragging bodies of the wounded, the dead, the hysterical out of what was left of RADA and the Victoria Club, reciting an Act of Contrition when a further stick of three bombs came raining down.

At 5 a.m. the raid died away. Dorothy had been told by a warden that Graham had been seen at the Victoria Club earlier that night covered in blood; but was reassured that it was probably not his own. "This was indeed local and domestic war," Graham thought, "like something out of *The Napoleon of Notting Hill*". He was in action, in the centre of things. This was his own personal Heroic Age. He would not have missed it for the world.

But there were no signs, as yet no signs at all, of a real job. And in September with the Blitz over, Graham's only usefulness in the War appeared to be over too. It was utterly frustrating.

Chapter XIX

Spy!

Elizabeth, Graham's youngest sister, was, at the outbreak of war, twenty-five years old, tall, attractive, efficient – and unmarried. A year earlier she had joined apparently the Foreign Office – in fact the Secret Intelligence Service. SIS operated not exactly under the aegis of, but in uneasy tandem with, the FO. She became the secretary of Colonel Stewart Menzies, the Head of Section II, SIS' military section.

SIS was a world of its own. Headquarters of this microcosm were to be found, most unmenacingly (but of course only by those in the know) at the Passport Control Office, a fine Queen Anne building situated, suitably enough, at 21 Queen Anne's Gate. There, on the top floor, 'C', the mysterious Head of the Secret Service, lived, worked, conspired and entertained. A concealed passage at the rear of Queen Anne's Gate connected his quarters with the much less elegant, much more anonymous Broadway Buildings (Nos. 54-55) on the fourth, fifth and sixth floor of which 'C's' ten Sections had their discreet, anonymous offices.

They worked from Broadway. But Intelligence came in from intelligence officers – spymasters – dotted all over Europe. There were SIS stations running agents in most of Europe's capitals. The Heads of Station, Britain's secret spymasters, worked invariably under the cover of Passport Control officers; and inevitably this became known. A rule of thumb had, therefore, grown up; that the Head of Station did not 'operate' against his host country. Thus the main Station keeping an eye on Nazi Germany, and the most heavily-manned, was at The Hague, capital of the neighbouring and neutral Kingdom of the Netherlands. It was all, in theory, very well organized.

Unfortunately however, The Hague had been rocked by a series of scandals. 'C' sent out the head of Section V, Counter Espionage, to investigate: Valentine Vivian, an intelligent, rather cultured, rather weak man, "a seedy figure" according to Kim Philby, with "carefully dressed crinkles in his hair and wet eyes". His investigations completed, 'Vee-Vee' left behind in The Hague a newly recruited member of his Section, a young man of twenty-seven fresh from the London School of Economics, Rodney Dennys. This was the man whom Elizabeth Greene was to marry.

Eventually – but not yet. First – despite Section V and its young representative's best efforts – there was to fall upon The Hague Station the most thunderous calamity of all time* that virtually wiped SIS off the slate, sinking its networks throughout Europe. This occurred shortly after the outbreak of war, and only five days after the (natural) death of 'C'. Thanks to a most ingenious and successful counter-intelligence coup, masterminded by the youthful Walter Schellenberg, the Abwehr ended up with an almost complete list not only of all British agents in Europe but of everyone working at Broadway – right down to the details of where and on which precise floor they had their offices.

In the panic that followed the Hague Station was practically closed down overnight. And by the following June, June 1940, when we seemed to be losing the war, there were for all practical purposes no SIS spy-rings or agent-runners left anywhere in Axis-controlled Europe.

A year later, however, SIS, reformed, was recruiting again. Stewart Menzies, Elizabeth's boss, had succeeded as 'C' rather than the rumbustious Claude Dansey, founder of the 'Z' networks,† who had confidently expected the post. Section V, Counter Espionage, expanded. On January 15th 1941 'Vee Vee' was kicked upstairs, his place taken as Head of Section by another former Indian policeman, Felix Cowgill whose "most conspicuous positive quality", Kim Philby recalls, (having listed his negative ones, including the "suspicious and bristling front" he presented to the outer world), was, apart from personal charm, "a fiendish capacity for work". The aim now was war by Section V on their rival service, the Abwehr: not a killing war, but a war of bribery, of passing false information, of discrediting or turning their agents, of infiltration, of blackmail, of intrigue and the double-cross, to be fought out in the neutral countries of Europe, in particular in the two truly neutral countries: Switzerland and Portugal.

Graham Greene was invited to an Intelligence Service party in Westminster sometime in the first half of 1941. It was, for a blitzed Londoner like himself, a

* The previous scandal had been the suicide, on September 4th 1936, of the Head of Station, Major Hugh Dalton, who was being blackmailed – and justifiably so. But the calamity was the successful trap set by the Abwehr for Dalton's successor, Major Richard Stevens. Lured to the Dutch/German border at Venlo, Stevens was 'snatched' on November 9th 1939, taken to a Nazi interrogation centre, and successfully (without torture, it must be said) interrogated. In other words two months after the declaration of war the Secret Service officer best informed about and most concerned with secret operations against the enemy was now in that very enemy's hands. Panic ensued.

† The 'Z' Organisation was a sort of parallel, unofficial Secret Service that the previous 'C' had set up, post-Munich, among British businessmen with interests or contacts abroad; about which the official Heads of Station had, till the outbreak of war, known nothing. One of the chief constellations in the 'Z' firmament was, fascinatingly enough, Alexander Korda and *London Films*. Unfortunately on the outbreak of war the local heads of the 'Z' networks were ordered to reveal their existence to the startled local Heads of Station. The result was that, at Venlo, the head of the 'Z' network in Holland, a poncey businessman, was kidnapped too; and, like his more official opposite number, revealed all under interrogation.

feast of opulence; the tables groaned with artichokes, whitebait, quail and enormous quantities of drink. There were lots of grey-haired men jovially speaking Russian to each other: the former Heads of Station in eastern Europe. The host indeed had been at one stage imprisoned in Russia. Graham found himself in the hall kissing the Belgrade Head of Station's secretary. "Aha," said a bald-headed major with a slight foreign accent, "You're Greene, aren't you? You've got your sister's urges. But she prefers the Senior Service." It was all very raffish and rather attractive. By early autumn Greene had been recruited; so had Malcolm Muggeridge. Muggeridge and Greene had been spending many nights in London together, plotting precisely such a release. They both felt they had Elizabeth to thank. But their official recruiter at Broadway was the avuncular Leslie Nicholson, "a sort of Father Browne of espionage", who had been till the outbreak of war Head of Station in Riga.*

That same month, September, a younger man by almost ten years than either of those two were also recruited: Kim Philby. Kim was amiable, self-deprecating, hard-drinking; and he had already had some fifteen months of training with a sabotage outfit, Section 'D' – D for Destruction, Philby said. All three – Philby, Muggeridge and Greene – were allotted to the expanding Section V.

Graham Greene had been sent, on recruitment, down to St. Albans to learn what Section V was all about, to familiarise himself with codes and procedures and security and transmitters and all the rest of the caboodle. It was there that he first met Kim. Kim and Graham spent a lot of their free time buying each other drinks in the St. Albans pubs. Thus – and there – began a lifelong, and most significant, friendship. "No-one could ever have a better chief than Kim Philby," wrote Graham Greene later. "He worked harder than anyone and never gave the impression of labour. He was always relaxed, and completely unflappable." Graham quickly became an almost unconditional fan of the younger man – as did so many others in the Service.

Philby was in charge – or was at any rate soon to be in charge – of Section V's Iberian sub-section; just as Rodney Dennys was in charge of Section V's Dutch sub-section. But whereas Philby was to stay in England, at headquarters, Greene and Muggeridge, older and therefore, it was no doubt thought, more responsible and self-sufficient officers were to be sent overseas, more or less on their own. The

* Leslie Nicholson had taken over as Head of Station, Riga, in February 1934, that is to say three months before Graham's visit there. It seems almost inevitable that they met there at the time. Certainly Malcolm Muggeridge, extricated from the Field Security Police "through the good offices of a friend – actually Graham Greene" and told to report to SIS, was met there by Nicholson's "kindly, twinkling and unassuming countenance". Riga has recently been described by the American expert Thomas Powers as being at the time "the world capital of espionage directed against the Bolshevik régime".

news soon spread. He would be going out to West Africa at the beginning of November for the Colonial Office, Graham told his friends.

This was somewhat premature: and slightly wrong. True Graham was due to go out to Africa, and indeed to West Africa; but things did not go as swiftly or as simply as had been hoped. The principle was exactly the same as in Europe: that SIS men should be stationed in neutral countries, and for exactly the same reasons. Thus Malcolm Muggeridge was sent out to a neutral colony, Portuguese East Africa, and stationed as Vice-Consul in Lourenço Marques where he intrigued rather dangerously and rather successfully against the Italian consul, General Campini, and the German consul, General Leopold Wurtz.

Graham Greene was destined for much the same role on the other side of Africa; but in, indeed, the only nominally independent country in the whole continent: Liberia. Monrovia was of course the obvious choice of "Station" for Graham. But unfortunately the Liberian Government remembered the man and his book. They had *not* liked *Journey Without Maps*. They refused to give their diplomatic *agrément* to Mr. Greene's appointment as Vice-Consul. SIS scratched their collective heads. Monrovia was out. There was a very good chap already *en poste* in Dakar, the capital of French West Africa. So what did that leave?

Taking a deep breath, SIS decided to kick out their Head of Station, Lisbon, a former MI5 man named Richman Stopford, an awkward cuss, who had, in this most sensitive of posts, to be replaced; and to send him far far away: to Lagos in Nigeria. Admittedly this was MI5 territory; but MI5 would just have to learn to live with SIS: and if there was to be an SIS Station in one British West African enclave, why not in another? So Stopford to Nigeria therefore, and Greene to Sierra Leone. But Stopford would obviously have to be given seniority: and Nigeria was a real country whereas Sierra Leone was just an outpost of the Empire. Greene, therefore, Head of Station, Freetown, to report to Stopford, Head of Station, Lagos: all shipshape and Bristol fashion.

Except that Greene would have to be given official status of some sort in a British colony, and high enough to allow him to pull his weight when need be. Better put him into uniform, therefore. So they sent Graham Greene on a course to correct his deficiencies: to learn the ranks and the drill.

He literally learnt the drill. He learnt, at any rate, how to salute with a cane: how to recognize the ranks: what initials meant which: the organization of divisions and brigades, tactical exercises – officer's basic training of a sort. It was all a bit of a farce. but it became, by all accounts,* more like a fiasco when an RAOC sergeant attempted to teach him to ride a motor bike. Graham had never had much *rapport* with machinery; and he twice nearly killed himself. Both he and his superiors had second thoughts about putting him into uniform. A new plain-

* There is in fact, only one: Graham Greene's own, to Ronald Matthews.

clothes 'cover' was chosen. He would, in the Colony, be working, officially at least, for the local police, the Special Branch.

Finally, therefore, it was not till December 9th 1941, two days after Pearl Harbour, that Graham Greene set out on his wartime adventures. Once again, as on the eve of his previous voyage out to the "Coast", seven years earlier, he breakfasted at the Adelphi Hotel in Liverpool. Once again he was sailing in an Elder Dempster steamer. This time of course the atmosphere was very different. There were a four hour submarine-watch and a four hour machine-gun manning anti-aircraft watch each day for the twelve passengers, life-boat drill taken seriously, a certain nervousness, and a convoy of seven ships. By December 23rd they were at long last free of the cold and the fog, in warm sunshine off the African coast. Then came a jittery two days where between Dakar and Freetown the coast juts out to meet the Brazilian bulge. "That Atlantic Channel" noted Graham, "is the happy hunting-ground for submarines." But there were no submarine scares; and next day Graham celebrated his daughter Lucy's birthday – she was eight – by buying champagne all round. Typically enough, he had begun by rather disliking his fellow passengers, but now: "I feel scared", he recorded in his journal, "of the loneliness I shall feel when I leave the ship. Have given up drinking gin," he added – "it's too depressing."

Finally, on January 3rd 1942 they were there, safely there and Graham turned rhapsodic, loneliness and presentiments all forgotten.

"Very hot," he wrote. "About 10 a.m. in the mist and heat of the hills behind Freetown. Before noon we had entered the boom. The great bay crowded with shipping. The strange bubble-like mountains, the yellow beaches, the absurd Anglican cathedral built of laterite bricks in the shape of a Norman Church. It felt odd and poetic and encouraging coming back after so many years, a shape imposing itself on life again after chaos. It was like seeing a place you've dreamed of. Even the sweet hot smell of the land – is it the starved greenery and the red soil, the bougainvillea, the smoke from the huts in the Kru town, or the fires in the bush clearing the ground for planting – was strangely familiar."

Greene, it might be said, (but not of course by him) was back in Greeneland.

* * *

Graham should not have kept a diary. It was a military offence in wartime. But most called-up writers tended to; and certainly compared to Evelyn Waugh's diary Graham's is the merest collection of jottings; and in any case ceases entirely for the rest of the war once he got properly settled into his job in Freetown. But first, after a mere ten days in Sierra Leone, he flew to Nigeria. He landed at Lagos on January 14th; and there he spent at least two months.

They were not happy months, or particularly interesting months, and the whole purpose of the stay in Lagos is obscure – to train Greene on the job, presumably, under the general supervision of "S" – Richman Stopford. He certainly worked in the SIS office. But the general futility of the job in this total wartime backwater seems to have impressed him more than any potential usefulness. His relations with Richman Stopford were not good. Part of the trouble was Graham's inability to disguise his contempt for the ignorant and the pompous. He had to unbend a little, of course, or he would have had no social life at all. He noted down rather pathetically in his diary a series of obscene puns for conversational purposes – it was the only way he could remember them.

He went around with Bingly, Forbes, Benton, Gillespie, Hayes, Trasdie, Director of Propaganda Middle East, and Wormell – a name that stuck in his memory. None of them were in any form of secret work. Those who were, were referred to by their initials only; and of these the most infuriatingly unplaceable is "LP". Graham shared a bungalow with LP; and every evening they would stalk cockroaches with the light of electric torches and the help of gym-shoes. Each scored one point for a proper kill, half a point for flushing the cockroach away. They would tot up each other's score before turning in, and felt acute disappointment if no cockroaches at all were there to be hunted. The 'game' was to be replayed again, ill-temperedly, in literature: in a deservedly famous scene that was, for some reason, to capture the reading public's imagination.

LP apparently suffered from deafness, was shy, and refused to be seduced by the local tarts when Graham and "C" took him to the Royal Hotel Roof Garden. But who was LP and how did he react when, six years later, he appeared – and it must have been unmistakeable to him and to everyone who had known them both in Lagos – as the prototype of the despicable Wilson in *The Heart of the Matter*? A mystery... that remains to be solved.

Meanwhile a stream of rather depressed letters from Dorothy reached Graham in Lagos, and this did not help his already low morale.

His 'military' course in England had actually taken place in Oxford, and he had been lodged at Pembroke College, taken over by Intelligence for training purposes; so there, before departure, he had been very close to his family, to Vivien and the children. But there is no reference in his jotted diary notes to any letters or cables to or from his wife. His emotional life appears at the time to have been entirely centred on Dorothy (with whom of course he had shared the highly emotional experience of the Blitz). As for Vivien, her role in his absence abroad was to handle his literary affairs and liaise with the agency.

His morale became even lower when he returned to Sierra Leone. Compared to Lagos, and indeed even to Accra, capital of the Gold Coast, Freetown was generally considered a hell-hole, small, hot and overcrowded, with a particularly stupid white population.

It was in this ambience that Graham lived and worked. He lived, insalubriously, in a two-storey iron-roofed house built by a Syrian, condemned by the Health officials, on grounds that in the rainy season became a mosquito-infested swamp.

Above him was Hill Station, Freetown's European quarter. Between his house and the sea stretched a few acres of scrub, used as an open-air lavatory by the natives living in huts nearby. In the heat of the day the vultures settled on the house-top and when one ponderously took off, the whole iron roof shook and clanged.

At 4.30 p.m. his boy brought tea. Then Graham would take a solitary stroll up the disused railway track running below Hill Station. That was the best time of the day, 'the hour of content', with the sun sinking over the ocean and before his eyes the tin roofs and the pink laterite roads, a wide view of Freetown bay, the harbour and the shipping, rosy in the evening light.

By dusk he was home. He took his daily bath before six o'clock, the 'rat hour' and then it was time for the first drink of the evening, whisky or pink gin.

Graham's cover was that of a plain-clothes detective, his apparent brief to keep an eye on subversive activities and activists, and he functioned therefore from police headquarters. It was there, beside the law-courts, a stone's throw from the low balconied Secretariat in James Street, up the hill from the tin-roofed brothel where the grinning girls offered jig-a-jig for ten bob, that Graham had his office: a table, two kitchen chairs, a filing cabinet and a safe in which he kept both his secret funds and the code-books and one-time pads that would be used for composing, in the XB code, his five-figure-group code messages to Broadway. It was there, from the Commissioner's own hands, that he would collect his cables from London or Lagos; and it was there that he would, with one finger, type out his own notes and reports.

Coded messages winged their way between Graham Greene and, on the other side of Africa, Malcolm Muggeridge in Portuguese East. There was one last-minute panic when SIS decided to persuade the Navy to intercept a Portuguese liner passing by Freetown outside territorial waters. This was an unusual, indeed illegal procedure but it was thought that there was an important German agent, a Swiss businessman, on board. The Colonial Secretary had to be persuaded to agree too. A pretext was duly found; and, while with all the other passengers the Swiss was subjected to long hours of queueing at the purser's office for passport control, Graham Greene searched his cabin and abstracted, among other papers, his notebook. This he took to his own office and there laboriously typed out a copy of the entries before replacing it. To his fascinated amazement it contained the name and address of Denyse Clairouin, his missing agent. Another little inexplicable mystery of wartime. The ship, and the Swiss, were allowed to proceed on their way. Graham in a coded cable asked London for news of Denyse on personal grounds. He received no reply.

But, apart from this odd episode, it was a dirty business searching people's cabins, going through their (usually totally harmless) private mail and poking around in their personal possessions. Its initial fascination soon waned; and as for the industrial diamonds (theoretically the object of all these searches) none were ever found. It was an even dirtier business, he found, when he was ordered to use emotional blackmail on a Scandinavian seaman to persuade him to work not for the Germans but for the "right side" – ours. Disgusted with his own role, he backed out. If Graham continued to lend an occasional hand it was not out of any sentiment of goodwill for MI5 or their repellent methods in general but simply because he had struck up a close personal friendship with the Commissioner of Police. Indeed, during these rather lonely months, the Commissioner had become his best friend. Graham admired his professionalism and his humanity and above all his sympathy for the African. Back from the execution of an African which he was forced *ex officio* to attend, the subdued Commissioner told Graham – and it was a phrase that struck him – "After a hanging I can't eat meat for a week".

Such namby-pamby sentiments proved that the Commissioner had been *en poste* too long – twenty-seven years Graham later said, probably exaggerating. He had a wife in England with whom he did not get on. Sierra Leone – as per ex-MI5 sources – "drove people dotty". In this case it was a combination of Sierra Leone and MI5 and, perhaps general unhappiness and wartime stress that drove the Commissioner dotty. But certainly it was an MI5 visiting team that proved the last straw. Two MI5 men arrived in August of 1942. The senior, an urbane barrister, was billeted with the Commissioner; the junior, a slimy little fellow, with Graham Greene. Graham – perhaps trained by too many inspections of cabins and personal papers – read his guest's diary, and was not pleased to find his house described as a rat hole and himself as being not the man for the job. Meanwhile, at Police Headquarters, a nasty little scene had taken place. The Commissioner was already cracking up. He was dressed correctly, in uniform – except for the fact that he was still wearing his pyjama top. "Dirty little spy," he yelled at Graham's guest. "I don't tolerate spies here. Get out of my office!" That might have passed; nobody liked Graham's guest: the Senior Prefect, Graham nicknamed him. But that night the Commissioner's own guest, the urbane barrister, had to face a repetition of the scene but far worse. The house-boys fled in terror as the Commissioner, a big man, began ranting and roaring against "spies", beating his chest, and acting in general as if he had totally lost control of his senses – so much so that the senior MI5 man had to barricade himself in his bedroom as his host paced to and fro cursing and muttering all night. Understandably enough both MI5 men ended up *chez* Graham – where next day they received a handsome letter of apology from the Commissioner. Stress, overwork, the climate, a temporary outburst – the senior MI5 man and Graham agreed to hush the matter up. But in a small colony like Freetown it was inevitably a public event when the senior policeman goes berserk. Rightly or wrongly – probably rightly – the 'Senior Prefect' put in a report; and on November 12th 1942 the Colonial Office minuted that the Commissioner of Police, Sierra Leone, Captain PT Brodie, "retires at end of leave". Graham, with whom loyalty to his friends over-rode all other considerations, never forgave MI5.

Can it be mere coincidence that it is on the very same date, November 12th, that Graham Greene's creation, the protagonist of *The Heart of the Matter*, Major Scobie, Assistant Commissioner of Police, Sierra Leone makes the final entry in his fictional diary – and retires from life?

★ ★ ★

All the same for his first six months in Freetown – that is to say from April to September 1942 – Graham was, in his own way, happy. That was very largely because he was living not in the present and in the frustrating reality of a largely futile task but in the immediate past and the passion of creativity. He was – in those first six months at Freetown – writing and completing another book.*

Not that this meant that he had skimped on his official job. In professional terms French West Africa, Vichy-ruled, was Graham's 'target'; and his particular task the gathering of all possible details about French military bases, troop concentrations, garrisons, commanders and orders of battle in that particular Colony of French West Africa that clamped itself around Sierra Leone (and neighbouring Liberia too) like a descending hand: French Guinea.

'Filthy Freddie', the so-called 'Food Controller', had suggested, originally, that Graham station himself up the line on the border with French Guinea, to control his cross-border agents – a suggestion that filled Graham with unspeakable gloom. In fact there seems to have been only one agent, an illiterate Mohammedan codenamed 'Wagon' who could count only on his fingers, who brought back dubious information about the defenses of the French airfields, and whose one indication of direction was: "towards Mecca". Graham did make the occasional trip up to Pendembu and Kailahun. The local Vichy District Commissioners were of course perfectly well aware of what this tall thin Englishman who called himself Special Branch was up to. Indeed they may have taken a certain glee – who knows? – in arranging for 'Wagon' to pass false information about their "heavily-defended" positions on to the British.

Head of Station Freetown's relations with Head of Station Lagos were already strained by bitter arguments about expenses. Lagos was meant to send Freetown a

* This was not *The Heart of the Matter*. It was to be another five years before Graham distilled his own experiences during his wartime year at Freetown, and the Commissioner's, into that novel of notoriety. The Freetown book was another spy thriller, his second; twitchily entitled *The Ministry of Fear*, set against the background of the Blitz in London; and far more deserving of the epithet "phantasmagoric" than had been his first comparatively relaxed spy thriller, *The Confidential Agent*. By that same date of November 12th two complete copies of the typescript of *The Ministry of Fear* had reached London, to be sent off immediately by the agency, one to Heinemanns and the other to Paramount Films. Who on December 21st bought the film rights for a very satisfying £2250. The subsequent film was to be made by one of Graham's most admired directors, Fritz Lang; but the end result satisfied neither novelist nor director.

monthly cash allowance by bag; and receive, by bag, Freetown's written monthly report back. On one occasion Stopford, furious about Greene's charge of 5/- a day expenses for tinned rather than market food on trek, stopped the monthly cash bag. It was all very petty and trivial. But then the whole of Graham's job was petty and trivial, in the sense that any information he might obtain was unlikely in actual fact to be of any practical use whatsoever. For the chances of the Free French "invading" Vichy French territory in West Africa (or of Vichy invading Sierra Leone, also much feared), became, as the war progressed, ever more remote.

Indeed, by November, that dramatic November of 1942, when so many fictional and factual, public and private events occurred,* when Graham had been in West Africa for less than a year, his 'target' ceased to exist. The Governor General of French West Africa announced, on November 23rd, from his palace in Dakar, the *ralliement* of all his territories to the cause of Free France. Whether therefore a hut at an airbase in French Guinea contained a tank (as 'Wagon' had reported) or old boots (as Graham suspected) was now a matter of purely technical interest to the war effort, seeing that French Guinea was now an ally, not a potential enemy, and there could be no question of bombarding or of capturing either the armoured fighting vehicle or the footwear. Graham spent Christmas at Freetown. But in effect, though not as yet in actual fact, his mission on the Coast was over. It had been a dull time.†

* * *

Thus in Sierra Leone Graham had been playing the role not of a Section V man, Counter Espionage, but rather of a traditional SIS Head of Station, the gathering

* On November 3rd the Eighth Army under Montgomery broke Rommel and the *Afrika Korps* at El Alamein.

On November 4th Graham's father had died, at Incents, aged 77. *The Times* obituary referred to his "qualities of tact, kindness and consideration" and his love for Berkhamsted School, "the place which he had served so faithfully and so well". The news reached Graham in a particularly upsetting way, via first a telegram to announce that his father was dead, then a telegram to say that his father was rather ill. On November 8th two vast Anglo-American flotillas launched a massive invasion of French North Africa, at Oran, Algiers and Casablanca. On November 9th Mr Greene was cremated in Kent. On November 11th, on Hitler's orders the Wehrmacht invaded the Unoccupied Zone in France. And on November 12th the two policemen, Captain Brodie in real life, and Major Scobie in literature, came to the end of the line in Sierra Leone.

† Was it, though, quite as dull and lonely as Graham Greene implies? In *The Heart of the Matter* Scobie has a doomed but passionate love affair with a 19 year-old war widow, Helen Rolt. Graham was not, of course, Scobie. But it is hard to imagine him remaining chaste – the local tarts apart – during those eighteen months in the tropics. Is there any evidence, one wonders, that a Helen Rolt of sorts did enter his life? Any evidence at all, bar the evidence, so often accurate in other cases, of literature?

of information on and about a neighbouring and potentially hostile country, 'France'. Real Section V men, like Trevor Wilson in French North Africa or Malcolm Muggeridge in Portuguese East Africa, were there to target the real enemy, the Germans and the Italians, a much more exciting and fruitful role. Malcolm Muggeridge for instance apparently had the fascinating but very tricky task of allowing himself to be approached and, apparently, suborned by the German Consul in Lourenço Marques – allowing himself in other words to appear to be a traitor – in order thereby to feed his German "controller" first "chicken-feed", then false information.* One can imagine with what delight Graham Greene would have played – had he had the chance – this intricate, treacherous game.

In London the opportunity of even more intricate and treacherous games, though of a different nature, was now awaiting him. In a certain sense his real 'secret war' was only now about to begin.

* Muggeridge makes no mention of this in his own memoirs. But his attempted suicide (which he attributes to a combination of *accidie* and emotional entanglement with a part-Greek night-club dancer) could more logically be ascribed to the stresses of such a double-cross. As the authors who report it (in *The Philby Conspiracy*) rightly say, "in these situations the relationship of espionage services with the enemy is morally hazardous… It is easy to see that operations of this sort can swiftly get altogether out of control."

Chapter XX

Konspiratsia in Ryder Street?

Hardish on the heels of his manuscript Graham Greene cleared out his office, burnt his code-books and returned to England. Precisely when he left Sierra Leone is not clear; and of the route and details of his voyage back there is no record; nor any account of his reunion with his wife and children, emotional no doubt after fifteen years of marriage and fifteen months of absence.

No sooner was he back – certainly by the end of February 1943 – than he was involved in a flurry of negotiations: about plays, about films, about short stories and indeed about new novels.* Wartime was boom time for books and publishers, agents and authors, alike. *The Ministry of Fear* came out almost immediately and soon sold 15,000 copies, by far and away Graham's best figures yet. It must have struck a chord in the hopes, fears and memories of the London public. It certainly struck many chords among the Greenes. For all over the bombed and blitzed city traitors and spies and Special Branch policemen and tall lean sardonic efficient men from MI5 stalk each other in a manner – violent death only added -highly reminiscent of the Ben Greene affair – and none too favourable to Ben's side at that. Prentice of Room 59, tweedy, merciless, long-legged might well be an idealized 'M'. Hilfe, the Austrian refugee who is in fact the leader of the Nazi spy ring, has an echo of Harold Kurtz. There is even a scrubby private detective

* The play of *Brighton Rock* opened in Blackpool on February 15th. A fortnight later Graham went to see it at the New Theatre in Oxford. He was horrified. He cared passionately about how his work was treated. He dashed off an enormously long letter to the agency demanding that his name be removed from the programme unless this scene was cut, that replaced, this dialogue changed etc. Hermione Baddeley's vulgar portrayal of Ida particularly infuriated him. But he found the young actor who played Pinkie admirable – though over-violent. This was Richard Attenborough. The part – and therefore, indirectly, Graham Greene – launched his career.

Another famous actor's career had also indirectly been launched by Graham Greene in Paramount's version of *A Gun For Sale*. The setting was changed from Nottwich to California, and the then-unknown Alan Ladd played a gangster who was substituted for Raven. It opened while Graham was still in Africa, an excellent film, a great success on both sides of the Atlantic. Graham didn't like it either (though Vivien, invited to the Leicester Square *première*, was thrilled by it). But he minded less about the films of his thrillers than the plays of his books.

agency, the Orthotex of Chancery Lane, that sounds very like that which Tooter used in real life to attempt to track down Kurtz. On the other hand the traitors, the spies, the would-be collaborators are, Hilfe apart, very much more like Ben Greene's friends and colleagues of the British People's Party: a pretentious doctor with a noble face, a self-important Church of England clergyman, the seedy second-hand bookseller, Lady Dunwoody's husband and son, and Mrs Bellairs the spiritualist medium.[*]

Graham, after a dutiful visit to his widowed mother at Incents and a dutiful ten days' holiday with his wife and children in Devon, moved back into Gower Mews, reunited with a Dorothy presumably delighted to see him back safe and sound and to whom he presented, in a special box, charmingly inscribed with his love, the 68,400-word-long MSS of his Freetown Novel. To the world at large and to his wife in particular he announced that his address in London would be c/o the Reform Club and that he would be working a six-day week of about ten hours a day as far ahead as he could see; and to the disappointed agency that he did not know if he would *ever* write another novel. He astounded Heinemann's by actually sending them back a cheque they had paid him in anticipation – an almost unheard-of thing for an author to do. Vivien had had enough of acting as his unpaid secretary and allowed herself a brief outburst of petulance: Never again! she wrote to Laurence Pollinger. All mail would go in a suitcase to the Reform Club, she would rather char for a living![†] Perhaps she suspected more than she let on about Graham's way of life.

During the next fifteen months, that is to say from March 1943 to April 1944, Graham Greene appears, for the first time in his writing life, to have written nothing: no novels, no filmscripts, no plays, no non-fiction books, no drafts even – nothing. This is so unusual, so unlike him, that one has to conclude that for those fifteen months he was indeed working ten hours a day for six days a week. If so, he was working extremely hard. But what precisely was he doing? There is no correspondence, no journal; and only the occasional later reference to files, files and more files. A picture of his life and work has to be built up therefore mainly from outside sources. What is absolutely clear, however, is that he was

[*] Could Mrs Bellairs' sinister house on Campden Hill, "old and unrenovated", be based on Sir Roger Hollis' house at No. 6 Campden Hill Square "dark, unwelcoming and very untidy" per Chapman Pincher? Roger Hollis was the younger brother of Christopher Hollis, a contemporary of Graham's at Balliol, and a Catholic; a writer too for The Tablet, certainly an acquaintance. It is, therefore, possible.

[†] Graham had been pretty petulant himself the previous June when an ecstatic Vivien had spent 16/- in wiring Freetown to announce that he had been awarded the Hawthornden Prize (and £100) for *The Power and The Glory*. And he had pestered her endlessly from long range about the *Brighton Rock* play. In his despondency over the outcome he tended to blame her, most unfairly, for having made a hash of things.

working at headquarters for Section V in the Iberian sub-section ; and that his immediate boss was Kim Philby.

"Graham Greene was brought back," Kim was to write, "to reinforce Section V from Freetown where he had supposedly been watching the intrigues of the Vichy French. He will forgive me for confessing that I cannot recall any startling achievements of his in West Africa*; perhaps the Vichy French were not intriguing?... Happily Graham was posted, where I put him in charge of Portugal."

That is to say, if Philby is telling the truth (and there seems to be no reason to doubt him in this particular instance), Graham was in charge at the London end of the assessment and distribution of the vital information pouring in to Section V from Section V's outstation in Lisbon.

French North Africa – Algiers – had been placed under Philby's control too after the successful invasion and partial liberation in November. The Algiers Station had been run by Trevor Wilson, "a short unaccountable man with a toothbrush moustache" whom Malcolm Muggeridge judged to be "about the ablest intelligence officer I met in the war, with an instinctive *flair* for his work, including all the deceits and double-crosses involved." Trevor Wilson was a Section V man, like both Malcolm Muggeridge and indeed Kim Philby "whom he enormously admired and endlessly praised". Muggeridge had been posted, with the shift in the fortunes of war in Africa, from his remote outstation in Portuguese East, to Algiers to reinforce the existing team. Graham dealt with their cables in London, and from this period dates, therefore, Graham's long friendship with Trevor Wilson, a man after his own heart. At SIS Headquarters in Algiers, a large Arab house overlooking the city, Muggeridge met another agent 'Adrian Hunter' – in fact a von Strachwitz.

Otto John was constantly in Lisbon, in contact with Ralph Jarvis, Head of Section V there, claiming to represent a group of German generals and officers planning to overthrow Hitler and thus end the war. Barbara Greene was in Germany. A von Strachwitz was with Section V in Algiers. Graham had turned down, for reasons of work, Heinemann's new contract on April 29th. On March 13th the German conspirators made their first, foiled attempt on Hitler's life. On March 27th Barbara married, in Germany, another von Strachwitz. Six months later Count Albrecht Bernstorff was present at a notorious Berlin conspiratorial meeting of the Kreisau Circle ("Frau Solf's tea party") that was to lead, the following January, to his arrest by the *Sicherheitdienst*. Elizabeth Greene was working directly for 'C' at Broadway. It may all have been coincidence.

* Though Kim does mention Graham's famous brothel plan (which was reluctantly turned down) for setting up a brothel at Bissau in Portuguese Guinea and enticing into it unsuspecting Vichy French visitors plus the two lonely Germans who were keeping a watch on British shipping from the nearby neutral base.

Admittedly Section V dealt with counter-espionage, the battle against the Abwehr, rather than with conspiracies against the enemy Head of State. But when Admiral Canaris, the Head of the Abwehr, was himself in almost direct contact with SIS, via the Head of Station, Berne, and the Abwehr was therefore possibly, objectively speaking,(as indeed Otto John claimed), an ally, – why then the tortuous intricacy of the whole business, involving as it did layer upon layer of treachery and disloyalty, cannot fail to have fascinated a man so attracted by the complexities of duty and betrayal as Graham Greene.

Even more intricate in design was the Ostro Ring, an instance of the supreme triumph of fantasy over reality; and as such it most certainly came to fascinate Graham.

During the course of 1943 it was becoming clear to the Iberian sub-section that they had trouble. Major von Auenrode, the Abwehr chief in Lisbon, had developed an extraordinary source, codename 'Ostro', who had agents placed almost worldwide: throughout neutral Europe, in the British Isles, in America. The information von Auenrode was receiving from 'Ostro' was worryingly accurate. Kim Philby himself, the sub-section head, went out to Lisbon to track it down.

The ringleader of the Ostro Ring, Kim and his team discovered, was a Czech businessman, based in Portugal, Paul Fidurmug by name. The information he had been supplying to the Abwehr was mainly derived from published material – newspapers, company reports, specialized journals, what-have-you – with a certain amount of imaginative guesswork added, the whole rehashed and served up to the Abwehr as reports emanating from whole networks of imaginary agents and sub-agents. That in itself was not surprising. The Spanish Press Attaché in London, Angel Alcazar, had in 1941 done much the same; and in 1942 the XX Committee, the famous Double Cross Committee, had taken a leaf out of Alcazar's book, playing back another Spaniard, codename 'Garbo', and the Yugoslav Dusko Popov,* with their strings of sub-agents and fictitious reports, to Abwehr headquarters. But the icing on the cake was, in the affair of the Ostro Ring, that for all these agents and sub-agents, pure figments of his fertile brain, Fidurmug was claiming, and receiving, substantial fees, payments, bribes and expenses. In other words he was running with great profit to himself an entirely imaginary business – financed *in toto* by the unsuspecting German Secret Service. Nothing could have appealed to the sense of the ridiculous of Englishmen like Kim Philby or Graham Greene more. Having rumbled 'Ostro', they let him and his 'Ring' run – at von Auenrode's expense.

This was not altogether wise, because it so happened that 'Ostro', out of pure

* 'Garbo' was first arrested, then 'turned'. Popov, though initially recruited by the Abwehr, volunteered his services to the British, deliberately choosing the role of double-agent that Graham Greene (who certainly came to know and admire Popov) had himself yearned after.

logical deduction, was to report, correctly, that Operation Overlord, the invasion of Europe, would be launched against the Normandy beaches. Had he been believed, 'Ostro' would have done the Germans the greatest service of the war and ruined all the Allies' carefully-calculated and enormously expensive deception plans, designed to focus German attention (as indeed they successfully did) on the Straits of Calais. But by then, by the early summer of 1944 even the Abwehr had begun to smell a rat, and 'Ostro' was discredited. By then in any case the matter was of minor interest to Graham Greene. He was on the point of leaving SIS. But he certainly remembered 'Ostro'.

★★★

Antonia White had joined the Political Intelligence Department of the Foreign Office in 1943. She was working in the French Section and, in May, trying unsuccessfully to get in touch with Graham. He was not in Oxford, he was not in London. In fact he was probably working, and possibly living, down in St. Albans, in one or other of Section V's country houses.★ Certainly it was in a train carriage going down to St Albans or to Bletchley that Graham and John Cairncross first met. Somewhere around this period, however – the precise date is obscure – Section V, by this time some 120 strong, migrated back to London, to offices at 14 Ryder Street very near Piccadilly. This was a brisk stroll from Broadway but extremely close, five minutes' away only, to MI5's new headquarters at 57 St James's Street.

Back in London Graham Greene moved out of Gower Mews, from the heart to the edge of Bloomsbury, to 18 Gordon Square. In Ryder Street for the next twelve months he shared a comfortable set of offices with the Iberian sub-section. It was not large. It consisted, secretaries apart, of five men: Kim Philby in charge, Tim Milne, his number two almost since the beginning, Graham Greene the new addition, and two others.† They drank together in the King's Arms behind St. James's Street. It was a cosy little world – till the Americans arrived.

Legend had it that the men of OSS landed at Bristol Airport heavily laden with revolvers; and, demanding transport to London, announced: "We are the American Secret Service". It did not happen quite like that. The first two Americans who did indeed land at Bristol Airport on April 13th 1943 were both

★ After Munich 'C', deciding, reasonably enough, that war was inevitable and that London would be bombed, set about acquiring a startling number of country houses, rather like a traditional Duke, though within striking distance of London: Bletchley Park for the Code and Ciphers people; then Hanslope Park; Whaddon Chase; and, for Section D, first The Frythe and next Brickendonbury Hall; finally, for Section V, on Lord Verulam's estate near St Albans, Prae Wood and Glenalmond, with Central Registry in St Albans itself in a large house called Brescia.

† Who were the "two others" who shared, so intimately, Graham Greene and Kim Philby's work? Any information would be most welcome.

civilians and Yale academics. The British rather enjoyed making up myths about their American colleagues. In fact they were younger men, these Americans, and comparatively inexperienced, quiet and well-mannered and they had come to learn from their *rusé* British colleagues the arts and crafts of counter-espionage. OSS itself, the forerunner of the CIA, had only been in existence for a year. SIS, the old boys, treated the OSS in general with a measure of benevolent patronage and controlled contempt. At Ryder Street itself personal relationships were good, if wary. Norman Pearson, of Yale University, would often trot down from his offices on the upper floor, Room 51, to chat about English Literature with Graham Greene. There was the occasional rather schoolboyish practical joke played on the OSS men[*] but no indication of the slightest anti-American feeling either on Graham Greene or even on Kim Philby's part. Indeed if one of his superiors criticized Norman Pearson on the grounds that he was a "Machiavellian outspoken Anglophile", those were exactly the trio of qualities that both Kim and Graham did most appreciate.

But there were other OSS operatives out in the field who were not so genteel; and certainly tensions at Ryder Street grew high in August 1943 when Donald Downes of the OSS launched from French North Africa and therefore in full view, so to speak, of the Iberian sub-section via their Algiers Station, a gang of ex-Civil War anti-Franco Spanish exiles upon the coast of Malaga. The whole operation must have reminded Graham Greene irresistibly (but he never mentions it) of those landings of the cloaked revolutionaries of General Torrijos in Carlyle's day that so fascinated him. Like *that* operation, like that *Episode*, it all went horribly wrong. Indeed this was the worst single OSS disaster of the whole war. Downes, wild with anger, concluding that "a full-grown Foreign Office rat" had been involved, blamed SIS for deliberately sabotaging the operation in order to undermine OSS.[†] It was by no means all sweetness, literature, jolly japes and light at Ryder Street.

★ ★ ★

[*] Described by its author (Graham Greene) in a little-known autobiographical essay, "Room 51". Among the Anglophiles *not* mentioned by Graham Greene was James Jesus Angleton who was, years later, in Washington to play such a cat-and-mouse game with Kim Philby.

[†] This seems unlikely. But the whole episode raises fascinating questions about the role of Kim Philby. For Downes was very much of a leftist, his Spanish exiles were mainly Communist, and though the professed aim of the operation was to set up an information network inside Spain reporting to North Africa, in fact Downes and his men were aiming, in the long-term, at the overthrow of the Franco régime. If indeed Kim Philby was (as he later claimed) at the time a convinced Communist and working for the Russians, this is an operation he would have tended to support, not to sabotage. Interestingly, Downes' account of it was later published by Derek Verschoyle, Graham's old friend and colleague on *The Spectator*, who after the War set up a small publishing firm of his own.

At Ryder Street Graham was given, under Kim's general supervision, particular responsibility for the Azores. Churchill had long been hankering to seize the Azores; and, by 1943, the attacks on the Atlantic convoys by U-boat packs skulking in mid-Atlantic all around the archipelago gave the affair a new urgency. There were however 36,000 Portuguese troops and 300 pilots on the islands; and who knew whether they would not put up an embarrassing resistance against an unprovoked attack by their oldest ally? The Foreign Office cited the Treaty of 16 June 1373. "I cannot see," thundered Churchill, "there is any moral substance in the legalistic point involved in over-riding the neutrality of Portugal in respect of these Islands which are of no peace-time consequence but have now acquired vital war significance." Fortunately the naval commander in the Azores, Captain Ponteado, was "our staunch supporter".

It was Graham's job to find out who, among the Portuguese officers and officials and the resident Portuguese community, were *not* "our staunch supporters"; and also of course – it came to much the same thing – to draw up the Abwehr "order of battle" in the archipelago. Gradually, in the summer of 1943 Graham Greene built up the information and character-sketches needed for the SIS pamphlet "Who's Who in the Azores" that would be issued to the senior officers of the invading forces, and to the Intelligence people moving in in their wake. He added two introductory essays, and Kim contributed a third: the first but not the last time Graham and Philby were to cooperate in print.* Twelve copies of this mini-masterpiece were run off; as Graham Greene later said, probably the smallest print run of any of his written works.

But it all came to nothing. There was no 'Operation Lifebelt', no invasion. The Foreign Office insisted on the discreet approach, and the Foreign Office proved to be right. And so, happily, on 8th October, the Allies landed on the Azores and set up, discreetly and with Portuguese agreement and without bloodshed, their bases. It was a little triumph of diplomacy, and no doubt Graham Greene's *Who's Who* was useful enough in rooting out or interning the Abwehr's Honorary Consuls and arranging for the dismissal of anti-British military men among the Portuguese. All part of the war effort.

There was however a sequel to the Azores affair. It seems that Graham Greene "forgot" to send out an SIS man as Head of Station there *after* the Allied take-over. Perhaps he felt it was unnecessary; a pointless exercise. In any case there was a row: Graham's negligence had allowed MI5 to establish their control of the islands' security operations and this was something that SIS could never tolerate. Their

* Graham's sources included, for the record, Pearce who owned a small embroidery factory on Terceira; Trethaway, manager of the Europe and Azores Telegraph company, and other local 'friendlies'. The essays were: on the Portuguese system of administration; on local agriculture; and on wireless communications with the Azores. Unfortunately no copies of the document appear to have survived, not even in the FO archives.

Head of Station was eventually installed but had to report back to Broadway, ignominiously, on MI5's radio. The row became so serious that it looked at one stage as if Graham would be ignominiously dismissed. But Kim Philby defended him fiercely. Kim Philby saved him.

⋆⋆⋆

Nevertheless, some months later, Graham did resign. The 'authorised version' is as follows; and both Kim and Graham appear, in their memoirs, to have agreed upon it. The war was being won. The German menace was on the point of disappearing. A new enemy – or rather an old, reinvigorated enemy – loomed on the horizon: Soviet Russia. In 1944, therefore, 'C' decided to create a new Section, Section IX, to combat Russian espionage. It was designed in effect gradually to replace Section V, which in the increasing absence of any German espionage activity would quietly fade away. Section V had in practice become, during the five years of active war, a parallel Intelligence Service with its own codes and networks and files and personnel and traditions – almost as important as all the other Sections lumped together. It looked as if, in the emerging post-War world, Section IX would become equally important. The question of the hour therefore at Broadway and Ryder Street and perhaps even at Downing Street was this: who was going to run counter-espionage against the Russians? Who was going to be Section IX's big man? Who was going to be 'Control'?

At first there was a mere holding operation. A Captain Currie (shades of *The Confidential Agent* where a ridiculous character of exactly that name and title appears) was drafted in from MI5 (where they were thought to know more about Communists) with as his Number 2 an unfortunate SIS man from the Far East, Harry Steptoe. Steptoe had been Head of the (one-man) Station in Shanghai; arrested and interned after Pearl Harbour, then released with other Western diplomats in a complicated exchange deal carried out on neutral territory, in Portuguese East Africa. There Malcolm Muggeridge had taken him under his wing and comforted him. Muggeridge liked him: "a little cocksparrow of a man, with a bristling moustache, a high voice, monocle and a lot of suits, ties, hats and shoes" who nevertheless "knew the Secret Service through and through... and was a master-hand at letting fall the technical terms of espionage (letter-box, chicken-feed, cover, etc, etc) thereby giving an impression of effortless expertise". The incipient Section IX consisted only of Currie, Steptoe, one nice Wren and one rather odd secretary.

Who would take over as Section IX grew and expanded? The obvious man was Felix Cowgill, "a kindly conscientious nervous man" per Malcolm Muggeridge with "a fiendish capacity for work" per Kim Philby, the head of Section V; for Section V had been an enormous success. By the end of the War, 3,575 enemy agents had been identified and 675 – those in territory under British control –

arrested. The man who had masterminded counter-espionage operations against the Germans was the obvious choice to mastermind counter-espionage operations against the Russians.

But Philby decided – or had it decided for him – that he was the man for the job. This meant he would have to intrigue against his own boss, Cowgill.* He intrigued successfully. One element in his intriguing was the proposition made to Graham Greene that Greene should take his, Kim's place, as head of the Iberian sub-section of Section V. But Graham did not like the idea. It would have meant his promotion over the head of Philby's official (and long-standing) Number Two, Tim Milne, So, rather than allow himself to be "used" in this way by Kim, Graham resigned.

There are two rather puzzling features about this version of events. First of all there is the question of dates. Graham's official half-time release from government service came on Friday, July 13th 1944 (and he started half-time work as a civilian the following Monday, July 16th). Yet Felix Cowgill did not resign – in understandable disgust at being passed over in favour of Philby – till January 18th 1945. There is, therefore, a gap of months here that seems to make nonsense of the whole story.†

The second question of course is why Graham Greene's promotion over the head of Tim Milne should have helped Kim Philby at all. In the end Kim managed to achieve his aim perfectly well without it. It may simply have been that he considered Graham 'his man' (when in fact Graham much resented being anyone's man but his own) and that he was attempting to place 'his men' in all the dominant positions. Here we approach a very delicate area.

Certainly there were tremendous internal disputes within Section V (and the repercussions spread through the whole of SIS) about one vital point: how much 'secret' information should be handed over to our Russian Allies? For instance Section V had (via its radio intercepts and Bletchley Park) a complete picture of the German order of battle and planned operations on the Eastern Front. Surely

* "This brings me to an episode," Philby writes of the intrigue in his memoirs, "which will make sour reading, just as it makes sour writing." He tells us that Currie was "hampered by deafness", Steptoe "a near-mental case", Cowgill "bent on self-destruction", and the man he used, Vee Vee, Colonel Vivien, "enfeebled". But he makes no mention of Graham Greene. In the Introduction however Graham Greene writes, "I saw the beginning of this affair – indeed I resigned rather than accept the promotion which was one tiny cog in the machinery of this intrigue. I attributed it then to a personal drive for power, the only characteristic in Philby which I thought disagreeable". Malcolm Muggeridge confirms the story adding that Greene "indignantly refused."

† But perhaps we simply do not have enough dates. When precisely was Section IX formed under Currie? When did Currie retire? And when did Philby take over as Head of Section IX? There may have been a gap between the last two events. And Cowgill may in fact have left before his resignation became official. More precise information from whatever source on the chronology of these events would be welcome.

the obvious thing, it was argued, was to pass this on to the Russians. God knows we were already working hand in glove with the Americans, who were actually installed at Ryder Street. Surely it was only logical to give as much help to the Russians, who were doing so much more of the actual fighting against the Germans – pre-D-Day at least – than Americans and British combined.

This point of view, that seems only decent and commonsensical, was supported by many elements in Ryder Street. Indeed Malcolm Muggeridge remembers that it was only on this issue that Kim Philby, who always avoided arguments and worked like a calm professional, lost his temper and "spluttered and shouted that we were in duty bound to do everything in our power, whatever it might be, to support the Red Army including risking – if there was a risk – the security of the Bletchley material."

There lay the rub. Cowgill's policy throughout, which he imposed on Section V, was to protect the Bletchley material: ie to tell the Russians virtually nothing, for fear that via the Russians it might leak back to the Germans. "I argued," wrote Malcolm Muggeridge, "that such caution was legitimate, especially in view of the way the Russians had passed on to the Germans everything they knew about us and our intentions during the period of the Nazi-Soviet pact." So that was official policy. But it was horrifying. It meant, it seemed to many in Section V, condemning thousands of Russians to death unnecessarily. Some acted on their own initiative. John Cairncross, for instance, had been at Bletchley Park and moved up to Ryder Street in 1944. He surreptitiously passed 'secret' information onto the Russians' and when, years later, he was confronted with this 'treachery', was understandably proud that he had, by doing so, in general helped the Russians defeat the common enemy and in particular supplied them with information about Luftwaffe strength and dispositions before the vital Battle of Kursk. And Malcolm Muggeridge believes that it was the same thing with Philby: that it was not till this point of crisis, whatever his later inventions may have been, that Philby became a Soviet agent: that is to say that Philby too, like Cairncross, began of his own initiative passing on highly secret information to the Russians.

Long after these events, many years after the War, Graham Greene's personal address book still contained the postal addresses of two, and only two, ex-SIS colleagues: of Philby, the Third Man, in Moscow and of Cairncross, the Fifth Man, in Rome.* Did Greene too pass on information to the Russians? There is

* An *aide-memoire*. Burgess and Maclean disappeared on the weekend of May 26th 1951 to reappear in Moscow. Philby, suspected of being the "Third Man", for years successfully denied it, did not disappear (from Beirut) till January 1963; on June 1st admitted, in Moscow, that he was indeed the "Third Man". Sir Anthony Blunt, Surveyor of the Queen's Pictures, was revealed in 1964 to be the "Fourth Man". But mystery long surrounded the identity of the "Fifth Man". Sir Roger Hollis, Director-General of MI5, seemed to be the favourite (posthumous) candidate. It was not till 1992 that John Cairncross, thanks to the opening up of the KGB's First Directorate files, was definitely identified as the "Fifth Man". Cairncross is no longer living in Rome.

absolutely no proof that he did. But it is possible to imagine him knowing of Cairncross' and Philby's actions; and it is impossible to imagine him condemning them. He had admittedly turned against Russia at the time of the German-Soviet Pact and even more strongly at the time of the Russo-Finnish war. But by 1944 that was four or five years previous, and since June 1941 the Russians had borne the brunt of Nazi Germany's attacks; and Graham's basic sympathies were (and were always to remain) basically pro-communist and anti-bourgeois. It is impossible to imagine him ranging himself with the inflexible ex-Indian policeman Cowgill (who had written two long tomes on Communist subversion in our Indian Empire) or with the ungenerously suspicious (and suspiciously anti-Communist) Malcolm Muggeridge.*

Clearly we can never know for sure whether Graham Greene did or did not pass secret information on to the Soviets. Others in his office and in his organisation most certainly did – that is undeniable. Graham might have done – that is undeniable too. My own instinctive feeling, for what it is worth, is this: that Graham had indeed been approached in January 1925† and enrolled (in the vaguest sense) as a potential agent; that he had for obvious reasons, never been activated, never indeed been contacted since; that his political compass had oscillated wildly in the intervening years; but that a certain residual loyalty to the Party had survived. Let us postulate therefore that in 1943 and 1944 Graham Greene's emotional sympathies were with the Red Army and the USSR; that he knew that Kim Philby and John Cairncross were passing secret information on to the Soviets; that he approved; and that, in a minor way, he helped. But, all the same, he had no desire to go too far; to become too deeply embroiled. He was almost forty, and a family man *malgré lui*.

The conflicting pressures upon him would become intolerably strong, he could foresee, if he accepted promotion inside SIS and a senior position as head of a sub-section. Therefore, rather than being faced with a searing (and potentially hazardous) conflict of loyalties in the post-war world of espionage, he decided to resign from SIS. The temptation to follow Kim Philby would – if this line of reasoning is correct – have been strong and to someone of Graham's temperament in one way almost irresistible. Not strong enough, however; patriotism and

* Muggeridge's visceral anti-Communism dated from the six months he had spent in the USSR as the *Manchester Guardian's* correspondent in 1932. Thereafter he hated and despised Soviet Russia and its 'liberal supporters' in the west. Kim Philby (in the introduction to his own book of memoirs) thanks God (so to speak) that he avoided "the road leading me into the political position of the querulous outcast, of the Koestler-Crankshaw-Muggeridge variety, railing at the movement that had let me down, at the God that had failed *me*." Kim had a point; but perhaps he ought not to have added: "This seemed a ghastly fate, however lucrative it may have been." It would have been just as lucrative, more so in fact during the decade following 1932, for Muggeridge to have remained pro-Marxist.

† Cp pp 23-25 below

prudence alike indicated resistance. He would follow Kim's future career with interest and warm sympathy – but at a safer distance. He quit while he was still in a position to quit. He was wise.

His resignation made no appreciable difference. Philby went on to become Head of Section IX. Tim Milne succeeded him as head of the Iberian sub-section of Section V. John Cairncross stayed at Ryder Street till the end of the War when he joined the Treasury. Norman Pearson returned to Yale, to his never-to-be-finished *magnum opus* on Nathaniel Hawthorne. And James Jesus Angleton went on to Italy and to a career of 'mole-hunting' in the CIA – when it was eventually created. The spies dispersed. But the friendships, enmities, alliances, suspicions and betrayals that had begun in Ryder Street remained.

Chapter XXI

VE Day – Venus Anadyomene

It was June 1944; cold, dank and dismal.

The flying-bombs rained down on London, monstrous in size, apparently unstoppable. Graham admitted he was terrified. When a rocket hit nearby Russell Square, he and Dorothy took refuge in the cupboard under their stairs. But for all that he was delighted to be back in the thick of action once more. He had loathed the false bellicosity of the white colony in Sierra Leone, and yearned in vain for a bombardment of Freetown to test their courage and puncture their wind-baggery. But as before, during the Blitz, he could not bring himself to leave London, and Dorothy, to face the music alone, not even for a weekend in the country for which he longed.

Death did not come to him via a doodlebug;* or indeed in any other form. "I had always thought," Greene wrote later, "that war would bring death as a solution in one form or another, in the blitz, in a submarined ship, in Africa with a dose of blackwater." Wrong. The war did not thus solve, as he had been convinced it would, his emotional problems. Not only had nothing changed but things must have seemed to be even more devilishly complex than they were before. For "here I was alive" – and there was Dorothy, once again with him, in London (it sounds very much as if they were living together at 18 Gordon Square); and there too were his wife and children, no longer in London (which must have been a great relief) but at reasonable arm's length, a discreet distance away, in Oxford. So he made no difficult choice. He took no melodramatic decision. He simply, as so many men tend to do, accepted the situation as it was, and kept on his mistress without giving up his wife or neglecting his family. On the contrary he was making a thorough effort, now that he was leaving SIS, to get his family life organised and settled. Hitler's rockets were not the only terrifying things he had, in these endeavours, to face; there was also Miss Rendel, formidable

* Though it came to his designated successor at Ryder Street, Carlson, middle-aged and apparently a professional SIS man, who was killed at his home in Tulse Hill. Graham had not liked him; there was an (unexplained) enmity over the Azores.

headmistress of Rye St Antony,* the Catholic girls' school in Oxford, whom he had to try and persuade to keep on his daughter Caroline (as Lucy Caroline Greene had now become and was to remain– few Greenes ever seem to have been satisfied with their original Christian names). That distasteful interview was on June 25th. Two weeks later Graham again caught a train down to Oxford, much touched by the friendly sign chalked up on a Didcot signals box: "Welcome to Londoners". This was for a small house-warming party, to which he and Vivien had invited Reggie and Stella Weaver. For the house to be warmed, at No. 15 Beaumont Street in the centre of Oxford just opposite the Playhouse Theatre, was their own. Graham had bought it. It was to become, for the years that followed, the Greene family home.

What Vivien's reactions were to all this is not clear. Vivien, at least officially, knew nothing about Dorothy. She suspected, of course. She knew of Dorothy's existence as a friend of her husband's, and she can hardly have imagined that her marriage was going well when Graham's appearances at Beaumont Street gradually became less and less frequent, whittling away to perhaps one visit a month. But Vivien was by nature a conventional person and a dutiful wife. Her husband had fulfilled his duties: he had provided her with a nice home, and he paid the bills. If he chose to spend more time in London than most husbands, that was his affair and she was not going to pry into his personal life or listen to malicious gossip. For her part her duties were to bring up the children and to have a comfortable home and well-cooked meals waiting for him when he should reappear. When he did reappear, he was always polite and considerate. It seems that they both, by mutual consent, avoided the minefield of intimate discussion. There would have been no point in it: for what was there to discuss? Tasteless details that would cause them both pain, and to which there was in any case no solution. For divorce was out of the question. And, besides, Vivien was always a little afraid of her husband. Graham was a formidable character and not a man to accept being quizzed. So Vivien smiled placidly or cried quietly. But, underneath, the strain of keeping up appearances must have been immense.

As for Dorothy, she of course knew all about Vivien and the children; and in one way her position was far worse, the classic situation of a mistress who has to recognize, hopelessly, that her lover will never marry her. On the other hand she had much more of Graham's company than his wife and children enjoyed; she and he obviously got on extremely well and could relax together, a thing that Graham was rarely able to do in his tense relationship with Vivien. Dorothy and Graham shared the same tastes. For instance, they both enjoyed detective stories,

* Rye St. Antony's was the only private lay-run Catholic girls' school in England, at Headington in Oxford: not a good one. The present author's sister was there at a later date and learnt, she has always claimed, nothing.

particularly Victorian thrillers, and they read together Wilkie Collins' *The Moonstone* with such enjoyment that they decided to build up a collection. Collecting second-hand books dealing with violent death from shabby second-hand bookshops was far more to Graham's taste than collecting, and prettifying, as Vivien loved to do, second-hand dolls-houses from country house nurseries.

Graham, who always enjoyed helping his friends in their professional careers, decided to help Dorothy too. Her pre-war 'farcical thriller' (which he had passed on to his agents at the time) had apparently come to nothing, and it was not as a writer that he saw her. But, sheltering from the doodlebombs, (perhaps in that staircase cupboard at Gordon Square) they had the idea for a series of children's books. Dorothy would do the illustrations, and Graham would help her by writing the texts. He wrote them in pencil, in tiny notebooks. So came to be written *The Little Steam Roller*, "A Story of Adventure Mystery and Detection," *The Little Train*, *The Little Horse Bus* and *The Little Fire Engine*.* As Evelyn Waugh was to write when he received as a present from Graham a copy of *The Little Fire Engine*, "Thanks awfully… I agree you are greatest novelist of the century but am not absolutely sure I should recognize this from the dramatic intensity of the story, as the blurb promises."† The four stories were short, unimportant and, had they not been written by Graham Greene, would no doubt have been swept away without a trace in the vast flood of children's literature. It comes as little surprise that the four vehicles were failures, in turn hunted and hunter; or that the big businessmen who put in an appearance are rogues; or, come to that, that *The Little Steam Roller* starts its career in Africa, and *The Little Train* is dedicated to the guard of the Brighton Express. *The Little Train* was indeed not only the first to be published but was published by a different publisher from the other three: Eyre and Spottiswoode. And one possible reason, modesty apart, why it was published anonymously was that Graham Greene was at the time of its publication a director of that firm.

* * *

* The initial plan seems to have been to publish these little books under Dorothy's (working) name without revealing to the general public that the text was written by Graham Greene at all. Thus the first to be published (but not till 1948) *The Little Train* was simply marked "illustrated by Dorothy Craigie". The proof copy of the second, *The Little Fire Engine*, shows the same intention. But in fact the stories were not really good enough to go out without a famous writer's name attached; and *The Little Fire Engine*'s eventual title page read: "by the Author of *The Little Train*, Graham Greene. Illustrated by Dorothy Craigie." Thus anonymity was, for both, abandoned.

† On a postcard dated 8 November 1950. A week later Evelyn, making *amende honorable*, (he was always careful of Graham's susceptibilities) added, "My younger children speak endlessly about your fire-engine"; and two years later, on its publication, "Dear Graham, How very nice of you, to send me *The Little Horse Bus* and how clever of you to write it! You really are the most versatile of men."

Graham's half-time release from Ryder Street and SIS is dated July 14th 1944. The following Monday he began work with Eyre and Spottiswoode's, in Bedford Square. This was a career move that he had long been planning; and he was to work as a publisher for the next four years – at first half-time; then, when his final release from SIS came through officially six months later, full-time or almost.

Just three days after Graham began working for Eyre and Spottiswoode, on July 20th 1944, Germany's military aristocracy attempted to overthrow the Nazi régime. The details at the time seemed obscure and confused to most people in England. But SIS must have known how Count Klaus von Stauffenberg had almost succeeded in blowing up Hitler, Goering, Keitel, Bormann and the other leaders of the Third Reich in the *Wolfsschanz* bunker in East Prussia; how – miraculously, as it seemed – Hitler had survived; how the *coup* in Berlin had failed, how the *coup* in Paris* had at first succeeded, with the Wehrmacht carrying out wholesale arrests of the Gestapo, only to be abandoned thereafter. It was in a sense the culmination of SIS' efforts – though there is no indication at all that SIS was directly involved. On July 23rd, another three days later, the Nazi reaction began. Admiral Canaris was arrested on Hitler's orders. *That* must have caused a stir in Ryder Street: the Head of the Abwehr, their rival service, first disgraced and dismissed, now arrested. *That* SIS and particularly Section V could hardly fail to have seen as an indirect triumph. Though indeed by July 1944 the Abwehr as such no longer existed. Earlier in the year, following failure after intelligence failure (and culminating in Nicholas Elliot at Istanbul Station persuading two important Abwehr agent-runners, the Wermehrens, to defect) Admiral Canaris had been dismissed, the Abwehr amalgamated into the *Sicherheitdienst*; and Walter Schellenberg put in charge of the combined operations. Graham could therefore perfectly justifiably claim that he had left only when Section V's private war had been won.†

★ ★ ★

By this time Alexander Korda was back in London, though continually crossing the U-boat-infested Atlantic to rustle up financial support in America, playing gin

* The indications are that when Graham moved out of Ryder Street, he joined Antonia White at Bush House in the Political Intelligence Department. This was only on a half-time and a temporary basis; but it covered France – and of course Paris.

† But Walter Schellenberg, as operational commander of The Hague trap that had destroyed SIS' networks at the beginning of the War (cp pp 176), was certainly a more dangerous enemy than the double-dealing Canaris. Graham, with Hugh, was to strike a last blow for SIS when, in their joint anthology *The Spy's Bedside Book*, published many years later, they included a hilarious and apparently straightforward account by Walter Schellenberg of his own office in Berlin – its desk equipped with hidden twin machine-guns with which to spray unwanted visitors – not a device much used in Ryder Street.

rummy with Basil Dean on the troopship, the *Queen Mary*. Back with ten million dollars reputedly at his disposal, twenty-seven writers (including Evelyn Waugh) under contract, a Hungarian chef on the premises, Ralph Richardson and Vivien Leigh as his potential stars, Deborah Kerr under his wing – and had even in his munificence found a niche for Moura Budberg, now in her substantial fifties, still caring for an HG Wells almost at the last gasp of his long life, but as vivacious and entertaining and scandalous, though hardly as beautiful, as ever. To such a set-up Graham, particularly by contrast with the stodgy atmosphere of Eyre and Spottiswoode's, was inevitably attracted. But it was not quite the Korda of old; for Alex was continually having to report back in person to MGM and Louis B Mayer. Nonetheless Graham was put under contract to MGM London Films too (and, if Evelyn Waugh's contract is anything to go by, on what promised to be very generous terms: £2000 a year for twelve weeks' annual work).*

However it was to Alberto Cavalcanti, reasonably enough,† that he sent a thirteen-page 'film story' based on his own experiences at Ryder Street; or rather on the experiences of *Pani* Fidurmug and his 'Ostro' Ring.

Graham reversed the reality. In his story he made SIS the suckers; and substituted for the ingenious Czech a rather pathetic British salesman of Singer sewing machines; who however, for very different motives and without really meaning to, finds himself doing exactly the same thing: setting up a ring of imaginary agents, whose 'reports' he invents and forwards to London, claiming allowances and salaries for them at Broadway's expense, and gradually gaining an overweening confidence that is inevitably followed (as was indeed the case with 'Ostro') by suspicion, exposure and fall. But, as in 'Ostro's' case in real life, so in the case of Graham Greene's fictional hero, there is, by sheer chance, one report that turns out to be both vital and precise, even though, ironically, it comes too late to be believed. 'Ostro' had reported that the Allies would invade Normandy,

* Almost a "slave contract" Graham Greene dubbed it many decades later, with a distinct touch of retrospective grievance – though there seems nothing slavish in accepting a one-off outright payment, provided it is hefty, for a short minor work. Most writers have at one stage or other had to do so, have welcomed the money – and run to the bank. What stuck in Graham Greene's throat, though, was the fact that he had lost control of *all* the rights, a thing he hated.

† For Alberto Cavalcanti had read that passionate wartime short story of Graham's, "The Lieutenant Died Last"; had persuaded Michael Balcon's Ealing Studios to buy the film rights for £300; and had directed the resulting film, his own first feature film, *Went The Day Well*. It was a resounding success. As so often happens, a short story produced a better film than many a novel. Indeed in the present writer's view this is by far the best and most moving of all the many films produced from Graham Greene's stories or novels, *The Third Man* only excepted. In later life Graham was to claim never to have seen it and to have disliked the changes Cavalcanti had made. It is true that it came out in October 1943 when he was still in Freetown. Yet out of a minor story Cavalcanti, the Brazilian, constructed a saga that one reviewer rightly called "one of the most intense of all British war films" – and one that is still stirring to this very day.

as indeed happened; but his report was pushed aside as coming from a discredited fantasist. In almost exactly the same way Graham Greene's hero reports that the Germans are about to invade Poland, and gives their full (and correct) Order of Battle. He is of course disbelieved. But as it happens (and here Graham the storyteller diverges from Greene of Section V) he has been summoned back to Broadway for explanations and a slating when the news of the German invasion actually comes through. As a result, all is forgiven: Richard Tripp (Graham's hero) is given the OBE, appointed Chief Lecturer on the training course for SIS recruits, and is last seen preparing to give, in the final line of the story, a lecture – how Graham must have savoured the title after his own experiences in Freetown – on "How to Run a Station Abroad".

What is significant about this minor little film story is not simply that it formed the basis for a future famous novel, one of Graham Greene's best-loved and most popular, that merits perhaps more than any other the title of an 'Entertainment': *Our Man in Havana*. What is fascinating is that it reveals Graham Greene's own sardonic view of SIS, Section V, Broadway, Ryder Street, and the whole of his service there. No sooner, almost, was he free from it than he was turning round and mocking, as it were, the devil and all his works and pomps. Overweening credulity, he seems to be saying, that is the hallmark of any Secret Service; and any intelligent – or even unintelligent – outsider can make a fool of any Secret Service – German, British or whatever – almost without trying. Malcolm Muggeridge (who was to leave Section V in a far more casual manner than Graham, simply upping sticks in Paris and abandoning his post without even going through the formalities of resigning) must have loved it. One can imagine him and Graham chortling over the story, and its final twist, as they enjoyed another plate of sausages (Graham's invariable wartime offering) at Graham's digs in Bloomsbury.

But obviously other members of SIS would have appreciated it far less. It added a further insult that the setting was pre-war 'Latesthia', a transparent disguise for Latvia and the Baltic Stations in the years 1938-9 – shortly after, in other words, Greene had visited Riga and Tallinn: the implication being that the pre-war SIS, the SIS of the "old hands" prior to the recruitment of the new young wave of intellectuals like Muggeridge, Greene and Philby, had been particularly credulous, hypocritical, inefficient and indeed comic. As indeed was the case, in methods at any rate, though the consequences – as at The Hague – had hardly been risible. Leslie Nicholson, for all his puckish sense of humour, cannot have been thrilled.

The film was never made. Cavalcanti submitted it to the British Board of Film Censors; and the British Board of Film Censors in their turn submitted it to Broadway. No certificate could be issued, Cavalcanti was told, for a film mocking the Secret Service. In the end, of course, the film was indeed to be made: starring Alec Guinness as the 'hero', Wormold (ex-Tripp), and Noel Coward, superbly, as the Vee-Vee/Cowgill figure; and most successful the mockery was to be too. But that was under a different title, by a different director, and in a different epoch, fifteen years later.

For MGM London Films Graham meanwhile planned a much more ambitious project; not a synopsis of thirteen pages but a long-short story of 20-25,000 words, resurrecting an idea he had first put to William Cameron Menzies back in 1936.* Originally the story was to have been set against the background of the Spanish Civil War. Now Graham transposed it to Occupied France, set against the background of the Resistance. He wrote it rapidly; and the typescript, some 110 pages in all, was delivered before the end of the year. It was a weak story; the logical holes and coincidences are too much for even the most hardened Greene fan to swallow, and it was never made (possibly because Korda was soon in deep waters financially once again, and had to resign the chairmanship of MGM London Films). But the beginning was strong – ten men held as hostages by the Germans faced with a decimation order – (hence the title) and Part One, twenty-seven pages long, is by far the best part of the book – for a book it was, eventually, to become.†

What is significant, and in itself rather fascinating, is that this, almost alone of all Graham Greene's stories, does not have a single English-speaking character in

* William Cameron Menzies, an art director most famous for the 1924 production of *The Thief of Bagdad*, had been brought over to England in 1936, at the height of Korda's success, to direct seven features for London Films; and of these *Four Dark Hours* (alias *The Green Cockatoo*), Graham's first screenplay, the "sleazy little Soho thriller", was one. It was on December 26th 1936 when Graham was down at Denham Studios and working on the Soho thriller that he first discussed this other idea with Menzies. Interestingly the eventual title given to this new idea, when it materialized years later, was that of a film Graham had reviewed earlier that same month, on December 11th: *The Tenth Man*, directed by Hurst, based on a short story by Somerset Maugham. Either the title stuck in Graham's subconscious; or, perhaps, he derived his whole idea from the title in the first place.

† This was indeed Graham Greene's *The Tenth Man*, not published till 1985, almost half a century after the idea had first come to him. The history of this whole affair is almost gothic in its complications. Briefly, Graham put the idea aside in 1936, only to revive it in 1944 and to write it (under the "slave contract") as a film story, not a novel or a novella. It was never produced. It lay, unused and forgotten, in the archives of MGM. What is fascinating is that *The Tenth Man* was written four years before *The Third Man*, the one remaining in obscurity, the other leaping into fame. A hoary American film researcher spotted it eventually in the early Eighties – an unknown, unpublished Graham Greene, with that strikingly reminiscent title: an amazing find. Anthony Blond, the daredevil British publisher, acquired the rights, approached Graham Greene in a slow-motion mating dance (metaphorically speaking) over the lunch tables at Antibes, charmed him out of creating a hullabaloo; and *The Tenth Man* (plus the 13 pages of the original Ostro Ring film idea, and indeed an Introduction by Graham Greene) was eventually published by Anthony Blond and The Bodley Head jointly in the United Kingdom; and by Louise Dennys, Elizabeth's daughter, Graham's niece, in Canada under the imprint of Lester and Orpen Dennys a year later in 1986 – somewhat to the bafflement of the reading public who never quite seemed to grasp where and how this latest novel, apparently of his old age, fitted in in the Graham Greene canon.

it. The young German officer apart (who announces to the hostages that they must select one of their own number for execution at dawn), all the speaking roles are French. The hero, the villain, the heroine – all are French. The setting is France. The deaths are of Frenchmen. The only English thing about *The Tenth Man* is the language in which it is written. And certain elements in the writing – the descriptions in particular of liberated Paris, with its "silent little bicycle taxis gliding by, the shabbiness of awnings and the strange faces" – certainly give the impression that the author has just been there.

He had two reasons to go back; the first that he was certainly running, in August, (and presumably for the FO) a journal to be distributed in liberated France called *Choix*; secondly his persistent worries over Denyse Clairouin.

He was right to be worried. Denyse Clairouin was apparently a British agent in the Resistance; indeed she may have been working for one of SIS' networks; or possibly for one of the more extensive SOE networks that Claude Dansey so horribly betrayed. However that may be,* she had been arrested by the Germans and died, or was to die, in a concentration camp. If Graham did indeed visit liberated Paris, was her fate known? Possibly she may still have been alive. Her flat, or her office (perhaps both) had been in Miromesnil; as an obeisance to her, Graham chooses that address for Louis Chavel's Parisian flat in *The Tenth Man*.

On the other hand he may not have crossed the Channel. Paris was liberated on August 25th. Malcolm Muggeridge was certainly there, in British uniform (which had a certain rarity value, as he soon found); and Trevor Wilson too. Either could have brought back reports to Graham Greene on conditions in Paris, and indeed on the whereabouts of Denyse Clairouin. Trevor Wilson, Muggeridge wrote, "was in his element, having acquired a long *poilu* greatcoat which swept the ground, the perfect companion for a Liberation". Together they attended the famous and moving Thanksgiving Service for the Liberation held at Notre-Dame and attended by General de Gaulle. Together they stayed at SIS' unofficial Paris headquarters, Victor Rothschild's mansion on Avenue Marigny. Together they 'rescued' PG Wodehouse from the uncomfortable aftermath of his unfortunate jokily pro-Nazi broadcasts. And alone Malcolm fulfilled a special commission given him by Graham, who, knowing that he was going to Paris, had asked him "to seek out François Mauriac and get him to agree to English translations of his books, to be brought out in a uniform edition by Eyre and Spottiswoode. This I gladly agree to do, and in the very early days of the Liberation made a special point of calling at the office of Mauriac's publisher, Grasset."

This, were it to be successful, would be Graham Greene's first major coup as a publisher. He had always admired Mauriac; and when *The Viper's Nest* had first appeared in its English translation in 1932, "I turned my back," wrote Graham,

* Any further information about Denyse Clairouin, her life, her Resistance record, her death, would be most welcome.

"on everything I had written up to then, especially on Conrad". "Grasset," Muggeridge found, had been "suffering from acute *ennuis*, having published during the occupation numerous volumes with a decidedly collaborationist flavour." Monsieur Grasset had therefore wisely retired *pro tem* to a psychiatric asylum. Madame Grasset, however, a fiery red-headed lady who was running the firm in her husband's absence, "pronounced herself wholly in favour of the translation project, which she commended to Mauriac, and it was arranged that I should go to see him". His own Resistance record, Muggeridge found, was impeccable, his company enormously stimulating, and his stories particularly about the French Academy (to which he had been elected in 1933, the year following the success of *The Viper's Nest*) hilariously funny. And, Muggeridge concludes, "In due course Mauriac's novels appeared under the Eyre and Spottiswoode imprint, brilliantly translated into English by Gerard Hopkins, and proved a great success."

It would therefore have been logical enough, after the opening move but before the happy conclusion of a signed contract, for Graham to have gone over to Paris himself sometime between the Liberation and the early spring of 1945 while Malcolm was still there; and thus to begin his friendship with this frail, intense man, almost twenty years his elder, that was to continue at least until the end of Mauriac's novel-writing career. The 'hero' of Greene's *The Tenth Man* is like the 'hero' of Mauriac's *The Viper's Nest* both a lawyer and named Louis;★ and this is perhaps one more slight indication that such a visit, and such a meeting, did take place.

★ ★ ★

Denyse Clairouin was not the only friend whom Graham Greene had lost in the War. Nordahl Grieg had been shot down on a bombing raid over Berlin. And now, as the war in Europe drew towards its close, another old acquaintance went to his death; again, like Denyse and Nordahl a foreigner – for Graham's English friends seem all to have been spared.

Count Albrecht Bernstorff had survived the fearsome reprisals that followed the failed Plot of July 20th, in which so many of his caste – thousands rather than hundreds – had been liquidated. Von Moltke of the Kreisau Circle, arrested simultaneously, was executed on January 23rd 1945. But still Bernstorff survived. Admiral Canaris was hanged on April 1945. But still the fat Count, his fifty-fifth birthday just past, was allowed to live. Finally, though, on the night of April 22nd, with Russian troops closing in on the centre of Berlin, Bernstorff and 19 other prisoners were marched from their gaol on Lehrterstrasse to Gestapo headquarters

★ But from where did Graham Greene derive the name of his story's main setting, St Jean de Brinac? Not from the map of France. Possibly from a Mauriac novel?

at Prinz Albrechtstrasse. Intercepted by an SS detachment, lined up against a wall, all twenty were shot.

Thus perished almost at the edge of salvation Graham's original and most genial and inoffensive spymaster, in the final conflagration of the Axis, only days before Mussolini's corpse was strung up by Italian partisans at Milan and before Hitler committed suicide in the *Führerbunker*, and before, at midnight on May 8th 1945, the War in Europe came to its long-awaited end.

★ ★ ★

There is no record of how Graham celebrated VE Day – perhaps at Oxford with his wife Vivien and children, or at Crowborough with his mother Marion, or more probably and logically in the Bloomsbury and Soho pubs with his mistress Dorothy, at the Horseshoe Tavern next to The Dominion Cinema in the Charing Cross Road frequented by Maclaren-Ross and his girlfriends, and by Arthur Calder-Marshall and his lovely husky-voiced wife Ara. But there *is* a record, written later, of how one of his fictional characters spent it: Sarah, Henry's wife, Bendrix' lover.

> "*8 May 1945*
> Went down to St James's Park in the evening to watch them celebrate V.E. day. It was very quiet beside the floodlit water between the Horse Guards and the Palace. Nobody shouted or sang or got drunk. People sat on the grass in twos, holding hands. I suppose they were happy because this was peace and there were no more bombs…
>
> Then the Royal Family came out on the balcony and the crowd sang very decorously. They weren't leaders like Hitler, Stalin, Churchill, Roosevelt: they were just a family who hadn't done any harm to anybody… I wanted to begin again. I wanted to be one of a family too."

Could this have been how Graham Greene spent VE Day? Could this have been Graham himself on the evening of VE Day sitting on the grass, holding hands with Dorothy his hopelessly loyal mistress or with Vivien his legally wedded wife – or, more likely, alone? Observant, a little melancholic, quietly reflective… There was certainly much for him in his personal life to meditate about.

Or was it the original of Sarah? For, though little did he know it, a third woman was about to enter Graham Greene's life – *une femme de trente ans*, a woman such as he had never known before, beautiful, quick-witted, warm-hearted, passionate too, famous indeed for her sexual expertise – and, most importantly, rich. Rich to a degree previously unknown to Graham; rich to a degree that literally enabled her to satisfy her slightest whim; most dazzlingly beautiful and most dazzlingly rich: Catherine.

Postscript

What do I think of Graham Greene?

Let me quote a description by Marie-Christine Bellosta: "un aventurier fabulateur d'une énergie peu commune, dur en affaires, égoïste en amour, invariable en politique, audacieux mais avisé, provocateur mais aimant la discrétion."

In fact she was writing not of Graham Greene but of his near-contemporary and her own countryman, Céline. But the description seems, in its essentials, to fit: that is, almost exactly, what I (who have, like any biographer, lived closely with 'my' man for many years) think of Graham Greene. Not an ordinary man, not a comfortable man, not a reliable man – but an adventurer, with all the vices and virtues of an adventurer; above all, as in Céline's case, a man of quite exceptional energy.

He is now poised (though he has as yet no inkling of it) on the edge not only of a great love but of a great literary success; and indeed of what he could previously only have dreamt of, ever-increasing and worldwide fame. How does he handle it? It will be a pleasure to recount…

Acknowledgements

A great number of people have greatly helped in the preparation of this book over a considerable number of years – it must be a decade now since the idea was first suggested to me and since, hesitantly, I took it up. Not all of them necessarily want their help to be acknowledged; indeed some have with considerable stress requested that their names should nowhere be mentioned. But above all, first and foremost, I would like to acknowledge the help of two people without whom, as they say, the book would never have seen the light of day. In the first place Gwendoline Marsh who has seen it – and myself – through so many crises with, always (well, almost always) uplifting good humour, plus courage, equanimity, resourcefulness, energy, audacity when needed, ruthlessness when vital, and the readiness to turn her hand to anyone and anything. The second is Kate Fraser who has typed out what must seem to her to be innumerable versions of this book with only the mildest of sighs; who must be the most reliable and conscientious transformer of the potential into reality whom any author could ever hope to ask for.

Unfortunately, in this decade, many of those who, I think, would have been interested to see this book in print have died; my thanks, nevertheless go, to the late Malcolm Muggeridge, the late Peter Quennell, the late Sir Harold Acton, the late Countess von Strachwitz (Barbara Greene) and the late Patricia Cockburn all of whom gave me both interviews and permission to quote from their books (or, in the case of Patricia Cockburn, to be more precise from her husband, Claud's books – he had died some years earlier). I would also like to thank for permission to reproduce copyright material the following journals and newspapers: *The Times*, *The Sunday Times*, *The Daily Telegraph*, *The Sunday Telegraph*, *The Observer*, *Daily Mail*, *Daily Express*, *The Graphic*, *The Spectator*, *The New Statesman*, *The Tablet*, *Cherwell* and *The New York Herald Tribune*.

My thanks are also due to the following for help, information, encouragement, hospitality, permission to reproduce copyright material, criticism; or some or all of these combined: in England to Gillon Aitken, Tania Alexander, Mark Amory, Peter Ackroyd, Lady Clare Asquith, Rupert Allason MP, Nicholas Bagnall, Ann Brewster, Richard Cox-Johnson, Sophie and James Dugdale, Lucy Dynevor, Sonia Land, Mark Le Fanu, Teresa Newman, Lucinda McNeile, Edward and Wiz

Mortimer, Sally Patience, Felix Pryor, Alan Ross, Dr AL Rowse, Professor PE Russell, Dom Martin Salmon, Dom Alberic Stacpoole, Father Vincent Turner, SJ Hugo Vickers, Suzanne von Pflügl, Auberon Waugh, Dr Patrick Weaver, John Wilkins; plus 'Tooter' Greene and indeed Mrs Vivien Greene; in France to Alan Adair, Pierre and Catherine Gremion, Kasia Greenwood, Suzanne Lipinska, Ghislaine Lipinska, Priscilla Malraux, Tania Mendonsa, Phyllis Springer, Jacqueline Tolstoy; elsewhere in Europe to Jenepher Bramble, John Cairncross, Christianne Höjer, Paddy and Cliona Marsh, Cynthia Thomas, Anton von Knorring; in the USA to Elaine Davenport, Pamela Haylock, Horace and Penny Judson, Anne Fremantle, Professor Roger Lewis, Stephanie Nathan, Jonathan and Gail Taylor, to the staff of the Georgetown University Library, the Berg Collection at the New York Public Library, the Butler Library at Columbia University, and above all the Humanities Research Centre at the University of Austin, Texas, and especially to its Librarian, Cathy Henderson; in Latin America and the Caribbean to Dudley Ankerson of the British Embassy in Mexico, to Mr John Palmer at the time British Ambassador in Cuba, to the British Consul in Haiti and many others there who in the present turmoil of that country may prefer to remain unnamed, to John Carlin in Mexico City, to Señor Nicola Cedillo in Ciudad del Mais; and indeed to the *guerrilleros* of the FAR, the *Fuerzas Armadas Revolucionarias* in Guatemala, temporary kidnapping on the Belize highway by whom gave us a genuine taste, for an anxious morning, of what it must have been like in Mexico of the Thirties, for Graham Greene to have travelled *his* lawless roads.

I am sure there are many many others whom I should have included on this list; and I ask them to forgive me; as I do any person or organisation whose copyright I may unwittingly have infringed; both faults which I hope can be remedied in the future.

Finally may I express my gratitude in advance to all those readers of this present volume who, hopefully, will be stimulated or provoked to write in and reinforce, or contradict, the hypotheses herein put forward – or simply to add information? It is part of a biographer's difficulties, part of his joys too, that very often the most interesting insights are contributed only *after* the work has been published.

Notes and Sources

How to give precise references to quotations from Graham Greene's published works? The puzzle is in the page numbers. Take, for instance, *The Basement Room* – published (in the United Kingdom alone) in three different hardback editions, plus one paperback, under its original title; and then again in hardback and in paperback under its film title. Six different editions, with page numbers differing in each edition: a morass.

Fortunately Graham Greene almost always divided his books into Parts and his chapters into either headed or numbered sub-sections. This has suggested a solution. References are therefore given not to any particular page in any particular edition of any particular work but to that section of the work from which the citation is taken. What this may lack in precision it will make up for in consistency.

* * *

GG in the reference notes that follow stands, obviously, for Graham Greene; and CC and MM for his contemporaries, Claud Cockburn and Malcolm Muggeridge. Other less alliterative authors are given their full names – except for EW which has become by now almost accepted literary shorthand for Evelyn Waugh. *Op Cit.* refers to books in Section II of the short bibliography that follows.

Prologue: A Sort of Death

All Fools Day 1991 It need hardly be said that this first paragraph is sourceless.

Graham Greene's Funeral Evening Standard, April 8th 1991; Guardian, April 9th, 1991.

When my daughter Caroline telephoned… 'Mandrake', Sunday Telegraph, April 7th 1991. Cp also Jane Thynne, Daily Telegraph, December 10th 1992.

The Requiem Mass Author's notes. Daily Telegraph, June 7th 1991.

A scarcely avuncular act A.N. Wilson, Daily Mail, April 6th 1991.

Chapter One: Greene Blood

three Greenes These would have been (had the scene imagined ever taken place) Sir Edward Greene, Bt, MP for Bury St. Edmunds; his elder son, Walter Greene, MP for the Chesterton Division of Cambridgeshire; and their first cousin Henry Greene, MP for Shropshire – whose father, Benjamin Buck, richest of all the Greenes, had been a High Sheriff, a Governor of the Bank of England, owner of a manor in Berkshire, of a mansion in Kensington Park Gardens, and of plantations in Mauritius.

All this wealth derived from Benjamin Greene who in 1799 aged 19 had taken over the Westgate Street brewery in Bury St Edmunds. The Greene wealth still flows, almost two hundred years later, from their shares in what has become an ever-expanding successful brewery conglomerate, Greene King. It is still based in Bury St. Edmunds and East Anglia.

a large family Benjamin the Brewer died in 1860, mid-Victorian times, leaving eight married children: four sons and four daughters. They married 'sensibly' – Smiths, Smythies, Wilsons, Lakes, Lanes, Burrells, Raymonds dot the family tree, a surprising number of them the sons and daughters of clergymen. Marion's grandfather, the Reverend Carleton's father John, a solicitor of Bedford, was one of the less successful of Benjamin the Brewer's four sons. William Greene, her husband Charles' father, also of Bedford, was another. The wealth and the status seemed to go to the other two sons of Benjamin the Brewer: Benjamin Buck and Edward. Edward indeed became MP for Stowmarket during his father's lifetime; and himself fathered the first Baronet. This may have led to a certain distance between the various branches of the Greene clan. Certainly the Greenes on both sides of Graham's ancestry were less grand and powerful than the other two branches of the family had become. It is a fascinating story of a clan climbing the social scale with great rapidity over a comparatively short period of time – Forsythian, almost.

There Graham shared a room… GG's first accounts of his childhood and youth can be found in his two pre-war travel books: scattered throughout *Journey Without Maps*, concentrated in the opening section of *The Lawless Roads*. Then comes a long gap, ended by "Part One – Personal Prologue" – the four pages that form the title essay of *The Lost Childhood and Other Essays* published in 1951. It was not till many, many years later that he pulled all of them together (plus other independently-published autobiographical essays and fragments such as *The Revenge*) into the first volume of his autobiography, *A Sort of Life*. The eleven chapters of this book take GG from his first memories of a dead dog in a pram (which seem suspiciously close to a self-parody in verse he previously published under an assumed name in a *New Statesman* competition) to the acceptance by Heinemann's of *Stamboul Train*.

Some deep unhealed traumatic wound Sean O'Faolain, Op.Cit. (1)

A savage land ... under occupation GG, A Sort of Life, 3,1

From that moment ... saw that it was so. GG, The Lost Childhood

But the indications are... These include: the inscription on the Reverend Carleton's tombstone in the churchyard at Great Barford; the entries in *Crockford's*; semi-jocular references in GG's autobiographical works that gradually become more explicit.

One of the few interviews John Cornwall, The Tablet, 23rd Sept. 1989. (But it is worth noting that John Cornwall entitled his obituary in the same journal, 13th April 1991, "A Catholic to the Last" and argued very strongly that this was so.)

No knowing that he had ever read In October 1972 GG wrote to his antiquarian bookseller friend David Low to ask him to keep a weather eye open for any books or pamphlets written by his grandfather. The letter indicates that he had never read any of the Reverend Carleton's writings.

The small human viciousness... GG, Journey Without Maps, Part III, Chapter Three, The Seedy Level.

His talk ... unaffected pleasure Peter Quennell, Op.Cit., P.98

Oxford, far more than his childhood Though GG wrote *of* his childhood, he did not write in the mode of a child; rather the contrary. The general point is elaborated at the end of the next chapter.

Footnotes

p3 At Berkhamsted... GG quoted by Marie-Françoise Allain, Op. Cit,p.30

p5 Halting at one of the pubs... lacerated imagination Sean O'Faolain, Ibid.

p10 It's amazing... low whistle CC, Op.Cit, p.37

p12 Which would have been a disaster GG, A Sort of Life, 4,2.

Chapter Two : Balliol Man

God be with you, Balliol men Hilaire Belloc, Collected Verses

The Trial of Pan GG, Oxford Outlook, Feb 1923

The Curate of Stow in the Wold GG, The Improbable Tale of the Archbishop of Canterbridge, Cherwell, Nov. 15, 1924

That Easter Vacation Raymond... Raymond Greene, Op.Cit.

A constant fear... GG, Weekly Westminster Gazette, Aug. 25, 1923. Reprinted in Reflections.

It is the poverty ... apathetic air. GG, Ibid

Sought out... cannot answer Peter Quennell, Op.Cit., pp.112-113

Was in the widest... mark of doom CC, Op. Cit.,

A deliberate insult ... GG, Oxford Outlook, June 1924. Reprinted in Reflections.

Footnotes

p17 Little prancing fawn... Harold Acton, Op,Cit., p.126
These public schoolboys ... AL Rowse, Op.Cit., p.24

p21 Short himself.... majestic persona Peter Quennell, Op.Cit., p.65

Chapter Three : Enter Vivienne, Softly

Did, or did not Graham Greene really attempt suicide while at Oxford? In the original version of this book the Russian Roulette episode was analysed (as mentioned in the Preface) in great detail: here it is relegated to a mere footnote.

The reasons for scepticism are several; and most varied. First, from the point of view of an historian, is the difficulty with chronology: when precisely did the six alleged attempts take place; why; and how do they fit in with the other known events of Graham's life at Oxford? His own varied accounts are inconsistent as to the dates; and are therefore impossible to link with any satisfactory explanation of motive. Secondly, there is the evidence of his contemporaries: neither Claud Cockburn nor Peter Quennell, the two who had known him longest, believed the story. Thirdly there are practical difficulties concerning the revolver – and the bullets – allegedly involved. Fourthly there is the psychological – and literary – aspect: if Graham Greene invented the story, why did he invent it? Rivalry – of a very curious sort if so – with Conrad and Henry James?

In the end, of course, as with all failed attempts at suicide witnessed by no-one, there is no knowing the truth, or otherwise, of the legend. Those who are sceptical, like the present author, might care to consider the explanation provided by the Commissioner in *Dr Fischer of Geneva: or The Bomb Party*.

What I remember ... open to the world AL Rowse, Op.Cit., pp.206-207

Mr Graham Greene ... Songs of the years CC, Isis,February 1925

I think the work very beautiful... GK Chesterton, Foreword to Vivienne Browning, Op.Cit.

All the work of my young daughter ... Muriel Dayrell-Browning, Note,Ibid

I'll meet my Fate in Devon... Vivienne Browning, Ibid

Fourteen long years on earth!... Vivienne Browning, Ibid

Brought up a non-Catholic What seems to have happened is that Muriel abandoned the Church, either on her marriage or on her separation – which apparently occurred in Rhodesia. But Vivienne, on returning to England and thereby making contact with her grandparents, converted to – or returned to – the Faith. This was probably in 1920, when she was aged 14 or 15, a year before the publication of her book of poems; her mother remaining a non-believer. It is not clear whether Vivienne was baptised at birth or upon being received into the Church in her teens.

Has visited and candidly commented... Beverley Nichols' own entry in Who's Who

This is the attractive title... CC, Isis, April 29, 1925

Admitting that Mr Graham Greene ... adolescent hysteria Harold Acton, Cherwell, May 9, 1925

Plainly Mr Greene ... lodgings in Thorncliffe Road Harold Acton, Cherwell, May 23, 1925

The end of Greene's career as a poet: This is debatable in the sense that a long poem, Sad Cure; The Life and Death of John Perry-Perkins, was published in three consecutive issues (early 1926) of The Cherwell after Graham had gone down; and he tried, but failed, to get Basil Blackwell to publish another volume of verse with that title. A swan song, perhaps. And two more volumes of his verse were privately printed in the Fifties. Rumour has it that they are pornographic – and if Norman Douglas had any influence upon them, rumour could well be true.

Footnotes

p30 How we make our timorous advance to death by GG, Babbling April, First Poem

Will it be mist and death GG, Ibid, Last Poem

p33 Babbling April's rarity value Vivienne's personal copy, sold at auction by Sotheby's after Graham's death, fetched £1200...

Chapter Four: Warily To Rome

I have been in dance halls and cabarets... Herbert Greene, Op.Cit.

Footnotes

p37 *The Episode* was inspired not only by Conrad's *The Arrow of Gold* but also, even more directly, by Carlyle's *Life of John Sterling*. It is set in London, against the background of the Carlist Wars; and tells how certain young English idealists supported a disastrous invasion of southern Spain by a group of London-based Spanish exiles. The extraordinary thing about it is how it prefigured so much yet to come in GG's own life: the indirect connection with the Cambridge Apostles, the more direct connection with another failed invasion of Spain inspired by the OSS – and, weirdest of all, the fact that the leader of the Spanish exiles was a General named Torrijos – exactly the name of the General whom Graham Greene so notoriously got to know in the Seventies.

The whereabouts of the manuscript of *The Episode* was for years a mystery. It has now apparently, since GG's death, joined the manuscript of *Anthony Sant* at Texas…

p43 The first published account of his conditional baptism GG, Journey Without Maps, Part II, I, New Country

In his autobiography GG, A Sort of Life, 9,2.

Chapter Five: Adam and Eve

Many of his friends: For instance Edith Sitwell, a great friend in later life, an acquaintance since Oxford days. Dear Graham Greene, she wrote, what a great priest you would have made. Yours always, Edith Sitwell.

His second cousin Christopher Isherwood: Emily Greene, elder sister of Sir Walter Greene, the second Baronet, had a daughter Kathleen who married Frank Isherwood, Christopher's father. Christopher Isherwood was thus a great-great-great grandson of Benjamin the Brewer – one remove further away than Graham.

Under the name of Elizabeth: Undoubtedly a portrait of Vivienne; but given the name of Graham's favourite, and younger, sister; which she, Elizabeth Greene, and the rest of the family, cannot fail to have noticed. Has this any significance? No-one can doubt that Greene was name-conscious, as Professor Stratford (in his splendid essay, 'Unlocking The Potting Shed') has stressed.

The peace of God GG, The Man Within, Part One, 2

God, you're respectable GG, Ibid,

Footnotes

p46 A touching short story GG, Twenty One Stories, The Blue Film.

Chapter Six: Novelist!

Neurotic and cowardly...the physical GG, The Man Within, Part One, 3

slim, long-legged... GG, Ibid, Part Two, 9

You are a funny boy... show you. GG, Ibid, Part Two, 7

Have you enjoyed yourself... animal in him. GG, Ibid, Part Two, 9

For a day we are disgusted...all over again GG, Ibid, Part Two, 9

He felt no fear of death...self-loathing. GG, Ibid, Part Two, 9

To their younger literary contemporaries Such as Clemence Dane

Mr Geoffrey Dawson had perfected... CC, Op.Cit, p.74

A rash and unfortunate decision. Reported by GG, A Sort of Life, 10,7

I can foresee... success with this book EW, The Graphic, Oct 25 1930 (Gallagher P.101)

Footnotes

p53 lower I believe we've got a winner ...young Greene. Cecil Roberts, Op.Cit.,p.136

The bearer of this note... agent to be you. David Higham, Op.Cit., p.170

p57 upper did a spell in the Home Room CC, Op,Cit., p.72

Chapter Seven: Enter Annette, Secretly

His second false dawn His first had been the enthusiastic acceptance of his very first novel, Anthony Sant, by AD Peters.

This is the one for me GG, England Made Me, Part One, 1.

(The evidence is ambiguous) See the second volume of GG's autobiography, *Ways of Escape* 1,6. This volume (in 9 chapters, 35 sub-sections and an epilogue) consists almost entirely of the Introductions to Heinemann's Collected Edition of GG's Works (over twenty of them in all) occasionally touched up – as in the case of 1,6; which is basically the Introduction to *England Made Me* – and 'linked' by various essays on GG's friends, such as Herbert Read and Evelyn Waugh, plus other sub-sections on his world travels.

Although he has never... pleading his own Philip Stratford, Op,Cit., p.90

It made no difference to me... chose an adventure story. GG., A Sort of Life, II,4

If in fact Greene had not reread... As is proved conclusively by his private diaries at Texas.

Read it out to me, said Graham... this new route. Ronald Matthews, Op.Cit., p.150

It is through their inadequacies... Philip Stratford, Ibid., p120

Chapter Eight: £1738.3s.8d

Rupert Hart-Davis and Peggy Ashcroft: See Vincent Browne's account in his biography of JP Priestley. Bizarrely, Sheridan Morley's biography of Peggy Ashcroft, from which one might have expected a fuller account, does not so much as mention the fact that it was her affair with Priestley that brought her marriage with Rupert Hart-Davis to so premature an end.

a trick of his race... black oiled hair GG,Stamboul Train, Part Two, I.Cologne

Novelists like Ruby M. Ayres... a fur coat or thereabouts GG, Ibid, Part Two, I.Cologne

Back from St. Kitts Where the Greenes had had plantations too.

Bubbled over with literary energy. And with political energy too. Back in Oxford GG founded a branch of the Independent Labour Party, the ILP; a curious moment in his political career about which one would like to know more. At this period the ILP had its own Members of Parliament, very much more militant than the Labour Party, and even than the CPGB.

Footnotes

p71 bottom JS Thomas...gave him a pipe GG, A Sort of Life, 11,5.

Chapter Nine: Enter Moura, Boldly

Her haggard sunken face GG, It's a Battlefield, 3.

In her brain Mr Surrogate knew... GG, Ibid.

My uncle Graham Greene... GG, Introduction, Ibid.

The book is heavy... John Atkins, Op,Cit., p.41. The reference to a 'social conscience' is interesting; and presumably ties up with GG joining the ILP – see above. It 'later disappears'; and indeed the ILP was only a very passing phase. GG's first cousins Ben and Felix were active in left-wing politics at this time; more committed too. Both had stood, unsuccessfully, for Parliament.

She was young and pretty... GG, It's a Battlefield, 4.

With comic hopefulness...don't turn up. GG, Ibid.

A film synopsis... in a dozen pages cp GG, The Tenth Man, where it is published.

Chapter Ten: Brothers and Sisters – and Cousin Barbara

Those who would understand Moura... Tania Alexander, Op.Cit.,p.48

A normal sexual relationship ...neither solemn nor dull GG, The Old School, The Last Word

Anthony was someone I knew very well... GG, Introduction, England Made Me

I was quite satisfied...the real thing. GG, Ways of Escape, 1,6

She might have been waiting...helped to kill him GG, England Made Me, Part One, 1

With the possible exception of Sarah GG, Ways of Escape, Ibid.

She's the goods... in the half light GG, England Made Me, Ibid.

When I pushed the button...nobody came up GG, England Made Me, Part Six, 1.

Why don't you come to Liberia... Barbara Greene, Op. Cit., p.1

Far from comforting Barbara Greene, Ibid, p.2

All my life... Barbara Greene, Ibid, p.48/49

Tall and hefty Barbara Greene, Ibid, p.2

So I wept a little... Barbara Greene, Ibid, p.3

At last a daughter of mine... Reported by Barbara Greene, Ibid, Foreword

His brain frightened me... Barbara Greene, Ibid, p.6

Footnotes

p93 Vivienne has said To the present author

p96 There are intriguing references... John Atkins, Op.Cit., p.68

Though GG never acknowledges this publicly, he had read John Atkins' criticism most attentively. But numerous examples can be found. For instance, to take just one simple case, John Atkins remarks (p.25) on GG's incongruous and inflated style in *The Name of Action*; and quotes, to illustrate his point, the phrase, 'a revolver drooped like a parched flower to the pavement'. In *Ways of Escape* (1,2)

GG writes "Here are examples of my... terrible use of simile and metaphor, 'A revolver drooped like a parched flower to the pavement'." Much more importantly, to John Atkins can be attributed, I think, Greene's later disclaimers of being a Catholic novelist.

Chapter Eleven: Explorer!

The misgovernment of the native tribes: At the time of writing Liberia is once again engulfed in turmoil and civil war. One regrets the old days when Her Majesty's Government felt it a dereliction of duty not to intervene – particularly as the conflict has spread over into neighbouring Sierra Leone.

As Waugh and Fleming had been... Peter Fleming was appointed a Special Correspondent for The Times on his trip to China and Manchuko; Evelyn Waugh on his journey to Abyssinia for the Coronation of the Negus.

It was René Clair... this was it. GG, Journey Without Maps, Part I, Chapter Two, Dakar

On the roofs the vultures sat... GG, Ibid, Chapter Three, Freetown

He was somewhat vague and impractical... Barbara Greene, Op, Cit., p.7

There they stood in their flowing white robes... Barbara Greene, Ibid, p.8

I couldn't have imagined then... GG, Ibid, The Three Companions

One cannot continue long... GG, Ibid, Fashionable Wedding at St. George's Cathedral.

The Englishmen here... GG, Ibid, Up to Railhead.

I liked him at once... Barbara Greene, Ibid, p.13/14

We were now going to plunge... Barbara Greene, Ibid, p.17

Physically he did not look strong. Barbara Greene, Ibid, p.6

Graham from the beginning... Barbara Greene, Ibid, p.68

Slowly with many biting expressions... Barbara Greene, Ibid, p.135

A little taken aback GG, Ibid, Part II, Chapter Two, "Boss of the Whole Show"

Most intimate friend... black dreamy eyes Barbara Greene, Ibid, p.34

One of the loveliest things... GG, Ibid.

Who would have welcomed white intervention... GG, Ibid.

Everywhere in the north... GG, Ibid.

Rather absurd... GG, Ibid, Part III, Chapter Three, Black Mercenary

Handsome villain... too theatrical Barbara Greene, Ibid, p.160

We want some whisky ... a beautiful thought Barbara Greene, Ibid, pp.161-169

My cousin had certainly caught... Barbara Greene, Ibid, p.159

Graham looked ghastly... Barbara Greene, Ibid, p.170

I had supper by myself... Barbara Greene, Ibid, p.174

Had Graham Greene died there... His short story, 'A Chance for Mr Lever', published in 1936 imagines exactly that situation: an 'explorer' meeting a solitary black-vomiting death in the dank Liberian forest.

His pencilled diary... This is long, and at Texas. It parallels his book; and is the third source for the trip. It is a matter of great regret that I cannot, for legal reasons, quote Graham's exact pencilled words as he lay (as he thought) dying: for they are very moving, and show his character in an extremely good light.

Footnotes

p100 upper	I could only use it occasionally.	Barbara Greene, Ibid, p.17
p104	With all the wealth of phrase...	Barbara Greene, Ibid, p.202

Chapter Twelve: Clapham Common

(The film reviews in *The Spectator* were almost all reprinted in *The Pleasure Dome*)

One of the last times... enthralling subject of food. Barbara Greene, Op.Cit., P.60/61

He never opened the Meccano set again... GG, The Basement Room, 2

To all sorts of shy people... In particular, and most notoriously, John Hayward to TS Eliot, with whom for a number of years John Hayward shared a flat in Chelsea. Eliot's sudden and mishandled abandonment of their shared life shattered John Hayward's morale; and accounts for GG's starched but obscure condemnations of Eliot in later life. See Peter Ackroyd's much-admired biography of *TS Eliot* (Hamish Hamilton, 1984).

Birth and death simultaneously... GG, The Bear Fell Free

Greene fulminated like a John Knox... Anthony Powell, Op. Cit., p.77

The finest travel film... GG, *The Spectator*, July 5 1935

No other film actress... GG, *The Spectator*, October 11 1935

The Grierson/Rotha/Wright/Cavalcanti set... John Grierson's documentary masterpiece *Drifters* was followed by Basil Wright's lyrical *Song of Ceylon*; which Graham reviewed ecstatically on October 4th, 1935. Paul Rotha was famous for his book *The Film Till Now*. Graham was continually lunching and discussing projects with everyone connected with the GPO Film Unit. But Alberto Cavalcanti – 'Cav' – a decade older than the rest of them, was in fact the film director who would, in the end, do most for him.

Graham Greene and The Tablet... Douglas Woodruff had been a notable Oxford figure, President of the Union two terms before Graham came up. An OG and a rumbustious Catholic, married to an Acton, formerly Colonial Editor of The Times, he became Editor of The Tablet when its clerical proprietors were ousted by a group of Catholic laymen. Graham Greene, from this time onwards an occasional contributor, was eventually to become a Director of The Tablet Publishing Company himself.

Haunted by the awful tedium ...word-associations GG, Introduction, Journey Without Maps.

Two accounts... that coincide almost exactly Three, including GG's pencilled diary

Some critics... GG, Introduction, Brighton Rock.

There seemed to be a seediness... GG, Journey Without Maps, Part I, Chapter One, Blue Book

The seedy level... GG, Ibid, Part III, Chapter Four

This may explain the deep appeal of the seedy... GG, Ibid, Part III, Chapter Five, Return

Footnotes

p112 It leaves you with a vivid sense... GG, *The Spectator*, July 5, 1935

p115 Greeneland, perhaps... GG, Introduction, *The Ministry of Fear*

Chapter Thirteen: Among the 'Dark Aliens'

Murder didn't mean much to Raven... GG,. A Gun For Sale, 1,i

Old thin body... a skeleton... GG, Ibid, 4,iii

Oh, she said with a sigh... GG, Ibid, 8,v

Unbearable pain... vast desolation GG, Ibid, 7,ii

He's very ugly... GG, Ibid, 1,iii

The vast expensive Korda-Wells film...fancy GG, The Spectator, Feb 28 1936

The dialogue... Wells downward GG, Ibid, May 8 1936

England of course... ever emerge GG, Ibid, June 5 1936

The Quota Act The Quota Act(s) and the resulting 'Quota Quickies' led to a boom in film production in Britain: from only 26 features completed in 1926, the crisis year, to a record 212 in 1936.

From film-reviewing it was only a small step... GG, Introduction, The Pleasure Dome

When we were alone... on the platform GG, Ibid

Film historians... Halliwell's Film Companion

Herr Pommer... romantic hero with ease GG, The Spectator, March 5 1937

I was nicknamed Sugar... that merry plan Basil Dean, Op. Cit, pp 251,253

Hale knew... lonely man at a railway station GG, Brighton Rock, Part One, 1

I liked Kite... GG, Ibid, Part Five, 1

It had been Kite's territory... GG, Ibid

A much more complex undertaking... cp John Atkins' Chapter VIII where he praises *Brighton Rock* for its 'intensity of mood'; which is however closely related to the Boy's (and Greene's) 'loathing of sexuality'. A book written 'in hatred', he describes it as, and in a 'state of emotional upheaval'. As for the notoriously bizarre moral theology,' Greene's faith seems to be no closer to Christ than Hitler's was to Goethe... It is insulting that Pinkie should be presented to us, in all his evil, as our spiritual superior.' This is a bald summary of a many-stranded, complex and refreshingly unusual argument.

Footnotes

p121 bottom Told of vulgar plot... EW, *Diaries*, Nov 20 1936

Chapter Fourteen: Blood of The Martyrs

To the Writers and Poets... your answers Nancy Cunard, Op.Cit.

As an Englishman... EW in Ibid

The publication... in Spain a hundred years ago GG, The Spectator, Dec.1937

I am warning you, Greene… Herbert Greene, Op.Cit. p.18

Stanley Carr, an old Army friend Herbert Greene, ibid, p.12

I do not even know… Herbert Greene, Ibid., p.11

Mrs Guest may have more information… Herbert Greene, Ibid, p.286

Useful information…in contact Herbert Greene, Ibid

He is neither a Spaniard nor a Jap Herbert Greene, Ibid, p.13

A Spy Advertises GG and Hugh Greene, The Spy's Bedside Book, p.41

To anyone whom it might concern… Herbert Greene, Ibid

A model… never sombre GG, The Spectator, Nov 1 1935

His future writings… Cp, for example, the vivid and polemic reference to "No stench from Campion's quarters" in his March 1937 film review of *Fire Over England*, quoted in the previous chapter.

He came back to his own country… the reign of Elizabeth GG, The Lawless Roads, Prologue : 2, The Faith

Looking back on it… Peter Fleming ('Slingsby') Night and Day, July 8 1937

The traditional Denham mouse…Naughty Wimperis vein GG, Ibid, Sept 30 1937

Restless shoulders and the protuberant breasts GG, Ibid, Aug 26 1937

If ever there was a Christ-like man… dead pen GG, Ibid, Sept 16 1937

Swaggering stride… a complete totsy GG Ibid, Oct 28 1937

I suppose…an uninstructed one Anthony Powell, Op.Cit, p80

Counsel for the appellant… Present author, Lions Under The Throne (the first chapter of which describes in gruesome detail the tortures and trials suffered by Campion and his fellow Jesuits in the reign of Elizabeth.)

Footnotes

p129 upper I am not a Fascist… EW in Nancy Cunard, Op.Cit.

p132 upper the manuscript fell… Barbara Greene, Too Late to Turn Back, Introduction.

Chapter Fifteen: Alone in Hateful Mexico

You can't conceive, my child… GG, Brighton Rock, Part 7,11

With longing of New York...cinnamon sticks and cherries GG, The Lawless Roads, 7,

Old fiery half-blind Archbishop...Catholic Action in San Antonio GG, Ibid, 1, Catholic Action

I have never been in a country... GG, Ibid

On the strength of a happy mood... GG, Ibid, 2, Monterrey

A lovely town... guns on their hips GG, Ibid, 2, The Rebel State

Complete irresponsibility...lawless roads GG, Ibid, 2, Tour of the Catacombs

General Saturnino Cedillo... cp Dudley Ankerson's fine book (Op.Cit.)

Mufti, an old soft hat...one-sided GG, Ibid, 2, A Day at the General's

There had been one priest...we die like dogs GG, Ibid, 6, A Day in the Beautiful City

Oh... a whisky priest GG, Ibid, 6, A Victorian Adventurer

In the only possible hotel... GG, Ibid, 6, Garrido's Capital

That very Catholic City GG, Ibid, 7, Salto de Agua

A clerk I grew to loathe... GG, Ibid, 8, The Exile

Lay on the hard earth, almost happy GG, Ibid, 9, The Luck of the Road

England of the Conquest... GG, Ibid, 9, A Grove of Crosses

Con Amistad... his office GG, Ibid, 7, Night on the Plain

Footnotes

p147 The Catholic revolt, half expected by Graham then... Yet another general, General Pineda, was expected 'at any moment' in 'the very Catholic city', to lead an uprising that might result in the long-desired separation of Chiapas, Tabasco, Yucatan and Quintana Roo from the rest of Mexico. (This does not seem to be, at least not openly and not yet, the policy of the present-day Indian insurgents.) The General, a former President of Las Casas, never appeared.

p148 Sudden crazy action... GG, Ibid, 6, Journey Downhill

Chapter Sixteen: Reacting to Evelyn Waugh

Korda and the Secret Service... See Chapter Twenty. London Films was a near-perfect 'cover'; and Korda's love for Britain had all the fervour of a convert's.

I was, I suppose, thirteen years old... GG,The Lawless Roads, Prologue, 1, The Anarchists.

I find it impossible… hatred of freewill EW, The Spectator, March 10 1939

An entirely dreary book about Mexico… Sean O'Faolain, Op.Cit.(1)

There is a theory… On Pritchett and Waugh's influence: the present author's

So far as the author…martyrs died EW, Ibid

The black letters in silencio…a prison wall GG, Ibid, 7, Salto de Agua

With his hand on his stomach…a neighbour shot GG, The Power and The Glory, Part IV

Footnotes

p153 The chief of police… GG, *The Lawless Roads*, 6, A Day in the Beautiful City.

The Chief of Police GG, *The Power and the Glory*, part I, 2, The Capital

Chapter Seventeen: Enter Dorothy, Devotedly

Seeing me there… inner fatigue Julian Maclaren-Ross, Op.Cit., Excursions in Greeneland

When we rose… massacre of the innocent Julian Maclaren-Ross, Ibid

The connection with Berkhamsted was almost broken… Ben Greene, Uncle Eppy's eldest son, alone of the Greene clan, continued to live there with his Scots wife and three young children, a respected local employer and magistrate.

Who exactly might be the Squire… In fact very little land went with Harston House. The local landowners were the Hurrells and, increasingly, the neighbouring Walstons.

He must have been thirty-four… Julian Maclaren-Ross, Ibid.

A simple and kindly gentleman… GG, The Spectator, July 1938

Muggeridge story… Told by MM to the present author.

Hadn't so much as heard from her… GG, The Power and The Glory, Part IV

The setting may be London or Liberia… more variable climate Arthur Calder-Marshall, Horizon, Op.Cit.

A fascinating study… GG, The Spectator, August 1939

Footnotes

p157 middle handsome with black hair… Julian Maclaren-Ross, Ibid.

p157 bottom In that case, said Greene recovering... Julian Maclaren-Ross, Ibid.

p160 You couldn't have called a man like that... GG, The Great Jowett, Commentator speaking

p161 A typically Greenian passage... Cp, for example, GG, The Living Room passim

p162 top The place was stuffy... behind the bell: Glover GG, The Confidential Agent, Part One, The Hunted, IV

p162 middle It's religion... enormous success in Norway GG, Ibid, Part Two, The Hunter, III

Chapter Eighteen: Royal Marine Manqué

The Officers' Emergency Reserve... This was a semi-official body only. GG's name probably came up as a former Special Constable during the General Strike of 1926; as his brother Raymond had also been.

How do you visualize yourself... the infantry GG,Introduction, The Confidential Agent

The awful repetitions... GG, The Spectator, March 8 1940

D'you see that... a cenotaph Julian Maclaren-Ross, Op.Cit., A Story in Horizon

On Skate's agenda... men were coming home from work GG, Twenty-One Stories, Men at Work

Went to Ministry of Information... wanted to become a Marine EW, Diaries, May 1940

I will never forget... home had been destroyed... MM p.83 Op. Cit. (2) and p.317 for sentiment. This was 14 North Side, Clapham Common – not *totally* destroyed, as it still stands today; but clearly gutted enough to make it uninhabitable.

This was indeed local and domestic war... GG, Ways of Escape, 4,1.

Footnotes

p166 Needed a few more months... GG, Ibid, 3,2,

p167 bottom Coolly exploring... MM. Op.Cit (1) p.78

Chapter Nineteen : Spy!

A reedy figure... wet eyes Kim Philby, Op.Cit., p.34

Most conspicuous… capacity for work Kim Philby, Ibid, p.32

A sort of Father Browne of espionage… MM, Introduction, John Whitwell, Op.Cit.

No-one could ever he a better chief than Kim Philby… GG, Introduction, Kim Philby, Op.Cit.

That Atlantic Channel… too depressing GG, In Search of A Character, II, Convoy to Africa, 27 December 1941.

After a hanging… he could not eat meat for a fortnight GG, In Search of A Character, Congo Journal, Feb 28.

Very hot… strangely familiar. GG, Ibid, Convoy to Africa, 3 January 1942

ex-MI5 sources… As related to the present author.

Footnotes

p177 Through the good offices… unassuming countenance MM, pp 192-193,Op.Cit (1) edition

p185 In these situations… Bruce Page, David Leitch, Philip Knightley, Op.Cit., p.148

Chapter Twenty: Konspiratsia in Ryder Street?

Graham Greene was brought back… Kim Philby, Op.Cit., p.58

A short unaccountable man… endlessly praised MM. pp 192-193, Op.Cit. (1)

Machiavellian outspoken Anglophile… Donald Downes, Op.Cit.

A full-grown Foreign Office rat… Donald Downes, Ibid.

Not the last time Graham and Philby were to cooperate in print… The appearance of Kim Philby's book in 1968, five years after he had fled to the USSR and been publicly revealed as a traitor, created an enormous fuss at the time – particularly, perhaps, because *My Silent War* was so readable, so well-written, so astringent. But even more of a scandal, if possible, was created by the Preface to the book that GG contributed. No wonder this caused such offence all round. For GG compared Philby to Campion and the Catholic martyrs of the reign of Elizabeth, an analogy as provocative as it was baseless: for Campion and his fellow Jesuits betrayed no-one, but were themselves betrayed, and executed. They were much more in the position of the British agents whom Philby betrayed; and, unlike Campion and his fellows, Philby never risked the rack, disembowelling, castration and hanging. GG, when he wrote the Preface, had expatriated himself to France; and he probably underestimated the furore he would cause in England. Thereafter, without denying him, he tended to be much more cautious in his support for his old friend.

A little cocksparrow... effortless expertise MM, Ibid, pp 170-171

Spluttered and shouted...the Nazi-Soviet Pact MM, Ibid, p.188

Malcolm Muggeridge's belief that Philby only became a Soviet agent during the War: It has always seemed paradoxical that Philby's own account of his early recruitment at Cambridge has been so readily accepted even by experts in the field. It seems much more probable that this was a lying account, invented much later and convenient (as propaganda) for Philby and his Soviet masters; and that Philby, in the immediate pre-war period at any rate, was exactly what he seemed to be: a genuine pro-Fascist. He was certainly, despite his charm, a totally unscrupulous man; and a profound liar.

Chapter Twenty One: VE Day – Venus Anadyomene

Thanks awfully... EW, Letters, Nov.8 1950

This minor little film story... Published, together with The Tenth Man, in 1985.

It was never made Not for the cinema. But a television version was shown in the USA on December 4 1988 starring Anthony Hopkins as Chavel and Derek Jacobi as the false Jean Louis.

Silent little bicycle taxis... GG, The Tenth Man, Part Two, 7

Was in his element... Liberation MM, Ibid, p.210

To seek out Mauriac...Grasset. MM, Ibid, p.237

Grasset... a great success MM, Ibid.

8 May 1945... a family too. GG, The End of The Affair. Book Three, 5.

Footnotes

p200 lower — My younger children... EW, Letters, Nov.16 1950

Dear Graham... most versatile of men EW, Ibid, Nov.12 1952

p202 upper — Slave contract GG, Introduction, *The Tenth Man.*

p202 lower — All the many films produced from GG's stories or novels... Strictly speaking, The Third Man is not an exception; for *The Third Man* was written (exactly as *The Tenth Man* had been) originally as a film-story and only thereafter published as a novel – the 'Book of the Film', so to speak, in both cases, though only in one was the film actually made.

Short Bibliography[1]

This bibliography is divided into two sections. First come works by Graham Greene that are 'covered' in this volume;next comes a (fairly eclectic) list of works by other authors that are quoted or referred to in the text or which otherwise might be of interest to readers.

I Works By Graham Greene

(Published by Heinemann, *unless* otherwise stated. ★s indicate: available in Penguin.)

A. *POETRY:*

Babbling April Basil Blackwell May 1925

B. *NOVELS:*

★ *The Man Within* June 1929

The Name of Action October 1930

Rumour at Nightfall November 1931

★ *Stamboul Train* December 1932

★ *It's A Battlefield* January 1934

★ *England Made Me* June 1935

★ *A Gun For Sale* July 1936

★ *Brighton Rock* July 1938

★ *The Confidential Agent* September 1939

★ *The Power and The Glory* March 1940

★ *The Ministry of Fear* May 1943

C. *NOVELLAS AND CERTAIN SHORT STORIES:*

The End of the Party The Graphic, Jan 1932

The Bear Fell Free Grayson & Grayson 1935

The Basement Room[2] The Cresset Press 1935

Men At Work Penguin New Writing, No.9, Sept.1941

The Lieutenant Died Last Colliers 1940

The Revolver in the Corner Cupboard The Saturday Book, Hutchinsons 1946

The Revenge Time and Tide,Dec 1954

★ *The Tenth Man* The Bodley Head and Anthony Blond 1985

D. *AUTOBIOGRAPHY:*

★ *A Sort of Life*[3] The Bodley Head Sept 1971

★ *Ways of Escape* The Bodley Head Sept 1980

E. *TRAVEL BOOKS AND JOURNALS:*

Journey Without Maps[4] May 1936

★ *The Lawless Roads* Longmans 1939

The Londoners: A Journal of the Blitz The Month, Nov 1952

In Search of A Character[5] The Bodley Head 1961

F. *CHILDREN'S BOOKS:*

The Little Train Eyre and Spottiswoode 1947

The Little Fire Engine Max Parrish 1950

The Little Horse Bus Max Parrish 1952

The Little Steam Roller Max Parrish 1953

G. *MISCELLANEOUS:*

The Old School[6] Jonathan Cape 1934

British Dramatists[7] Collins 1942

The Great Jowett[8] The Bodley Head 1981

The Spy's Bedside Book[9] Hart-Davis 1957

Lord Rochester's Monkey[10] The Bodley Head 1974

H. *COLLECTIONS:*

Twenty Four Stories[11] The Cresset Press 1935

Nineteen Stories July 1947

* *Twenty One Stories* Nov 1954

* *The Last Word and Other Stories* Reinhardt Books 1990

The Lost Childhood and other Essays Eyre & Spottiswoode 1951

Collected Essays Penguin 1970

The Pleasure Dome[12] Secker & Warburg 1972

Reflections[13] Reinhardt Books 1990

Footnotes:

[1] This bibliography may seem none too short to some. But so enormous was Graham Greene's literary output that a whole academic industry has grown up in the bibliographical field alone. Compared to RA Wobbe's "*Graham Greene: A Bibliography and Guide to Research*" (Garland Publishing Inc New York and London, 1979) a massive 440 pages long, covering 'only' the period up to 1977, it is, therefore, skimpy indeed.

[2] Available in Penguin together with *The Third Man* (under its film title of *The Fallen Idol*)

[3] Now available together with *Ways of Escape* in a Penguin entitled *Fragments of Autobiography*

[4] Withdrawn in year of publication. Republished with new Preface and alterations in 1946; and again with a new Introduction and more changes in 1978.

[5] Includes his Journal *Convoy to West Africa* (first published in The Mint in 1946); and a later Journal, on his trip to the Congo in 1959.

[6] Edited (plus the final chapter contributed).

[7] One of 24 titles in the "Britain in Pictures" series.

[8] The text can be found in the Penguin edition of the *Collected Plays*

[9] Co-edited by Graham Greene and Hugh Greene

[10] The (very) delayed (coffee-table) edition of the Rochester biography.

[11] Eight by Graham Greene.

[12] The collection of most (but not all) of Graham Greene's film criticisms and writings; edited by John Russell Taylor; with an introduction by Graham Greene.

[13] A collection of over 70 of Graham Greene's occasional pieces including journalism, reviews, poems, speeches and forewords. Edited, with an introduction, by Judith Adamson.

2. Works by Other Authors

This is a short hotch-potch from a list that could be almost indefinitely extended. There are probably hundreds of critical works on Greene in scores of languages; and this makes no pretence to do more than scratch some varied surfaces.

Harold Acton *Memoirs of An Aesthete* Methuen 1948

Judith Adamson (1) *Graham Greene and Cinema* Pilgrim Books 1984
(2) *Graham Greene: The Dangerous Edge* Macmillans 1990

Tania Alexander *A Little of All These: An Estonian Childhood* Jonathan Cape 1987

Marie-Françoise Allain *The Other Man: Conversations with Graham Greene* The Bodley Head 1983

Kenneth Allott and Miriam Farris *The Art of Graham Greene* Russell & Russell 1951

Dudley Ankerson *Agrarian Warlord: Saturnino Cedillo* N. Illinois University Press 1984

Jocelyn Baines *Joseph Conrad: A Critical Biography* Weidenfield & Nicolson 1960

Marjorie Bowen *The Viper of Milan* London 1906

Andrew Boyle *The Climate of Treason* (2nd Edition) Hutchinson 1980

Vincent Browne *J.B. Priestley* Hamish Hamilton 1988

Arthur Calder-Marshall (1) *The Works of Graham Greene* Horizon, May 1950
(2) *The Magic of My Youth*[1] Hart-Davis 1951

Claud Cockburn *I Claud* Penguin 1967

Joseph Conrad *The Arrow of Gold* Dent 1924

Nancy Cunard (Ed) *Authors Take Sides* Left Review, 1937

Vivienne Dayrell-Browning *The Little Wings* Basil Blackwell 1921

Basil Dean *Mind's Eye* Hutchinson 1973

Donald Downes *Scarlet Thread Adventures in Wartime Espionage* Derek Verschoyle 1953

Peter Fleming (1) *Brazilian Adventure* Jonathan Cape 1933
(2) *One's Company: A Journey to China in 1933* Jonathan Cape 1934

Barbara Greene *Too Late to Look Back*[2] (2nd Edition) Settle & Benson 1981

Herbert Greene *Secret Agent in Spain* Robert Hale 1938

Raymond Greene *Moments of Being*[3] Heinemann 1974

Christopher Hawtree (Ed) *Night and Day* Chatto & Windus 1985

David Higham *Literary Gent* Jonathan Cape 1978

Julian Maclaren-Ross *Memoirs of the Forties* Alan Ross 1965

Ronald Matthews *Mon Ami Graham Greene* Desclée de Brouwer 1957

Anthony Mockler (1) *Lions Under the Throne*[4] Frederick Muller 1980
(2) *Haile Selassie's War* Oxford University Press 1984

Malcolm Muggeridge (1) *Chronicles of Wasted Times.* Collins 1973
Vol II: The Infernal Grove Fontana 1975
(2) *Like It Was: The Diaries of Malcolm Muggeridge*
Collins 1981

Sean O'Faolain (1) *The Vanishing Hero*[5] Eyre & Spottiswoode 1957
(2) *Vive Moi* Hart-Davis 1965

Bruce Page, David Leitch and Philip Knightley *Philby: The Spy Who Betrayed A Generation* André Deutsch 1968

Kim Philby *My Silent War*[6] McGibbon & Kee 1968

Anthony Powell *Faces in My Time* Heinemann 1980

David Pryce-Jones *Graham Greene* (2nd Edition) Oliver & Boyd 1973

Peter Quennell *The Marble Foot* Collins 1976

Cecil Roberts *The Bright Twenties* Hodder & Stoughton 1970

AL Rowse *A Cornishman at Oxford* Jonathan Cape 1965

Norman Sherry *The Life of Graham Greene : Vol One* Jonathan Cape 1989

Philip Stratford *Faith and Fiction*[7] University of Notre Dame Press, Illinois, 1964.

Martin Stannard *Evelyn Waugh: Vols I & II* Dent 1986 & 1992

Michael Tracey *A Variety of Lives: The Biography of Sir Hugh Greene* The Bodley Head 1988

Evelyn Waugh (1) *Rossetti: His Life and Works* Duckworths 1928
(2) *Decline and Fall* Chapman & Hall 1928
(3) *Edmund Campion: Jesuit and Martyr* Longman 1935
(4) *Waugh in Abyssinia* Longman 1936
(5) *Robbery Under Law: The Mexican Object Lesson* Chapman & Hall 1939
(6) *The Diaries of Evelyn Waugh* (Edited by Michael Davie) Weidenfeld & Nicolson 1976
(7) *The Letters of Evelyn Waugh* (Edited by Mark Amory) Weidenfeld & Nicolson 1980
(8) *The Essays, Articles and Reviews of Evelyn Waugh* (Edited by Donat Gallagher) Methuen 1983

John Whitwell[8] *British Agent* William Kimber 1966

Nigel West *MI6 British Secret Intelligence Service Operations 1909 – 1945* Weidenfeld & Nicolson 1983

Footnotes:
Has a chapter on Raoul Loveday, allegedly murdered by Aleister Crowley.[9]

Previously published as *Land Benighted* (Geoffrey Bles 1938)[2]

Tells the tale of the expedition to 'avenge' Raoul Loveday; plus much mountaineering.[3]

Subtitled *The Lord Chief Justices of England*. Has a chapter on Greene's bête noire, Hewart.[4]

Subtitled *Studies in the Novelists of the Twenties.* The relevant chapter is: 'Graham Greene: I Suffer; Therefore, I am.'[5]

With a (notorious) Introduction by Graham Greene[6]

Subtitled *Creative Process in Greene and Mauriac*[7]

"John Whitwell" is the pen name of Leslie Nicholson. Introduction by Malcolm Muggeridge.[8]

FILMS AND FILMOGRAPHY

1. *"Orient Express" – 1933/4*
   The film version of *Stamboul Train.*
   Produced and directed by Paul Martin.
   Starring Norman Foster as Carleton Myatt and Heather Angel as Coral Musker.

2. *"The Future's In The Air" – 1937 Strand Film Unit*
Commentary by Graham Greene
Directed by Alexander Shaw. Produced by Paul Rotha.

3. *"The New Britain" – 1940 Strand Film Unit*
Commentary by Graham Greene
Directed by Ralph Keene. Produced by Alexander Shaw.

4. *"Twenty One Days / Twenty One Days Together" – 1939/40 Columbia*
The film version of Galsworthy's short story "The First and the Last".
Screenplay by Graham Greene and Basil Dean.
Directed by Basil Dean. Produced by Alexander Korda.
Starring Laurence Olivier as Larry Durrant, Vivien Leigh as Wanda and Robert Newton as Tolly.

5. *"The Green Cockatoo/Four Dark Hours/Race Gang" – 1940 Fox*
From a Story by Graham Greene
Screenplay by Edward O Berkman and Arthur Wimperis.
Produced by William K Howard. Directed by William C Menzies.
Starring John Mills as Jim Connor, Robert Newton as Dave Connor, and René Ray as Eileen.

6. *"This Gun For Hire" – 1942 Paramount*
The film version of "A Gun For Sale"
Directed by Frank Tuttle. Screenplay by Albert Maltz and WR Burnett.
Starring Alan Ladd as Raven and Veronica Lake as Anne.

7. *"Went The Day Well" – 1943 Ealing*
The film version of Graham Greene's short story, "The Lieutenant Died Last".
Directed by Alberto Cavalcanti. Produced by Michael Balcon.
Screenplay by Angus MacPhail, John Dighton, Diana Morgan.
Starring Leslie Banks as the quisling/squire. Music by Sir William Walton.

8. *"The Ministry of Fear" – 1944 Paramount*
The film of the novel.
Directed by Fritz Lang. Producer and Screenplay: Seton I Miller.
Starring Ray Millard as Arthur Rowe and Marjorie Reynolds as Anna Hilfe.

9. *"The Confidential Agent" – 1945 Warner Bros.*
The film of the novel.
Directed by Herbert Shumlin. Producer and Screenplay: Robert Buckner.
Starring Charles Boyer as "D" and Lauren Bacall as Rose.